Psychotherapy with Adolescents and Their Families

Essential Treatment Strategies

Muriel Prince Warren

Crown House Publishing Limited
www.crownhouse.co.uk

First published in hardback under the title *Behavioral Management Guide: Essential Treatment Strategies for The Psychotherapy of Children, Their Parents, and Families* in 2002 (Original ISBN: 0-7657-0354-8; original LCCN: 2001045699).

This paperback edition published by

Crown House Publishing Ltd
Crown Buildings, Bancyfelin, Carmarthen, Wales, SA33 5ND, UK
www.crownhouse.co.uk

and

Crown House Publishing Company LLC
4 Berkeley Street, 1st Floor, Norwalk, CT 06850, USA
www.CHPUS.com

© 1999, 2005, Muriel Prince Warren

The right of Muriel Prince Warren to be identified as the author of this work has been asserted by her in accordance with the Copyright, Designs and Patents Act 1988.

All rights reserved. Except as permitted under current legislation no part of this work may be photocopied, stored in a retrieval system, published, performed in public, adapted, broadcast, transmitted, recorded or reproduced in any form or by any means, without the prior permission of the copyright owners. Enquiries should be addressed to Crown House Publishing Limited.

British Library of Cataloguing-in-Publication Data
A catalogue entry for this book is available from the British Library.

10-digit ISBN 1904424627
13-digit ISBN 978-190442462-8

LCCN 2004111441

Printed and bound in the United States

With Love for Howard, Joel, Jenny, and George

CONTENTS

PART I: INTRODUCTION

1 The Changing Face of Psychotherapy   3
   Managed Care and Adolescent Psychotherapy   3
   Medical Necessity   5
   When the Appeal Process Fails   6
   Treatment Planning   7
   How to Use This Guide   8

2 The Paper Trail   10
   The Outpatient Treatment Report (OTR)   11
   Other Forms and Reports   11

PART II: THE TREATMENT PLANS

3 Critical Incident Stress Management   15

4 Anxiety Disorders   37
   Acute Stress Disorder   37
   Generalized Anxiety Disorder   50
   Obsessive-Compulsive Disorder   61
   Post-traumatic Stress Disorder   71
   Separation Anxiety Disorder   83
   Social Phobia   95
   Specific Phobia   108

5 Behavior Disorders   121
   Attention Deficit/Hyperactivity Disorder   121
   Conduct Disorder   133
   Oppositional Defiant Disorder   135
   Disruptive Behavior Disorder NOS   136

6	**Bipolar Disorders**	**146**
	Bipolar I Disorder	146
	Bipolar Disorder NOS	149
	Bipolar II Disorder	151
	Cyclothymic Disorder	153
7	**Depressive Disorders**	**170**
	Major Depressive Disorder	170
	Dysthymic Disorder	172
	Depressive Disorder NOS	173
	Bereavement	187
8	**Eating Disorders**	**201**
	Anorexia Nervosa	201
	Bulimia Nervosa	203
9	**General Medical Conditions**	**216**
	Personality Change Due to a General Medical Condition	216
	Mental Disorder Not Otherwise Specified Due to a General Medical Condition	217
	Psychological Factors Affecting Medical Condition	218
10	**Impulse Control Disorders**	**232**
	Intermittent Explosive Disorder	232
	Kleptomania	246
	Pathological Gambling	258
	Trichotillomania	272
11	**Relational Problems**	**285**
	Parent–Adolescent Relational Problem	285
	Sibling Relational Problem	287
	Divorce or Separation-Related Problems	294
	Adolescent Abuse or Neglect	308
12	**Sleep Disorders**	**326**
	Dyssomnias	326
	Parasomnias	326
13	**Substance Disorders**	**342**
	Substance Dependence	342
	Substance Abuse	344

PART III: TREATMENT AIDS

14 Behavioral Techniques   **359**
    Bad Dreams   359
    Change   361
    Family Sculpturing   362
    Genograms   363
    Hypnosis   364
    Learning   365
    Relaxation   365
    Role-Playing   368

15 Therapeutic Games   **374**

16 Homework Assignments   **377**
    Automatic Thought Log   377
    The Steps to Constructing a Rational Response   379
    Challenging Cognitions   380
    Common Cognitive Distortions   381

17 Bibliotherapy   **382**
    Self-Help Books For Adolescents   382
    Self-Help Books For Parents and Families   393
    Videotapes   403
    Audiotapes   403

18 Self-Help Groups and 800 Numbers   **406**

19 Online Resources   **408**

PART IV: APPENDIX

20 Practice Management Reports   **417**
    Psychosocial Intake Report   418
    Outpatient Medical Management Report   419
    Payment and Session Monitor   421
    Progress Notes   424
    CPT Codes   426
    Discharge Summary   426

References   429
Index   435

ACKNOWLEDGMENTS

First and always I would like to thank Norma Pomerantz who has held my hand through the birth of each publication. I would also like to acknowledge my husband, Howard Matus, who gives me love and support in all that I undertake, and Bill O'Hanlon for his generous contributions to this book and to my life.

Special recognition goes to Dr. David I. Perry who spent many weekends with us researching and editing this manuscript, and to the many people who have encouraged me along the way, including Dr. Joseph Pirone, my first psychology teacher, whose brilliance has added shine to my life, and Dr. Irving Weisberg, who has taught me to keep things in perspective.

I am also indebted to Dr. Gabriel Stutman for sharing her ideas about the use of toys in working with learning disabled children, as well as to Dr. Judith Gordon, John Reiner, and Tina Rosenbaum at the Summit School who work with these children every day.

Most of all I am sincerely grateful to my patients and their families for all they have taught me about psychotherapy.

PART I
INTRODUCTION

1
THE CHANGING FACE OF PSYCHOTHERAPY

MANAGED CARE AND ADOLESCENT PSYCHOTHERAPY

The language of adolescent psychotherapy changed when therapists contracted with insurance companies and became "service providers." The process of treating adolescents was once regarded as a "talking cure" in which therapy was often non-directive and the emphasis was on the relationship between the client and the therapist. The therapist provided a safe holding environment to help the teenager, in a non-directive way, gain insights into his or her problems and their possible causes. Although this process worked over time, it was perceived by managed care as too lengthy and too expensive. They found it more expeditious to cover measurable, short-term behavioral changes rather than long-term structural change in the client's psyche.

The treatment goals and interventions in this book have been presented in cognitive, solution-focused language. The purpose "is to describe the treatment process in behavior-focused and measurable language, thereby allowing case managers to relate to what providers are trying to accomplish rather than being put off by psychoanalytic terms that may be foreign to their training or experience.

Managed care's overnight rise to dominance brought with it more than just behavioral management. A fundamental concern with cost-effectiveness led logically to the basic business techniques of project management: establishing long-term goals, choosing short-term tasks or objectives to get there, and tracking the process from start to finish. Suddenly, these terms were incorporated into the managed care lexicon and the more psychoanalytic-oriented, non-directive techniques were considered archaic. Gone were the concepts of "working through the resistance," "repetition compulsion," "maintaining a holding environment," and "exploring the underlying transference." Free association, a standard treatment mode since the early days of Freud, was replaced with a mode that could be charted step by step along a predetermined path to the final achievement of a treatment goal.

Psychotherapists, who had spent years studying the giants of psychiatry and mastering the proven techniques of maintaining a sound holding environment, listening, and intervening, suddenly discovered they could not talk to managed care case managers in terms they understood. The language of psychotherapy had changed. Mental disorders gave way to "behavioral impairments," patients became "clients," and psychotherapists became "service providers." Now, all terms that suggest long-term treatment, such as "psychoanalysis," "improve client's low self-esteem," or "enhance quality of life," are in danger of being labeled vague and not "medically necessary." Chances are that treatment authorization will be denied.

Managed care is concerned with Axis I impairments. These are disorders normally coded on Axis I of the Multiaxial Assessment System of the *Diagnostic and Statistical Manual of Mental Disorders* Fourth Edition (*DSM-IV*) published by the American Psychiatric Association. Managed care providers do not want to pay for the treatment of irresolvable diagnoses, and Axis II diagnoses are usually considered irresolvable by insurance companies. However, if you have a client with a personality disorder, the diagnosis can be coded as Axis II, and the behavioral symptoms coded and treated as Axis I impairments. Most, if not all, personality disorders also have Axis I impairments. Managed care providers are also concerned that therapists treating an adolescent for one long-term disorder may be fostering a dependent personality disorder. So, if managed care case managers spot a provider with a cluster of long-term clients, they are more apt to refer future clients to other providers who provide short-term treatment. Goals that are not achievable within three months should be avoided or replaced with more focused, resolvable goals. Managed care providers want quick, cost-effective change using modalities that are consistent with the client's needs. Most insurance companies accept behavioral, solution-focused, brief dynamic, group, medication management, or psychopharmacology. Prior approvals are normally required for evaluation of medication by a psychiatrist or for psychological testing. Some companies will pay for psychological testing, biofeedback, and hypnosis, sometimes referred to as relaxation technique. Check with each company before using these in your outpatient treatment reports. Most insurance companies find the term "relaxation technique" more acceptable than "hypnosis."

Another potential problem appears to be the idea of a therapeutic alliance between patient and therapist. Although many insurance case managers balk at the term therapeutic alliance, "research demonstrates that in successful cognitive-behavioral therapy, patients view the therapy relationship as 'crucial in helping them change'" (McGinn and

Sanderson, 1999, p. 6). The development of a positive therapeutic relationship is critical in psychotherapy and is considered to be most predictive of positive treatment outcome. The therapeutic relationship is even more important in the treatment of adolescents. "The therapist must make contact with the client, engage the client, and engender his or her trust if treatment is to be effective" (Knell, 1993, p. 46). The current focus appears to be on a more active role for the client in therapy. O'Hanlon (1987) echoes the view of Milton Erickson, noted hypnotherapist, that it is the therapist's responsibility "to create a climate, an atmosphere for change in which people change themselves" (p. 19). Rossi, Ryan, and Sharp (1983) use Erickson's analogy of the starting pistol at a race: "The therapist merely initiates the race by firing the starting pistol; it is the patient who must actually run and win the race" (pp. 102–3).

In adolescent psychotherapy, treatment often extends to parents in family sessions with or without the client present. William O'Hanlon, author of many books on brief, solution-focused therapy and Ericksonian hypnosis, (personal communication, 2000) explains that it is sometimes important to involve parents of adolescents in treatment in order to disrupt the maladaptive patterns of behavior in the family.

Insurance companies want clients to take a more active role in treatment. They encourage the use of homework assignments and self-help books, as well as referrals to self-help groups. Suggested homework assignments are included in Chapter 16 of this book, self-help books in Chapter 17, self-help groups and 800 numbers in Chapter 18 and online resources in Chapter 19.

Treatment frequency is usually crisis-driven. Once a week is standard and may temporarily be increased to twice a week. Some companies also may reduce sessions to every other week or once a month as a prelude to termination. Most insurance companies will allow up to 10 sessions per treatment plan. If you divide a complex goal into several simpler goals, it is more likely that a case manager will see gradual improvement and authorize further sessions. In the next treatment plan, you can request further sessions for another problem or part of the original problem that remains unresolved.

MEDICAL NECESSITY

Medical necessity is the criterion used by managed care companies to authorize treatment sessions. There are various definitions of medical necessity in use today. The term and its meaning are usually published in the insurance companies' provider manuals. Value Options, one of the nation's larger behavioral management organizations, defines medical necessity treatment as "that which is intended to prevent, diagnose, correct, cure, alleviate or preclude deterioration of a diagnosable condition (*ICD-9* or *DSM-IV*) that threatens life, causes pain or suffering, or results in illness or infirmity" (*Value Options Provider Handbook*, 1999, p. B-2). Medical necessity is usually limited to resolvable issues. The term resolvable is vague and subject to definition by the insurance company's case manager.

The *Value Options Provider Handbook* lists other qualifications as well. The treatment must also be:

1. Expected to improve the client's condition or level of functioning;
2. Consistent with the symptoms, diagnosis, and nationally accepted standards of care;
3. Representative of a safe level of service where no effective, less expensive treatment is available;
4. Not intended for the convenience of client or provider;
5. No more restrictive than necessary to balance safety, effectiveness, and efficiency (p. B-2).

Medical necessity is open to interpretation by a case manager who determines what is appropriate. In my private practice, one insurance company authorized 30 sessions for one patient and only 10 for another with the identical diagnosis.

Frager (2000) stresses that "Medical necessity determination is not a clinical decision, nor is it a clinical concept of relevance to practice. Despite the name ... it is a kind of code governing the rationing of sessions [and is] open to a good deal of speculation, depending on the benefit plan of the client and the purchaser's contract with the insurance managed care company" (p. 102). She adds, "Most medical necessity guidelines specify clearly that treatment must focus on symptom-reduction and restoration of functioning or the resolution of a specific problem.... It is the resolvability clause that managed care companies tend to use when they think they have paid for too many sessions and are looking for a way to deny treatment" (p. 108).

If you feel the authorization decision has been unfairly made, you can usually appeal. Most insurance companies provide for at least two levels of appeal. However, the process is different for each company and is usually outlined in the provider handbooks or available from the company's provider service center.

WHEN THE APPEAL PROCESS FAILS

It may seem as if insurance companies have the last word, but that is not always true. The National Association of Insurance Commissioners (NAIC) is an organization of insurance regulators from each of the

50 states, the four US territories, and the District of Columbia. NAIC helps insurance regulators protect the interests of insurance consumers. If you are an insurance subscriber or a provider who feels that you have been treated unfairly or has an insurance problem that defies resolution, NAIC is a good place to start. You may contact them at the following address:

National Association of Insurance Commissioners
2301 McGee (Suite 800)
Kansas City, MO 64108-2604
(816) 842-3600

They are also available online at www.naic.org. They may refer your problem to a funded consumer representative in your area or to your state insurance department. However, the process will eat up valuable treatment time and few complaints are filed because providers fear they will be removed from the insurance company's referral list in retribution.

TREATMENT PLANNING

Not long ago, plans for the psychotherapeutic treatment of a specific patient were characteristically general and sometimes vague. The idea was to get the patient better as quickly as possible given the time to work through the problem. The techniques used to bring about that change were limited only by the therapist's training and experience. Essentially, this was a "talking" therapy. Although it was usually effective over time, insurance companies and others criticized it as costly. Obviously, certain problems (i.e. personality disorders) can take a considerable amount of time to resolve in a traditional once-a-week therapy. As managed care rose to dominance in a society alarmed by skyrocketing medical costs, learning how to write formalized treatment plans became a *must* for physicians and psychotherapists, yet many practitioners had not developed the art of formal treatment planning during their extensive educational programs. This book is designed to fill that gap.

What is a Treatment Plan?

A formal treatment plan is a road map of treatment for a specific disorder that contains broad objectives, specific behavioral treatment goals designed to meet those objectives, and interventions by the therapist to achieve those goals. Together, these written elements build a solid, measurable approach to the treatment of a given disorder that effectively meets the demands for therapist accountability to insurance overseers and government regulators.

Building a Treatment Plan

The treatment plan starts with the intake psychosocial evaluation of the patient in which the patient's problem/s are defined and a diagnosis is established. In the initial evaluation session, the therapist and patient must agree on what issues to address in treatment. Other issues may emerge as treatment progresses.

The additional plan elements then flow logically from that database. Next, a list of broad, generalized objectives of treatment is formulated. This is a description of where you want to be when treatment has been completed, written in a manner that is understandable to the patient and quantifies for an insurance case manager what is going on in the treatment room. Once the objectives are in place, specific treatment goals to achieve those objectives are constructed in behavioral terms. It may take a number of goals to meet a given objective. With the generalized objectives and specific goals established, the therapist must address each goal in turn by constructing an appropriate intervention to meet the goal. The therapist must draw upon his or her training and experience to select an effective intervention.

HOW TO USE THIS GUIDE

This book is a guide for the development of a comprehensive treatment plan for adolescent patients and their families based on a presenting problem and diagnosis. Throughout the treatment plans provided in this book, the therapist is not, and should not be, limited to those objectives, goals, and interventions provided, but also should adapt the plan to the needs of his or her own practice. The plans in this book are provided as a guide. Each therapist should amend the plan to include his or her own objectives, goals, and interventions wherever possible.

In addition to the treatment plans, this guide includes essential instructions for tracking patient sessions and alerting you that outpatient treatment reports (OTRs) are due. It also provides tips on preparing the required treatment progress notes, and discharge summaries. The major diagnostic categories listed in the *DSM-IV* are discussed. Mental disorders are presented as behavioral problems that are more readily understood and accepted by managed care case managers. A comprehensive outline of broad, long-term treatment objectives, measurable, short-term behavioral goals, and possible interventions are provided. This book will take you step-by-step through the authorization process, show you how to monitor payments and authorization dates, and guide you through the required reports and progress notes with separate treatment plans, not only for the adolescent, but for the parents and the entire family as well.

2
THE PAPER TRAIL

Even in the electronic age, paper is still king. Under state law, the entire treatment process must be documented from the first phone call to the final discharge summary. If it is not documented, it never happened. In addition to the Outpatient Treatment Report (OTR), discussed below, the forms that you may need include: the Psychosocial Intake Report; Medical Management–Psychiatrist's Report; Payment and Session Monitor; Progress Notes; Billing—HCFA-1500 Form; and the Discharge Summary.

Chapter 20 contains sample forms and guidelines for their use. If you are a provider and have contracted with any of the managed care companies, be aware that they have a right to request any of these documents. Many insurance companies follow the guidelines prepared by the National Committee for Quality Assurance or the Institute for Healthcare Quality, organizations that have researched, developed, and written position papers on each diagnosis. The papers include a description, approved treatment usually psychotherapy and pharmacology with a strong emphasis on the cognitive behavioral, interpersonal, and brief dynamic treatment modalities.

While some insurance companies rely on professional research and consulting groups to determine the number of sessions to authorize for the treatment of a given disorder, other managed care companies have developed their own detailed formulas. Some claim to use "medical necessity," as discussed in Chapter 1, as the criterion.

Author and former case manager Susan Frager (personal communication, 2000) suggests that the number of sessions authorized depends heavily on the company that subscribes to managed care and the employee's insurance coverage. No matter which insurance company manages the benefits, everything hinges on the specific policy selected and the power of the subscribing company, she says.

THE OUTPATIENT TREATMENT REPORT (OTR)

This book will guide you in writing an effective outpatient treatment report. The first step is to make a multiaxial assessment. Based upon this assessment, you will establish both broad, long-term objectives and measurable short-term behavioral goals that can be met within a specific time frame. You must be able to estimate when you will reach a short-term behavioral goal, and how far away you are from achieving that goal at any given time. There is usually more than one short-term behavioral goal for each diagnosis. The goals must be concrete events; vague goals are unacceptable.

Part II of this book includes a list of suggested objectives, behavioral goals, and therapist's interventions for each major adolescent diagnosis. Choose those you consider appropriate for your client. Additionally, you can develop and include some of your own goals and interventions. Be sure they have been translated into behavioral terms and are measurable. Managed care companies expect treatment plans to include homework assignments and referrals to self-help groups. See Chapter 16 for suggested homework assignments, Chapter 18 for a listing of major self-help groups and 800 numbers, and Chapter 19 for online resources.

By following these guidelines, you will develop a viable behavioral treatment plan for every client, a smoother relationship with behavioral case managers, and outpatient treatment reports that assure optimum treatment certification for your clients. In actual practice, of course, treatment is considerably more complicated than the plans outlined in this book.

OTHER FORMS AND REPORTS

Other forms that may be helpful are contained in Chapter 20 and include a Payment and Session Monitor, a Psychiatrist's Medical Management Report, Progress Notes, Common Procedural Terminology (CPT) Billing Codes, and a Discharge Summary.

Progress Notes

Progress notes must be kept for each session. The notes must include the name of the client, the date, a summary of what transpired in the session including your intervention, and an evaluation of progress toward a treatment goal. The provider must sign the progress notes for each session. Dictated notes are considered preliminary until the transcription is reviewed and signed. A sample form is included in Chapter 20.

Billing

Despite substantial inroads in electronic billing, notably by Medicare and leading insurance carriers, the HCFA-1500 (12-90) is still the universal form for billing, and all insurance companies require that this form be filled out accurately and completely. If not, the form may simply be discarded. However, some insurance companies may return a form to you indicating the reason it has been rejected. Detailed instructions for filling out a HCFA form are contained in the *Clinical Social Worker Reference Guide* published by Empire Medicare Services. Providers must keep accurate records and be prepared to follow up by telephone or rebilling if they have not been paid within 60 days. Insurance companies frequently change claim addresses, misplace bills, pay incorrect fees, ignore some billed sessions, or claim authorized sessions are unauthorized and deny payment. See Chapter 20 for a review of the CPT billing codes in use today.

Discharge Summary

Some, but not all, insurance companies require discharge summaries. Since many companies are tracking your success rate and duration of treatment, it is a good idea to submit a discharge summary even if you suspect the client may return to treatment and you have authorized sessions left. (You can always reopen the case.) A typical discharge summary appears in Chapter 20.

PART II
THE TREATMENT PLANS

3
CRITICAL INCIDENT STRESS MANAGEMENT

In response to the many adolescents who have been traumatized by the September 11, 2001 attack on the World Trade Center and the reinforcing impact of the continuing war on terror in the United States and throughout the world, Critical Incident Stress Management (CISM) heads up our extensive list of treatment plans.

This is not a *DSM-IV* classification, but many of the symptoms of this disorder fall into Axis I behavioral impairments, and the diagnosis probably should be Post-traumatic Stress Disorder or Bereavement, depending on how the incident affected your patient. If he or she is suffering from the loss of a loved one, you will probably be dealing with both diagnoses.

Critical Incident Stress Management, in itself, is not psychotherapy, but a system of interventions designed to prevent or mitigate adverse psychological reactions. If crises and disasters become epidemic, we will need immediate, effective strategies to deal with our patients. Individual, family, and group interventions may be needed at any time and at any place with the goal of reducing fear and returning to normal functioning as much as possible.

In Critical Incident Stress Management, the patient has witnessed or experienced an actual or threatened event that placed him or her or another person in danger of death or serious injury, and reacted with feelings of intense horror, fear, or helplessness. No one who experiences a disaster in person or sees it on television is untouched by it. After a disaster, most people will pull together, but their effectiveness will be diminished. Many will not see the need for mental health services and may reject assistance of all types. This is a special time, and therapists need to put aside their usual methods and use a more practical, active outreach approach that is appropriate for each phase of the disaster.

Patients may react to disaster in a wide range of ways. They need to be reminded that grief reactions or disaster stress reactions are normal in times of crisis. In the beginning, people will need more practical advice than psychological help. There are four waves of assistance: (1) Coping and Stabilization with a focus on basic needs and safety; (2) Stress Management, including arousal reduction strategies and coping with current and future life circumstances; (3) Resolution of grief and trauma; and (4) Accommodation, Adaptation, Transformation, and Reconnection.

Behavioral Symptoms
(severity index: 1–mild; 2–moderate; 3–intense)

Severity

Emotional
1. Overwhelming fear or anxiety _____
2. Feels lost or overwhelmed _____
3. Depression _____
4. Guilt, grief _____
5. Excessive death anxiety _____
6. Feels detached from others _____
7. Range of feelings is restricted _____
8. Has increased sense of limited future _____
9. Irritable, displays outbursts of anger _____

Behavioral
10. Withdrawn from others _____
11. Experience sleep disturbances _____
12. Exhibits unusual behaviors _____
13. Changes eating patterns _____
14. Excessive silence or problems in communication _____
15. Changes work habits _____
16. Persistently reexperiences traumatic event as a dream or recollection _____
17. Has flashbacks of the event _____
18. Displays intense distress at cues reminiscent of the event _____
19. Avoids people, places, activities, and thoughts associated with the event _____

Cognitive
20. Poor concentration _____
21. Memory problems, poor attention span _____
22. Difficulty making decisions _____
23. Slowed problem solving _____
24. Difficulties with calculations _____
25. Unable to remember an important aspect of the event _____
26. Interest in usual activities is diminished _____
27. Is easily startled _____

Physical
28. Muscle tremors _____
29. Chest Pains _____
30. Gastrointestinal distress _____
31 Difficulty breathing _____
32. Headaches _____
33. Elevated blood pressure _____

CRITICAL INCIDENT STRESS MANAGEMENT TREATMENT PLAN

Patient: _____ Date: _____

I. OBJECTIVES OF TREATMENT *(select one or more)*

1. Identify if basic needs are being met (i.e., safety, food, shelter etc.)
2. If necessary, refer to Federal Emergency Management Assistance (FEMA)
3. Educate parents or caregivers about the cognitive, emotional, behavioral, and physical symptoms associated with being involved in a critical incident
4. If the adolescent has lost a loved one, use the Bereavement plan or Post-traumatic Stress Disorder plan in addition to this one
5. Help family regain internal and external control
6. Reduce cognitive, behavioral, emotional, and physical stress symptoms
7. Diminish symptoms of anxiety or survivor guilt
8. Help mourners through the grieving process
9. Teach strategies to reduce stressors to critical events
10. Identify stress reactions of significant others
11. Resolve feelings of despair and hopelessness
12. Help each family member to tell his or her story and identify how he or she is dealing with the trauma
13. Eliminate sleep disturbances and nightmares
14. Demonstrate appropriate communication skills (active listening, questioning, mirroring, paraphrasing)
15. Restore appetite, stop weight loss
16. Teach the Phoenix Model of dealing with Bereavement and crisis (i.e. Impact, Chaos, Adaptation, Equilibrium, and Transformation or Self-Actualization)
17. Encourage compliance with educational programs and referrals
18. Develop personal rituals to ensure safety and empowerment
19. Reframe irrational beliefs
20. Promote socialization, reconnection, reduce alienation
21. If appropriate, encourage family to develop spiritual side for grounding
22. Develop discharge plan for coping with everyday life

II. SHORT-TERM BEHAVIORAL GOALS AND INTERVENTIONS
(select the goals and interventions appropriate for your patient)

NOTE: Separate goals and interventions are provided for Parents, Adolescent, and Family

PARENTS' GOALS	THERAPIST'S INTERVENTIONS
Collaborate with the therapist to reduce stressors immediately associated with the event.	Establish therapeutic alliance with the parents, adolescent, or family as soon as possible to help them deal with overwhelming stressors of traumatic event(s).
Relate the traumatic event in detail and your reactive feelings to it.	Investigate the impact of the traumatic event on the parents and how it is affecting them.
Parents and family are treated for Bereavement plus CISM.	Assess problem with the parents and, if anyone in their family has died, revise diagnosis and see Bereavement plan to use with CISM.
Explain your needs to the therapist.	Investigate if basic needs are being met (i.e. food, clothing, shelter, safety etc.).
Follow-up with referral.	Refer to FEMA (see Online Resources, Chapter 19).
Describe flashbacks and their intensity.	Explore for flashbacks and assess intensity.
Understand the different types of trauma.	Help parents understand the different types of trauma. Type 1: Single unpredictable event. Type 2: Ongoing world event, sexual abuse, or domestic violence. Type 3: Individual—a brutal blow to psyche that breaks through one's defenses; Collective—a blow that damages social life and bonds between people.

PARENTS' GOALS	THERAPIST'S INTERVENTIONS
Become aware of ways to reduce stress during critical incidents or disasters. Learn how to reduce stressors to the critical event.	Educate parents about ways to reduce stressors to the critical event. 1. Structure time. Keep busy. 2. Don't label yourself crazy. It's normal to feel crazy under stress. 3. Talk to others. 4. Understand that attempting to numb pain with drugs, alcohol, or excessive food will just complicate problems. 5. Reach out and connect with others. 6. Show feelings. 7. Help coworkers and let them help you. 8. Write your feelings in a journal, especially during sleepless hours. 9. Do things that feel good. 10. Do not begin hoarding out of fear. It will cause more trouble for everyone. 11. Do not make any major life decisions. 12. Do not fight flashbacks. Talk about them. Realize they will become less painful over time. 13. Do things that help you feel you have some control over your life.

PARENTS' GOALS	THERAPIST'S INTERVENTIONS
	14. Listen carefully to traumatized persons.
	15. Do not deny reality, but reduce the time listening to radio and watching TV to avoid reinfecting yourself.
Learn to identify symptoms of stress reaction: emotional, behavioral, cognitive, or physical.	Help parents identify the stress reactions they and their children and adolescents are having to the traumatic event(s).
Help yourselves and your family move through a transitional period toward greater development.	Educate parents to understand the phases of the Phoenix Model: (1) Impact, (2) Chaos, (3) Adaptation, (4) Equilibrium, (5) Transformation (see *The Phoenix Phenomenon: Rising from the Ashes of Grief* in Bibliotherapy, Chapter 17).
Identify the Phoenix developmental stage your adolescent is in to help deal with the crisis.	Help parents identify where they are in the Phoenix Model and what to expect from themselves and their adolescent.
Understand you need to maintain stability, establish security measures, and begin to belong or reach out to others.	During the Impact stage, help them to understand the needs for food, shelter, sleep, safety, security, and preliminary belonging. Guide them in designing a support system.
Recognize the need to maintain physiological stability while acknowledging and expressing grief while resisting isolation.	During the Chaos stage there is still a need for food, shelter, sleep, safety, and security, but the major task is to maintain physiological stability and be able to talk about and acknowledge grief while staying connected and resisting isolation.

PARENTS' GOALS	THERAPIST'S INTERVENTIONS
Understand that during times of crisis and fear, there can also be growth.	The following stage of Adaptation is aimed at normalization. Remind parents that "Although the world is full of suffering … it is also full of overcoming it" (Helen Keller). Create a realistic outline to live in today's world while encouraging the expression of feelings.
Develop proactive strategies to reduce helplessness and hopelessness.	Help parents gain equilibrium and develop proactive strategies for living in the new world.
Look for ways to create meaning from the tragedy.	Help parents through the transformation stage by creating meaning from the grief and loss of life.
Confront thoughts of unrealistic or exaggerated consequences.	Guide parents in confronting distorted reactions to trigger situations.
Identify cognitive distortions.	Weigh the actions against evidence-based reality.
Learn to self-soothe rather than catastrophize.	Help parents develop coping mechanisms that are soothing rather than frightening, (i.e. staying in the "here and now." Even though this may be very difficult during times of critical disaster, help them see that what they worry about often doesn't happen, and what they don't know to worry about may happen.

PARENTS' GOALS	THERAPIST'S INTERVENTIONS
Enter treatment to help deal with your trauma and enhance the outcome of your adolescent's therapy.	Evaluate parents for anxiety problems related to traumatic event and refer for treatment or treat if appropriate. Refer to *Behavioral Management Guide: Essential Treatment Strategies for Adult Psychotherapy* (see Bibliotherapy, Chapter 17).
Develop awareness of how your personal theory influences cognition of the problem in your adolescent.	Explore parental theory of the crisis.
Learn to reach beyond automatic cognitive reactions in viewing the problem.	Expand parental perspective beyond limited cognitive reactions.
Learn how to help your adolescent deal with stressors.	Teach parents the laws of anxiety: anxiety is not dangerous or permanent; avoidance increases anxiety; confronting the problem can reduce anxiety; exposure can produce growth. Attempt to help them normalize life as much as possible.
Undergo treatment for individual problems, which, in turn, enhances the outcome of your adolescent's therapy.	Explore for parental psychopathology (i.e. anxiety, depression, marital discord etc.) and refer for treatment or treat as appropriate.
Learn how to deal with your adolescent's sleep disorder.	Investigate for sleep problems in adolescent and teach parents how to deal with the problem.
Learn diaphragmatic breathing as relaxation technique and teach adolescent to help in relaxation.	Teach parents diaphragmatic breathing to assist adolescent in relaxation (see "Relaxation," Behavioral Techniques, Chapter 14).

PARENTS' GOALS	THERAPIST'S INTERVENTIONS
Agree to allow therapist to confer with your adolescent's school to help in development of a comprehensive psychoeducational treatment plan.	After interviewing the adolescent, and with permission of the parents and the adolescent, confer with teachers and school administrators.
Comply with referrals for medical and psychiatric evaluations.	Provide referral for medical and psychiatric evaluations, if appropriate.
Develop new coping strategies.	Assign parents to read books to enhance coping skills such as *I Can't Get Over It* or *Life After Trauma: A Workbook for Healing* or *The Phoenix Phenomenon: Rising From the Ashes of Grief* (see Bibliotherapy, Chapter 17).
Cultivate new parenting skills and learn how to deal with your adolescent's anxiety.	Assign parents to read *Making Families Work and What to Do When They Don't* and *Trust After Trauma* (see Bibliotherapy, Chapter 17).
Monitor your adolescent's medication schedule and report all reactions or failures to take meds.	If adolescent is on meds, instruct parents on need for a regular schedule and feedback that may indicate the need for revised dosage.
Resolve separation and dependency issues and terminate treatment.	Develop a treatment termination plan and discuss issues of separation anxiety and dependency

ADOLESCENT'S GOALS	THERAPIST'S INTERVENTIONS
Develop a therapeutic relationship to help you through the traumatic event or loss of loved one.	Engage the adolescent in a therapeutic relationship to help deal with the traumatic event.
Identify how you are attempting to deal with the traumatic event.	Investigate the impact of the traumatic event and how the adolescent is affected by it.
Get help to deal with the crisis if you need it.	Determine if basic needs are being met (i.e. food, clothing, shelter, safety). If necessary, refer to FEMA (see Online Resources, Chapter 19).
Realize you can look to others for support.	Explore available support systems. Are there aunts, uncles, other relatives, or friends available to help the adolescent adjust to the emotional shock wave?
Understand the stages of trauma and be reassured that you will get through the grieving process.	Educate the adolescent about the stages of trauma: (1) shock, denial, disbelief; (2) anger, "why did it happen?"; (3) chaos, despair "How can it ever get better?"; (4) bargaining, "If I am a better person, things will improve." Help the adolescent reorganize and create a new life in order to reduce the effects of trauma.
Learn to identify the symptoms you are experiencing and recognize them as a response to trauma.	Help the adolescent identify his or her stress reactions: emotional, behavioral, cognitive, and physical.
Undergo treatment for symptoms.	See appropriate treatment plans for indicated disorders.

ADOLESCENT'S GOALS	THERAPIST'S INTERVENTIONS
Realize that human beings are not perfect and reduce stressors imposed on self.	Teach the adolescent that human beings are not perfect.
Determine the impact of the trauma on schoolwork.	Explore for academic problems related to the trauma and treat accordingly (refer to appropriate treatment plan).
Become aware of ways to reduce stress during critical incidents or disasters.	Educate the adolescent about ways to reduce stressors to the critical event.
Learn how to reduce stressors to the critical event.	1. Structure time. Keep busy. 2. Don't label yourself crazy. It's normal to feel crazy under stress. 3. Talk to others. 4. Understand that attempting to numb pain with drugs, alcohol, or excessive food just creates problems. 5. Reach out and connect with others. 6. Show feelings. 7. Help others and let them help you. 8. Write your feelings in a journal, especially during sleepless hours. 9. Do things that feel good. 10. Do not begin hoarding out of fear. It will cause more trouble for everyone. 11. Do not make any major life decisions.

ADOLESCENT'S GOALS	THERAPIST'S INTERVENTIONS
	12. Do not fight flashbacks. Talk about them. Realize they will be less painful over time.
	13. Do things that help you feel you have some control over life.
	14. Listen carefully to other traumatized persons.
	15. Do not deny reality, but reduce the time spent listening to radio or watching TV to avoid reinfecting yourself.
Learn how to manage the stages of grief.	Teach client to understand the phases of the Phoenix Model: (1) Impact; (2) Chaos; (3) Adaptation; (4) Equilibrium; (5) Transformation (see *The Phoenix Phenomenon: Rising from the Ashes of Grief* in Bibliotherapy, Chapter 17).
Learn to identify the Phoenix development stage you are in.	Help the adolescent identify where he or she is in the Phoenix Model and what to expect at this stage.
Recognize that you need to maintain stability and safety, and begin reaching out to others.	During the Impact phase, help the adolescent understand the need for food, clothing, shelter, safety, and sleep. Start a support system.
Recognize the need for psychological stability while being able to express grief.	During the Chaos phase, basic needs continue, but the major task is to maintain physiological stability and be able to talk about and acknowledge grief while staying connected and resisting isolation.

ADOLESCENT'S GOALS	THERAPIST'S INTERVENTIONS
Develop proactive strategies for living in the new world.	Help the adolescent regain equilibrium after the trauma by developing proactive strategies for reducing helplessness and hopelessness.
Look for ways to create meaning from the tragedy.	Guide the adolescent through the Transformation phase by attempting to find meaning in the grief and loss of life.
Develop a realistic outline for living in an uncertain world.	The following phase of Adaptation is aimed at normalization. Remind the client of Helen Keller's words, "Although the world is full of suffering, it is also full of overcoming it." Develop a realistic outline to live in today's world while encouraging the expression of feelings.
Confront thoughts of unrealistic or exaggerated consequences.	Guide the adolescent in confronting distorted reactions to trigger situations.
Identify and correct cognitive distortions	Weigh the actions against evidence-based reality.
Learn to self-soothe rather than catastrophize.	Help the adolescent develop coping mechanisms that are soothing rather than frightening (i.e. staying in the "here and now.") Even though this may be difficult during times of critical disaster, help the adolescent realize that what we worry about often doesn't happen and what we don't know to worry about may happen.

ADOLESCENT'S GOALS	THERAPIST'S INTERVENTIONS
Realize that others also feel bad when critical trauma incidents occur.	Explore for low self-esteem or survivor guilt, and explain it as a normal reaction to trauma.
Identify irrational beliefs.	Explore irrational beliefs about death.
Reframe beliefs about fears and anxieties.	Discuss the beliefs and develop rational alternatives.
Using relaxation techniques and guided imagery, learn to gain control over feelings.	Teach relaxation techniques and guided imagery to master anxieties (see "Relaxation," Behavioral Techniques, Chapter 14).
Understand anxiety and realize that avoidance does not help.	Teach the adolescent the laws of anxiety: anxiety is not dangerous or permanent; avoidance increases anxiety; confronting the problem can reduce anxiety; exposure can produce growth.
Communicate your life story to therapist.	Have the adolescent relate the story of his or her life.
Express suppressed feelings about saying goodbye to a loved one.	If appropriate, play *The Goodbye Game* to dispel myths and false ideas about death (see Therapeutic Games, Chapter 15).
Discuss personal coping mechanisms developed to handle stressful situations.	Investigate with the adolescent possible patterns of social withdrawal or becoming overly active as a way of dealing with feelings about trauma.

ADOLESCENT'S GOALS	THERAPIST'S INTERVENTIONS
Recognize and discuss how the family affects the problem.	Explore the family's impact on the problem. Are they supportive? Do they talk about the tragedy or pretend it never happened? Remind the adolescent that anxiety and uncertainty are normal parts of grief.
Learn positive self-talk.	Teach the adolescent positive self-talk to interrupt negative patterns.
Learn new techniques for relaxing and dealing with anxieties.	Teach diaphragmatic breathing to help the client relax and reduce stress (see "Relaxation," Behavioral Techniques, Chapter 14).
Agree to allow therapist to confer with your school to help in development of a comprehensive psychoeducational treatment plan.	Interview the adolescent to determine if he or she thinks the school should also be involved in helping.
Comply with referrals for medical and psychiatric evaluations.	Provide referrals for medical and psychiatric evaluations, if appropriate.
Develop new coping strategies.	Assign parents to read to client *I Can't Get Over It* or *Trust After Trauma* (see Bibliotherapy, Chapter 17).
Identify ways you have changed.	Investigate ways in which the adolescent has changed in attempt to create meaning for what he or she has gone through.
Shift focus of attention from problems to accomplishments.	Ask the adolescent to describe his or her accomplishments of the past week.

ADOLESCENT'S GOALS	THERAPIST'S INTERVENTIONS
Feel more confident as self-esteem improves.	Compliment the adolescent to provide positive reinforcement whenever possible.
Learn that grieving is a natural process and learn skills to cope.	Assign adolescent to read *I Can't Get Over It* or *Life After Trauma: A Workbook for Healing* (see Bibliotherapy, Chapter 17).
Learn ways to transform saddest moments into occasions for rebirth and transformation.	Assign the adolescent to read *The Phoenix Phenomenon: Rising From the Ashes of Grief* (see Bibliotherapy, Chapter 17).
Learn methods you can use to advocate for yourself.	Instruct the adolescent in the techniques of self-advocacy.
Understand that you can deal with these issues and bring treatment to a successful conclusion.	Develop a treatment termination plan and resolve issues of separation anxiety and dependency. Let them know you will be available should they ever need further counseling.

FAMILY'S GOALS	THERAPIST'S INTERVENTIONS
Improve communications among family members to reduce familial anxiety.	Conduct family sessions, to reduce alienation, improve communication skills, and enhance understanding of the trauma on the entire family.
Identify unsatisfied needs and get help.	Explore how basic needs are being met, (i.e. food, clothing, shelter, safety etc.) and if necessary refer family for FEMA (see Online Resources, Chapter 19).
Identify outside sources that can lend temporary support during the grieving process.	Identify if there are members of the extended family who can provide additional support.
Each family member shares his or her reaction to the loss.	Explore individual reactions to the trauma. See how each family member felt before and after the loss.
Family members understand the normal stages of grieving and what to expect from each other.	If the rest of the family is unfamiliar with the stages of grief, explain them using the Kubler-Ross Model: Denial, Anger, Bargaining, Depression, and Acceptance (Kubler-Ross, 1997), or the Phoenix Model: Impact, Chaos, Adaptation, Equilibrium, and Transformation.
Each family member shares his or her unique reaction to the critical incident.	Have the family members explore their individual feelings and response to the critical incident to give their sorrow words, which, in turn, can be cathartic.
Identify methods of coping with the disaster.	Discuss methods of coping.

FAMILY'S GOALS	THERAPIST'S INTERVENTIONS
Identify irrational thoughts related to death.	Explore irrational methods of coping in all family members. Do they feel guilty for the death? Blame each other?
Each family member identifies his or her unfinished business with the deceased and psychodynamically works through relevant issues that are unresolved.	If any family members died in the critical incident, use role-playing with an empty chair representing the deceased. Ask family members to express what they would like relate to the dead person. Include any unfinished business they would like to complete (see "Role-playing," Behavioral Techniques, Chapter 14).
Learn how to reduce stressors to the critical event.	1. Structure time. Keep Busy 2. Don't label yourself crazy. It's normal to feel crazy under stress. 3. Talk to others. 4. Understand that attempting to numb pain with alcohol, drugs, or excessive food will just complicate problems. 5. Reach out and connect with others. 6. Show feelings. 7. Help others and let them help you. 8. Write your feelings in a journal especially during sleepless hours. 9. Do things that feel good.

FAMILY'S GOALS	THERAPIST'S INTERVENTIONS
	10. Do not begin hoarding out of fear. It will cause more trouble.
	11. Do not make any major life decisions.
	12. Do not fight flashbacks. Talk about them. Realize they will become less painful over time.
	13. Do thing that help you feel you have some control over life.
	14. Listen carefully to other traumatized people.
	15. Do not deny reality, but reduce the time listening to radio or watching TV to avoid reinfecting yourself.
Expose hidden blame in order to resolve it.	Probe for hidden blame for the disaster.
Family members disclose survivor's guilt.	Explore for survivor's guilt and explain that it is a normal part of the grieving process.
Family realizes they can find hope through growth and adaptation.	Explain the phase of Adaptation and help family members realize their old lives have ended. Help them see the process as the birthplace of hope and transition.
Family members are empowered by realizing by trial and error they can take on new roles and grow.	Assist family in establishing equilibrium by taking on new roles and planning new lives even in times of crisis.
Stay in the "here and now" to reduce stress.	Realize that staying in the "here and now" will calm you down.

FAMILY'S GOALS	THERAPIST'S INTERVENTIONS
Recognize the uselessness of worry.	Reassure family members that worry is useless since what you worry about rarely happens.
Each family member strengthens himself by developing new, productive roles.	Help each family member build self-confidence through actual realistic achievements.
Each member individually develops a S.M.A.R.T. plan to help them get through the crisis.	Develop a S.M.A.R.T. action plan: Small, Measurable, Achievable, Realistic, Timeline goals (see "Change," Behavioral Techniques, Chapter 14).
Family members recognize they have the power to make important changes even if they seem small.	Help family members realize they have an opportunity to do some things differently.
Realize that major change is the result of small changes taken one at a time.	Help family members identify and prioritize achievable goals.
Identify individual transformation.	Have each member identify ways he or she has transformed since the tragedy.
Discuss the assigned books to enhance your understanding of grief.	Assign reading of *The Phoenix Phenomenon: Rising From the Ashes of Grief* (see Bibliotherapy, Chapter 17).
Make use of available community resources.	Refer family to available Community groups (see Self-Help Groups and 800 Numbers, Chapter 18, and Online Resources, Chapter 19).

FAMILY'S GOALS	THERAPIST'S INTERVENTIONS
Reduce negative communication.	Develop a system of positive reinforcement with family to help members interact better with each other and reduce scapegoating.
Work together to develop a treatment termination plan.	Discuss termination issues and develop a plan to terminate treatment.

4
ANXIETY DISORDERS

ACUTE STRESS DISORDER—(308.3)

Acute Stress Disorder is marked by anxiety, dissociation, and other symptoms within one month after an extreme traumatic event. Symptoms include at least three of the following: a sense of numbing, detachment, lack of emotional responsiveness, a reduction in awareness of one's surroundings, derealization, depersonalization, or dissociative amnesia. The traumatic event is persistently reexperienced, and situations that may trigger a remembrance of the event are actively avoided. The disturbance lasts for at least two days and usually does not endure for more than four weeks. During that time, the disorder may significantly interfere with the individual's normal functioning. A diagnosis of Post-traumatic Stress Disorder requires a history of more than one month. If the symptoms of Acute Stress Disorder persist, a revised diagnosis should be considered.

Behavioral Symptoms
(severity index: 1–mild; 2–moderate; 3–intense)

		Severity
1.	Numbing or lack of emotion	_____
2.	Feels dazed or disconnected	_____
3.	Derealization or depersonalization	_____
4.	Inability to recall an important part of the traumatic event	_____
5.	Recurring images, thoughts, dreams, or flashbacks of the event	_____
6.	Distress at reminders of the event	_____

7. Avoids people, places and things associated
   with the event   _____
8. Sleep problems, anxiety, irritability, lack of
   concentration, restlessness, or exaggerated vigilance   _____
9. Major impairment of daily activities   _____

ACUTE STRESS DISORDER TREATMENT PLAN

Patient: _____ Date: _____

I. OBJECTIVES OF TREATMENT *(select one or more)*

1. Educate parents about the disorder
2. Investigate family history of the disorder
3. Help family develop better coping skills
4. Reduce anxiety related to the disorder
5. Reduce other symptoms: restlessness, sleep problems, irritability, poor concentration, or excessive vigilance
6. Encourage compliance with educational programs and referrals
7. Reduce irrational beliefs
8. Restore realization and personification
9. Promote socialization
10. Eliminate need for avoidance of people, places, or things reminiscent of the trauma
11. Reduce alienation
12. Restore to optimum level of functioning
13. Develop discharge plan for coping with everyday life

II. SHORT-TERM BEHAVIORAL GOALS AND INTERVENTIONS
(select goals and interventions appropriate for your patient)

NOTE: Separate goals and interventions are provided for Parents, Adolescent, and Family

PARENTS' GOALS	THERAPIST'S INTERVENTIONS
Collaborate with therapist in development of a treatment plan.	Establish therapeutic alliance with parents to enhance outcome of treatment.
Undergo treatment for individual problems, which, in turn, enhances the outcome of therapy.	Explore for parental psychopathology (e.g. anxiety disorder, marital discord etc.) and refer for treatment or treat (see appropriate treatment plan.)

PARENTS' GOALS	THERAPIST'S INTERVENTIONS
Undergo testing and evaluation for possible medication.	If appropriate, refer parents for psychological testing and psychiatric evaluation.
Become aware of maladaptive messages you are sending to your adolescent.	Identify how parents deal with stress or anxiety.
Develop awareness of how your personal theory influences cognition of the problem.	Explore parental theory of the problem.
Learn the laws of anxiety: anxiety is not dangerous or permanent; avoidance increases anxiety; confronting the problem can reduce anxiety; exposure can produce growth.	Teach parents the laws of anxiety.
Examine distortions in reaction to the traumatic event stressors.	Discuss reactions to identify exaggerations and distortions.
Replace exaggerated reactions with positive reactions using evidence-based reality.	Reframe negative reactions with positive, reality-based reactions.
Help your adolescent practice coping skills in real-life situations. Report reactions and reward successes.	Instruct parents on how to help the adolescent challenge persons, places, things, and activities related to the traumatic event and record reactions. Reward successes.
Learn to reach beyond automatic cognitive reactions in viewing the problem.	Expand parental perspective beyond limited cognitive reactions.
Agree to allow therapist to confer with your adolescent's school to help in development of a comprehensive psycho-treatment plan.	If appropriate, request and receive parental permission to confer with the adolescent's teachers and school officials.

PARENTS' GOALS	THERAPIST'S INTERVENTIONS
Attend self-help group to improve parenting skills.	Evaluate parenting skills and, if necessary, refer to parenting skills group (see Self-Help Groups and 800 Numbers, Chapter 18, and Online Resources, Chapter 19).
Read about and improve parenting skills.	Assign reading of *Positive Parenting From A to Z* or *Your Anxious Child* (see Bibliotherapy, Chapter 17).
Discuss a treatment termination plan and resolve termination issues.	Develop a treatment termination plan and discuss issues of separation and dependency.

ADOLESCENT'S GOALS	THERAPIST'S INTERVENTIONS
Enter non-threatening therapeutic interaction geared to appropriate development level.	Engage the adolescent in age-appropriate therapeutic relationship.
Learn about diagnosis and develop realistic expectations of self.	Educate the adolescent about the diagnosis and discuss symptomatology so he or she can adjust self-expectations.
Describe the event that triggered the stress reaction.	Investigate with adolescent his or her reaction to the traumatic event.
Identify sleep problems.	Explore for sleep problems.
Learn that you can control nightmares and other sleep problems.	If the adolescent has sleep problems, use technique called "Bad Dreams" (see Behavioral Techniques, Chapter 14).
Observe new ways to deal with anxieties.	Use role-playing to help adolescent work through problems (see "Role-playing," Behavioral Techniques, Chapter 14).
Practice in session new ways to deal with anxieties.	Discuss new ways to deal with anxiety.
Learn that it is okay to feel anxious and face it anyway.	Praise client for appropriate facing of anxiety.
Recognize underlying feelings of anger or depression and express appropriately.	Explore for underlying feelings of anger or depression and treat (see appropriate treatment plan).
Realize others also feel bad and overcome the feeling.	Investigate for feelings of low self-esteem related to Acute Stress Disorder. Talk about how it feels and what to do about it.

ADOLESCENT'S GOALS	THERAPIST'S INTERVENTIONS
Understand how you increase anxiety by distorting reality.	Instruct the adolescent to maintain an Automatic Thought Log to help understand his or her cognitive distortions (see Homework Assignments, Chapter 16).
Identify irrational beliefs.	Explore irrational beliefs.
Reframe beliefs about stress.	Develop rational alternatives.
Learn from role-modeling and shape new behaviors.	Role-play situations that create acute stress and role-model new solutions (see "Role-playing," Behavioral Techniques, Chapter 14).
Using guided imagery and relaxation techniques, learn to gain control over feelings.	Use guided imagery and relaxation techniques to gain mastery over anxieties (see "Relaxation," Behavioral Techniques, Chapter 14).
Learn new methods for dealing with stressors.	With parents' permission, teach the adolescent relaxation technique or self-hypnosis to help deal with stress (see "Relaxation," and "Hypnosis," Behavioral Techniques, Chapter 14).
Understand anxiety and realize that avoidance does not help.	Teach client the laws of anxiety: anxiety is not dangerous or permanent; avoidance increases anxiety; confronting the problem can reduce anxiety; exposure can produce growth.
Communicate your life story to therapist.	Have the adolescent relate the story of his or her life.

ADOLESCENT'S GOALS	THERAPIST'S INTERVENTIONS
Express suppressed feelings in a non-threatening environment.	Play *The Talking, Feeling, Doing Game* to understand underlying processes in a non-threatening way (see Therapeutic Games, Chapter 15).
Understand how trauma may have contributed to existing disorder.	Explore the adolescent's background for trauma that may have exacerbated acute stress.
Discuss personal coping mechanisms developed to handle anxieties.	With the adolescent, investigate possible patterns of withdrawal used to avoid anxiety.
Understand how you misinterpreted events.	Explore for misinterpretations of environmental events and correct.
Recognize and relate how family impacts the problem.	Explore familial impact on the problem.
Recognize the patterns of your disorder and the possibility of changing how you deal with it.	Discuss the patterns of the adolescent's Acute Stress Disorder and focus on solutions.
Learn positive self-talk.	Teach the adolescent positive self-talk to interrupt negative patterns.
Learn new technique for dealing with anxiety.	Teach diaphragmatic breathing to control anxiety (see "Relaxation," Behavioral Techniques, Chapter 14).
Learn new relaxation techniques.	Assign the adolescent to read *Ready...Set...R.E.L.A.X.* or alternative (see Bibliotherapy, Chapter 17).

ADOLESCENT'S GOALS	THERAPIST'S INTERVENTIONS
Read the assigned material and discuss new ways to deal with Acute Stress Disorder.	Assign the adolescent to read *The Anxiety and Phobia Workbook* and discuss with you (see Bibliotherapy, Chapter 17).
Read about ways to avoid and work through fears.	Assign reading of *Smart Guide to Relieving Stress* (see Bibliotherapy, Chapter 17).
Read about various techniques for getting a good night's sleep.	Assign the adolescent to read *All I Want is a Good Night's Sleep* (see Bibliotherapy, Chapter 17).
Adolescent learns how self-hypnosis and focusing on what you want rather than what you don't will help relieve stress.	Teach adolescent self-hypnosis to use between sessions to reduce anxiety. Develop methods to stay in the "here and now" rather than the past or the future.
Learn new techniques for dealing with emotional difficulties.	Play with the *Positive Attitude Ball* or the *Less Stress Ball* to reduce stress and build positive attitudes (see Therapeutic Games, Chapter 15).
Shift focus of attention from problem to accomplishment.	Ask the adolescent to describe his or her accomplishments of the past week.
Feel more confident as self-esteem improves.	Compliment the adolescent to provide positive reinforcement whenever possible.
Through relaxation techniques or hypnosis, learn new methods to reduce acute stress.	With parental permission, use relaxation techniques or hypnosis to help client reduce stress. Provide audiotape for home use (see Behavioral Techniques, Chapter 14).

ADOLESCENT'S GOALS	THERAPIST'S INTERVENTIONS
Report results to therapist.	Provide positive reinforcement when the adolescent reports back that he or she has developed new ways to handle stressors. Praise attempt and reward success.
Learn positive problem solving and how to turn fear and stress into power and action.	Assign to read *Feel the Fear and Do It Anyway* or *From Panic to Power* (see Bibliotherapy, Chapter 17).
Learn methods that can be used to advocate for yourself.	Instruct the adolescent in the techniques of self-advocacy.
Understand that you can deal with these issues and bring treatment to an end successfully.	Develop a treatment termination plan and explain issues of separation anxiety and dependency.

FAMILY'S GOALS	THERAPIST'S INTERVENTIONS
Improve communications among family members.	Conduct family sessions or refer for family therapy to reduce anxieties and/or alienation, and improve communication skills within the family.
Cooperate in amplifying family genogram.	Amplify family genogram created in early parental session to help understand ways family deals with anxiety.
Discuss genogram openly to fully understand family history as it relates to aggression and anxiety.	Discuss genogram to reveal family history and possible family secrets dealing with anxiety.
Demonstrate boundaries, alliances, triangles, and emotional currents that may exacerbate the problem.	Explore family boundaries using sculpturing, a useful technique for understanding triangulation, alliances, and emotional currents (see "Family Sculpturing," Behavioral Techniques, Chapter 14).
Shift focus from problem to possible solutions.	Have family imagine a future without the problem and suggest actions that can be taken now to make that future possible.
Think about what treatment outcome would look like. Explain what you would like to see change in other family members when treatment is completed.	Ask family members to think about what they might want to say about each other when treatment is completed.
Family realizes they have the power to make important changes even if they seem small.	Help family realize they have an opportunity to do some things differently.

FAMILY'S GOALS	THERAPIST'S INTERVENTIONS
Family members are empowered. They recognize that they can create positive change.	Ask family members to relate what they have accomplished in the past week.
Realize that major change is the result of small steps taken one at a time.	Help family identify and prioritize achievable goals.
Enhance understanding of condition and see how other families have handled similar problems.	Assign homework reading *Smart Guide to Relieving Stress*, *The Worry Control Workshop*, or *Do One Thing Different* to find new solutions (see Bibliotherapy, Chapter 17).
Make use of available community resources.	Refer family to available resources in the community (see Self-Help Groups and 800 Numbers, Chapter 18).
Family works together to develop a treatment termination plan.	Discuss termination issues and develop a plan to terminate treatment.
Review discharge plan with therapist. Understand that recovery is not only possible, but also expected.	Address the discharge plan, showing the adolescent that recovery is expected.
Read and understand book on acute stress and discuss with therapist.	Assign the adolescent to read recommended self-help book and discuss, (see *The Worry Control Workshop*, Bibliotherapy, Chapter 17).
Learn new methods to deal with stress and your body.	Assign the adolescent to use home audiotape to reduce anger and improve outlook (see or *Peaceful Body, Quiet Mind*, Bibliotherapy, Chapter 17).

FAMILY'S GOALS	THERAPIST'S INTERVENTIONS
Cooperate with homework assignments. Reduce irrational thinking	Provide homework assignments that reduce stress and challenge irrational cognitions (see Homework Assignments, Chapter 16).
Discuss and resolve treatment termination issues with therapist.	With the adolescent, explore treatment termination issues, separation anxiety, and dependence and resolve.

GENERALIZED ANXIETY DISORDER—(300.02)

Generalized Anxiety Disorder is characterized by excessive anxiety and worry about various events and activities over a six-month period. In adolescents, anxiety and worry must be accompanied by one additional symptom to qualify for this diagnosis. Symptoms include restlessness, irritability, tires easily, difficulty concentrating, muscle tension, or disturbed sleep. Usually, the duration or intensity of the anxiety or worry is out of proportion with the likelihood of the anticipated or feared event. Adolescents with this disorder tend to worry about their competence or quality of their performance in routine activities at school, sporting events, or at home. Concerns may focus on punctuality or catastrophic events like earthquakes or nuclear war. Clients may be insecure, overly conforming, and perfectionistic. They are often overanxious in seeking approval and require constant reassurance. Individuals with Generalized Anxiety Disorder frequently also suffer from major depression or other anxiety disorders. In addition, certain medical conditions can mimic Generalized Anxiety Disorder making differential diagnosis difficult.

Behavioral Symptoms
(severity index: 1–mild; 2–moderate; 3–intense)

To qualify for this diagnosis, patients must experience *excessive anxiety or worry more days than not for six months or more, PLUS one of the following:*

		Severity
1.	Feels restless	_____
2.	Fatigues easily	_____
3.	Has difficulty concentrating	_____
4.	Is often irritable	_____
5.	Displays muscular tension	_____
6.	Has difficulty getting to sleep and staying asleep	_____
7.	Complains about multiple physical problems	_____
8.	Symptoms impair adolescent's daily activities	_____

GENERALIZED ANXIETY DISORDER TREATMENT PLAN

Patient: _____   Date: _____

I. OBJECTIVES OF TREATMENT
(select one or more)

1. Educate parents about disorder
2. Investigate family history of the disorder
3. Help family develop better coping skills
4. Reduce pervasive anxiety and worry
5. Diminish symptoms of anxiety (i.e. restlessness, fatigue, difficulty concentrating, irritability, somatization, or sleep disturbance)
6. Encourage compliance with educational programs and referrals
7. Reduce irrational beliefs
8. Promote socialization
9. Reduce alienation
10. Restore adolescent and family to optimum level of functioning
11. Develop discharge plan for coping with everyday life

II. SHORT-TERM BEHAVIORAL GOALS AND INTERVENTIONS
(select goals and interventions appropriate for your patient)

NOTE: Separate goals and interventions are provided for Parents, Adolescent, and Family

PARENTS' GOALS	THERAPIST'S INTERVENTIONS
Parents collaborate with therapist in development of a treatment plan.	Establish therapeutic alliance with parents to enhance outcome of treatment.
Help therapist understand the development of the adolescent's anxiety problems.	Assess problem with parents and record a comprehensive history of the adolescent's development and anxiety problems.

PARENTS' GOALS	THERAPIST'S INTERVENTIONS
Become aware of the diagnosis and what to appropriately expect from their adolescent.	Educate parents about the diagnosis.
Cooperate in building a genogram to identify familial history and its relationship to anxiety problems.	Construct a genogram to better understand the family history and define how family deals with anxiety and its impact on the adolescent (see Behavioral Techniques, Chapter 14).
Enter treatment for Generalized Anxiety Disorder, if appropriate, to enhance outcome of your adolescent's therapy.	Evaluate parents for anxiety problems and treat or refer for treatment if appropriate.
Develop awareness of how your personal theory influences cognition of the problem in your adolescent.	Explore parental theory of the problem.
Recognize fears and feelings of negative self-blame related to the problem.	Evaluate parents' fears and negative feelings of self-blame for the adolescent's problem.
Learn to reach beyond automatic cognitive reactions in viewing the problem.	Expand parental perspective beyond limited cognitive reactions.
Parents learn to help their adolescent deal with stressors.	Teach parents the laws of anxiety: anxiety is not dangerous or permanent; avoidance increases anxiety; confronting the problem can reduce anxiety; exposure can produce growth.
Parents learn to deal with sleep disorder of their adolescent.	Investigate for sleep problems in the adolescent, and teach parents how to deal with problem.

PARENTS' GOALS	THERAPIST'S INTERVENTIONS
Confront thoughts of exaggerated and unrealistic consequences—"what ifs?"	Guide parents in confronting distorted reactions to trigger situations.
Identify cognitive distortions.	Weigh the reactions against evidence-based reality.
Restructure distortions with evidence- based consequences.	With parents, reframe distortions with reality-based reactions to stressors.
Learn diaphragmatic breathing as relaxation technique and teach their adolescent to help in relaxation.	Teach parents diaphragmatic breathing to assist the adolescent in relaxation (see Behavioral Techniques, Chapter 14).
Agree to allow therapist to confer with the adolescent's school to help in development of a comprehensive psycho-educational treatment plan.	Request and receive parental permission to confer with the adolescent's teachers and school administrators.
Comply with referral for medical and psychiatric evaluations.	Provide referral for medical and psychiatric evaluations if appropriate.
Parents develop new parenting skills.	Assign parents to read books on how to deal with their anxiety and increase parenting skills, such as *Making Families Work and What to Do When They Don't* and others (see Bibliotherapy, Chapter 17).
Monitor your adolescent's medication schedule and report all reactions or failures to take meds.	If adolescent is on meds, instruct parents on need for a regular schedule and feedback that may indicate need for revised dosage.

PARENTS' GOALS	THERAPIST'S INTERVENTIONS
Meet with other parents who are experiencing similar difficulties, and share solutions for coping with the problem.	Refer parents to self-help group or group on parenting skills (see Self-Help Groups and 800 Numbers, Chapter 18, and Online Resources, Chapter 19).
Read about anxiety disorders to better understand how to cope.	Assign books on anxiety disorders such as *Your Anxious Child* (see Bibliotherapy, Chapter 17).
Discuss a treatment termination plan and resolve related issues.	Develop a treatment termination plan and discuss issues of separation anxiety and dependency.

ADOLESCENT'S GOALS	THERAPIST'S INTERVENTIONS
Enter non-threatening therapeutic interaction geared to appropriate developmental age.	Engage the adolescent in an age-appropriate therapeutic relationship.
Learn about diagnosis and develop realistic expectations of self.	Educate the adolescent about the diagnosis and discuss symptomatology so he or she can adjust self-expectations.
Understand underlying dynamics which lead to maladaptive behavior and stress,	Explore ways in which anxieties manifest themselves (e.g. need for perfection, worry about nuclear war or catastrophe, over-conformance), and clarify underlying dynamics.
Realize that human beings are not perfect, and reduce stressors imposed on self.	Teach the adolescent that human beings are not perfect.
Recognize underlying feelings of anger or depression and express appropriately.	Explore for underlying feelings of anger or depression (see appropriate treatment plan).
Begin to see new role models deal with anxieties.	Shape the adolescent's behavior by role-playing new ways to deal with anxiety (see Behavioral Techniques, Chapter 14).
Learn acceptable expression of feelings.	Explore socially acceptable expression of feelings about anxieties.
Work out stressful events psychodramatically in a safe environment.	Role-play stressful events to help the adolescent handle fears successfully (see Behavioral Techniques, Chapter 14).

ADOLESCENT'S GOALS	THERAPIST'S INTERVENTIONS
Realize others also feel bad and overcome the feeling.	Investigate for feelings of low esteem related to anxiety.
Begin to see possible solutions.	Discuss how to deal with negative feelings.
Identify irrational beliefs.	Explore irrational beliefs about fears and anxieties.
Reframe beliefs about fears and anxieties.	Change irrational beliefs by exploring rational alternatives.
Learn from role modeling and shape new behaviors.	Role model appropriate behavior.
Using guided imagery and relaxation techniques to gain control over feelings.	Teach relaxation techniques and guided imagery to master anxieties (see "Relaxation," Behavioral Techniques, Chapter 14).
Understand anxiety and realize that avoidance does not help.	Teach the adolescent the laws of anxiety: anxiety is not dangerous or permanent; avoidance increases anxiety; confronting the problem can reduce anxiety; exposure can produce growth.
Communicate your life story to therapist.	Have the adolescent relate the story of his or her life.
Use immediate feedback to change ways of thinking.	Assign the adolescent to keep an Automatic Thought Log to challenge distorted cognitions and replace them with evidence-based reality (see Homework Assignments, Chapter 16).
Understand how trauma may have contributed to existing disorder.	Explore the adolescent's background for trauma that may have exacerbated the disorder.

ADOLESCENT'S GOALS	THERAPIST'S INTERVENTIONS
Discuss personal coping mechanisms developed to handle the disorder.	With the adolescent, investigate possible patterns of withdrawal used to avoid anxieties.
Recognize and relate how family impacts the problem.	Explore familial impact on the problem.
Learn positive self-talk.	Teach client positive self-talk to interrupt negative patterns.
Learn new technique for dealing with anxiety.	Teach diaphragmatic breathing to control anxiety (see Behavioral Techniques, Chapter 14).
Recognize that thoughts create feelings and identify ways to use positive thinking to replace negative feelings.	Use *The Talking, Feeling, Doing Game* or *The Ungame* to teach how positive self-talk can help control emotional difficulties (see Therapeutic Games, Chapter 15).
Shift focus of attention from problem to accomplishment.	Ask the adolescent to describe his or her accomplishments for the past week.
Feel more confident as self-esteem improves.	Compliment the adolescent to provide positive reinforcement whenever possible.
Communicate problematic feelings to develop new skills or options.	Recommend routine exercise to help the adolescent relieve anxiety.
Attempt to use new control skills in school.	Urge the adolescent to use new control skills in the classroom setting.

ADOLESCENT'S GOALS	THERAPIST'S INTERVENTIONS
Report results to therapist.	Provide positive reinforcement when the adolescent reports back that he or she has challenged anxiety-provoking situations. Praise attempt and reward success.
Read assigned book.	Assign to read *Smart Guide to Relieving Stress* or *The Worry Control Workshop* (see Bibliotherapy, Chapter 17).
Learn new strategies to control thoughts that contribute to unhealthy anxiety.	Assign to read *How to Control Your Anxiety Before It Controls You* (see Bibliotherapy, Chapter 17).
Learn methods that can be used to advocate for yourself.	Instruct the adolescent in the techniques of self-advocacy.
Understand that you can deal with these issues and bring treatment to an end successfully.	Develop a treatment termination plan and explain issues of separation anxiety and dependency.

FAMILY'S GOALS	THERAPIST'S INTERVENTIONS
Improve communications among family members to reduce familial anxiety.	Conduct family sessions or refer for family therapy to reduce anger and/or alienation, and improve communication skills.
Cooperate in amplifying parental genogram.	Amplify genogram created in first parental session to help understand family history.
Discuss genogram openly to fully understand family history as it relates to anxiety.	Discuss genogram to reveal family history and possible family secrets dealing with anxiety(see Behavioral Technique, Chapter 14).
Demonstrate boundaries, alliances, triangles, and emotional currents thatexacerbate the anxieties.	Explore family boundaries using sculpturing, a useful technique for understanding triangulation, alliances, and emotional currents (see Behavioral Techniques, Chapter 14).
Shift focus from problem to possible solution.	Have family imagine a future without the problem and suggest actions that can be taken now to make that future possible.
Think about what treatment outcome would look like. Explain what you would like to see change in other family members when treatment is completed.	Ask family members to think about what they might want to say about each other when treatment is completed.
Family member realizes they have the power to make important changes even if they seem small.	Help family realize they have an opportunity to do some things differently.

FAMILY'S GOALS	THERAPIST'S INTERVENTIONS
Family members are empowered. They recognize that they can create positive change.	Ask family members to relate what they have accomplished in the past week.
Realize that major change is the result of small steps taken one at a time.	Help family identify and prioritize achievable goals.
Enhance understanding of condition and see how other families have handled similar problems.	Assign homework reading *Making Families Work and What to Do When They Don't* (see Bibliotherapy, Chapter 17).
Make use of available community resources.	Refer family to available resources in the community. (see Self-Help Groups and 800 Numbers, Chapter 18, and Online Resources, Chapter 19).
Reduce negative communication.	Develop a system of positive reinforcement with family to interact better with each other and reduce scapegoating.
Family works together to develop a treatment termination plan.	Discuss termination issues and develop a plan to terminate treatment.

OBSESSIVE-COMPULSIVE DISORDER—(300.3)

Obsessive-Compulsive Disorder (OCD) is marked by persistent and time-consuming obsessions or compulsions that cause significant distress or impairment in everyday activities. Obsessions are inappropriate and intrusive (ego-dystonic) ideas, thoughts, impulses, and images that cause anxiety or distress. These may take the form of thoughts about contamination, repeated doubts, the need for a specific pattern of order, sexual imagery, or aggressive impulses. Compulsions are repetitive behaviors or mental acts designed to relieve anxiety or distress, or to prevent a dreaded event. Common compulsions including washing and cleaning, counting, checking, and other repeated actions. Most adults realize that the obsessions or compulsions are excessive and unrealistic. Although the disorder may begin in childhood, it is more common in adolescence or early adulthood, appearing earlier in males than in females.

Behavior Symptoms
(severity index: 1–mild; 2–moderate; 3–intense)

Severity

Obsessions
1. Intrusive, inappropriate thoughts, impulses, or images that cause anxiety or distress.   _____
2. The thoughts, impulses, or images are not just excessive worries about real-life problems.   _____
3. Wards off or suppresses these stimuli by ritualized thought or action   _____
4. The adolescent recognizes the stimuli as the products of his or her own mind.   _____

Compulsions
1. The adolescent is driven to act out repetitive physical or mental tasks to reduce or eliminate distress or to prevent a dreaded event   _____
2. The behavior is not connected in a realistic way with the event   _____
3. The adolescent recognizes that the obsessions or compulsions are excessive or unrealistic   _____
4. The obsessions and compulsions are time-consuming, cause distress, and interfere with the adolescent's daily activities   _____

OBSESSIVE-COMPULSIVE DISORDER TREATMENT PLAN

I. OBJECTIVES OF TREATMENT
(select one or more)

1. Educate parents about the disorder
2. Investigate family history of the disorder
3. Help family develop better coping skills
4. Reduce anxiety related to the disorder
5. Ameliorate obsessive thoughts, impulses, and images that cause anxiety or distress
6. Encourage compliance with educational programs and referrals
7. Reduce or eliminate the excessive and unrealistic compulsions that interfere with the adolescent's daily activities
8. Reduce irrational beliefs
9. Promote socialization
10. Reduce alienation
11. Restore the adolescent to optimal level of functioning
12. Develop discharge plan for coping with everyday life

II. SHORT-TERM BEHAVIORAL GOALS AND INTERVENTIONS
(select the goals and interventions that are appropriate for your patient)

NOTE: Separate goals and interventions are provided for Parents, Adolescent, and Family

PARENTS' GOALS	THERAPIST'S INTERVENTIONS
Parents collaborate with therapist in development of a treatment plan.	Establish therapeutic alliance with parents to enhance outcome of treatment.
Help therapist understand your adolescent's development and accurately assess problem.	Discuss problem with parents and record a comprehensive history of the adolescent's development in order to assess Obsessive-Compulsive Disorder.

PARENTS' GOALS	THERAPIST'S INTERVENTIONS
Become aware of the diagnosis and what to appropriately expect from your adolescent.	Educate parents about the diagnosis.
Cooperate in building a genogram to identify familial history and its relationship to the disorder.	Construct a genogram to better understand the family history and its impact on the client (see Behavioral Techniques, Chapter 14).
Develop awareness of how your personal theory influences cognition of the problem.	Explore parental theory of the problem.
Recognize fears and feelings of negative self-blame related to the problem.	Evaluate parents' fears and negative feelings of self-blame for the adolescent's problem.
Learn to reach beyond automatic cognitive reactions in viewing the problem.	Expand parental perspective beyond limited cognitive reactions.
Undergo treatment for underlying problems that may exacerbate your adolescent's condition.	Explore for underlying problems in parents, (e.g. anxiety, depression) and treat or refer for therapy.
Comply with referral.	If appropriate, refer parents for psychological evaluation.
Agree to allow therapist to confer with your adolescent's school to help in development of a comprehensive psycho-educational treatment plan.	If appropriate, after interviewing adolescent, and with his or her consent, request and receive parental permission to confer with the adolescent's teachers and school administrators.
Comply with referral for psychological testing of your adolescent.	Provide referral for psychological testing of the adolescent to determine intellectual capabilities and rule out other diagnostic considerations.

PARENTS' GOALS	THERAPIST'S INTERVENTIONS
Agree to psychiatric evaluation, if necessary, after the adolescent is interviewed.	Provide referral for psychiatric evaluation and possible medication if indicated.
Meet with other parents who are experiencing similar difficulties and share solutions for coping with the problem.	Refer parents to self-help group.
Read about Obsessive-Compulsive Disorder to help your adolescent develop coping strategies to foster healing.	Assign reading of *The OCD Workbook* or *Stop Obsessing: How to Overcome Your Obsessions and Compulsions* (see Bibliotherapy, Chapter 17).
Make use of community resources.	Educate parents about available community resources (see Self-Help Groups and 800 Numbers, Chapter 18, and Online Resources, Chapter 19).
Discuss and approve a treatment termination plan and resolve termination issues.	Develop a treatment termination plan and discuss issues of separation anxiety and dependency.

ADOLESCENT'S GOALS	THERAPIST'S INTERVENTIONS
Enter non-threatening therapeutic interaction geared to appropriate developmental age.	Engage the adolescent in an age-appropriate therapeutic relationship to enhance outcome of treatment.
Communicate the story of your life with therapist.	Have the adolescent relate the story of his or her life.
Learn about diagnosis and develop realistic expectations of self.	Educate the adolescent about the diagnosis and discuss symptomatology so he or she can understand the nature of Obsessive-Compulsive Disorder.
Identify automatic thoughts and behaviors.	Have the adolescent list his or her automatic thoughts and ritualized behaviors.
Evaluate automatic thoughts for cognitive distortions.	Point out cognitive distortions and ritualized actions.
Replace distorted thinking with evidence-based reality.	Reframe the distortions based on available evidence.
Identify ritualized actions you use to ward off anxiety.	Identify and monitor the adolescent's ritualized actions.
Understand anxiety and realize that avoidance does not help.	Teach the adolescent the laws of anxiety: anxiety is not dangerous or permanent; avoidance increases anxiety; confronting the problem can reduce anxiety; exposure can produce growth.
Psychodramatically work through the stressors that lead to OCD behavior.	Role-play stressful events that lead to ritualized actions to help the adolescent understand the underlying dynamics and explore more appropriate behaviors (see "Role-playing," Behavioral Techniques, Chapter 14).

ADOLESCENT'S GOALS	THERAPIST'S INTERVENTIONS
Learn that it is okay to express feelings.	Reward and/or praise the adolescent for expressing feelings appropriately.
Recognize underlying feelings of anger or depression and express appropriately.	Explore for underlying feelings of anger or depression and treat if necessary (see appropriate treatment plan).
Realize others also feel bad and overcome the feeling.	Investigate for feelings of low esteem related to Obsessive-Compulsive Disorder.
Begin to see possible solutions.	Discuss effective ways to deal with obsessions and compulsions.
Identify irrational beliefs.	Explore irrational beliefs about the disorder.
Reframe irrational thoughts and develop rational alternatives.	Discuss the irrational beliefs and develop rational alternatives.
Learn from role modeling and shape new behaviors.	Role model appropriate behavior.
Learn to identify irrational thoughts and reframe them with evidence-based reality.	Assign the "Challenging Cognitions Worksheet" combined with "Common Misconceptions in Obsessive-Compulsive Disorder" to help identify and reframe distortions (see Homework Assignments, Chapter 16).
Express suppressed feelings in a non-threatening environment.	Play *The Talking, Feeling, Doing Game* to understand underlying processes in a non-threatening way (see Therapeutic Games, Chapter 15).

ADOLESCENT'S GOALS	THERAPIST'S INTERVENTIONS
Understand how trauma may have contributed to existing disorder.	Explore the adolescent's background for trauma that may have exacerbated the disorder.
Discuss personal coping mechanisms developed to handle the disorder.	Investigate possible patterns of withdrawal used to avoid Obsessive-Compulsive Disorder with the adolescent.
Recognize and relate how family impacts the problem.	Explore familial impact on the problem.
Learn positive self-talk.	Teach the adolescent positive self-talk to interrupt obsessions/compulsions.
Learn new technique for dealing with aggression.	Teach diaphragmatic breathing to control anxiety (see Behavioral Techniques, Chapter 14).
Recognize that thinking affects feelings, and replace cognitive errors with positive thinking.	Use *The Talking, Feeling, Doing Game* to teach the adolescent how to identify negative feelings and replace them with positive thinking (see Therapeutic Games, Chapter 15).
Shift focus of attention from problem to accomplishment.	Ask the adolescent to describe his or her accomplishments for the past week.
Feel more confident as self-esteem improves.	Compliment the adolescent to provide positive reinforcement whenever possible.
Understand that regular aerobic exercise produces endorphins that naturally reduce stress.	Recommend routine exercise to help relieve stress.

ADOLESCENT'S GOALS	THERAPIST'S INTERVENTIONS
Attempt to use new control skills in school.	Urge the adolescent to use new control skills in the classroom setting.
Report results to therapist.	Provide positive reinforcement when the adolescent reports back that he or she has exercised control in school. Praise attempt and reward success.
Learn positive problem solving and how other people have overcome obstacles.	Assign the adolescent to read *The OCD Workbook* (see Bibliotherapy, Chapter 17).
Learn methods that can be used to advocate for yourself.	Instruct the adolescent in the techniques of self-advocacy.
Understand that you can deal with these issues and bring treatment to an end successfully.	Develop a treatment termination plan and explain issues of separation anxiety and dependency.

FAMILY'S GOALS	THERAPIST'S INTERVENTIONS
Improve communications among family members.	Conduct family sessions or refer for family therapy to reduce anger and/or alienation, and improve communication skills within the family.
Cooperate in amplifying family genogram.	Amplify family genogram created in parent and adolescent sessions to help understand family history (see Behavioral Techniques, Chapter 14).
Discuss genogram openly to fully understand family history as it relates to OCD.	Discuss genogram to reveal family history and possible family secrets dealing with OCD.
Demonstrate boundaries, alliances, triangles, and emotional currents that may exacerbate the problem.	Explore family boundaries using sculpturing, a useful technique for understanding triangulation, alliances, and emotional currents (see "Family Sculpturing," Behavioral Techniques, Chapter 14).
Shift focus from problem to possible solutions.	Have family imagine a future without the problem and suggest actions that can be taken now to make that future possible.
Think about what treatment outcome would look like. Explain what you would like to see change in other family members when treatment is completed.	Ask family members to think about what they might want to say about each other when treatment is completed.
Family members realize they have the power to make important changes even if they seem small.	Help family realize they have an opportunity to do some things differently.

FAMILY'S GOALS	THERAPIST'S INTERVENTIONS
Family members are empowered. They recognize that they can create positive change.	Ask family members to relate what they have accomplished in the past week.
Realize that major change is the result of small steps taken one at a time.	Help family identify and prioritize achievable goals.
Enhance understanding of condition and learn specific coping strategies to help the adolescent heal.	Assign homework reading *The Anxiety and Phobia Workbook* (see Bibliotherapy, Chapter 17).
Make use of available community resources.	Refer family to available resources in the community (see Self-Help Groups and 800 Numbers, Chapter 18, and Online Resources, Chapter 19).
Reduce negative communication.	Develop a system of positive reinforcement with family to interact better with each other and reduce scapegoating.
Family works together to develop a treatment termination plan.	Discuss termination issues and develop plan to terminate treatment.

POST-TRAUMATIC STRESS DISORDER—(309.81)

Specify: Acute: < 3 months
Chronic: > 3 months
Delayed onset: after 6 months

Post-traumatic Stress Disorder is characterized by development of typical stress symptoms following experience of an event that involves potentially severe personal injury or loss of life. Witnessing such a life-threatening event happening to another person, especially a close friend or relative, may also trigger the symptoms. The individual's response to the event includes intense fear, helplessness, or horror. In adolescents, the response may include disorganized or agitated behavior. Other symptoms include the persistent reexperience of the event, persistent avoidance of stimuli associated with the event, the numbing of general responsiveness (emotional anesthesia), or increased arousal. Traumatic events may include violent personal attack, physical or sexual attack, mugging, robbery, severe auto accidents, natural disasters, or being diagnosed with a life-threatening illness. In adolescents, traumatic events may include sexual experience that is developmentally inappropriate without threat of injury or death. The symptoms must persist for more than a month and cause significant distress or impairment in important areas of functioning. Studies show that children and adolescents whose parents do not overreact fare better in treatment.

Behavioral Symptoms
(severity index: 1–mild; 2–moderate; 3–intense)

                                                                    Severity

1. Persistently reexperiences the traumatic event as a recollection or dream _____
2. Has flashbacks of the event _____
3. Displays intense distress at cues which are reminiscent of the event _____
4. Avoids people, places, activities and thoughts associated with the event _____
5. Unable to remember an important aspect of the event _____
6. Interest in usual activities is diminished _____
7. Feels detached from others _____
8. Range of feelings is restricted _____
9. Has increased sense of limited future _____

10. Has problem falling asleep or maintaining sleep _____
11. Irritable, displays outbursts of anger _____
12. Unable to concentrate _____
13. Is easily startled _____

POST-TRAUMATIC STRESS DISORDER TREATMENT PLAN

Patient: _____   Date: _____

I. OBJECTIVES OF TREATMENT
(select one or more)

1. Educate parents about disorder
2. Investigate how family deals with anxiety
3. Reduce pervasive anxiety and worry
4. Help family develop better coping skills
5. Eliminate stressors associated with the traumatic event
6. Diminish symptoms associated with the event (i.e. restlessness, fatigue, difficulty concentrating, irritability, somatization, sleep disturbance)
7. Encourage compliance with educational programs and referrals
8. Reduce irrational beliefs
9. Promote socialization
10. Reduce alienation
11. Restore adolescent and family to level of functioning before the event

II. SHORT-TERM BEHAVIORAL GOALS AND INTERVENTIONS
(select the goals and interventions that are appropriate for your patient)

NOTE: Separate goals and interventions are provided for Parents, Adolescent, and Family

PARENTS' GOALS	THERAPIST'S INTERVENTIONS
Parents collaborate with therapist in development of a treatment plan.	Establish therapeutic alliance with parents to enhance outcome of treatment.
Relate in detail the traumatic event and your reactive feelings to it.	Investigate with parents the traumatic event and their feelings and reactions.
Help therapist understand your adolescent's development of anxiety related to the traumatic event.	Assess problem with parents and record a comprehensive history of the event.

PARENTS' GOALS	THERAPIST'S INTERVENTIONS
Describe your adolescent's flashbacks and their intensity.	Explore parents' perception of flashbacks in adolescent and assess intensity.
Become aware of the diagnosis and what to appropriately expect from the your adolescent.	Educate parents about Post-traumatic Stress Disorder.
Cooperate in building a genogram to identify familial history and its relationship to anxiety problems.	Construct a genogram to better understand the family history and define how family deals with anxiety and its impact on the adolescent (see Behavioral Techniques, Chapter 14).
Enter treatment to help you deal with your adolescent's trauma and enhance outcome of his or her therapy.	Evaluate parents for anxiety problems related to traumatic event and refer for treatment if appropriate.
Develop awareness of how your personal theory influences cognition of the problem in your adolescent.	Explore parental theory of the problem.
Recognize fears and feelings of negative self-blame related to the problem.	Evaluate parents' fears and negative feelings of self-blame for the adolescent's problem.
Learn to reach beyond automatic cognitive reactions in viewing the problem.	Expand parental perspective beyond limited cognitive reactions.
Learn how to help their adolescent deal with stressors.	Teach parents the laws of anxiety: anxiety is not dangerous or permanent; avoidance increases anxiety; confronting the problem can reduce anxiety; exposure can produce growth.

PARENTS' GOALS	THERAPIST'S INTERVENTIONS
Undergo treatment for individual problems, which, in turn, enhances outcome of your adolescent's therapy.	Explore for parental psychopathology (e.g. anxiety, depression, marital discord, etc.) and refer for treatment.
Parents learn to deal with their adolescent's sleep disorder.	Investigate for sleep problems in the adolescent, and teach parents how to deal with the problem.
Confront thoughts of exaggerated and unrealistic consequences.	Guide parents in confronting distorted reactions to trigger situations.
Identify cognitive distortions	Weigh the reactions against evidence-based reality.
Restructure distortions with evidence-based consequences	With parents, reframe distortions with reality-based reactions to stressors.
Learn diaphragmatic breathing as relaxation technique and teach your adolescent to help in relaxation.	Teach parents diaphragmatic breathing to assist the adolescent in relaxation (see Behavioral Techniques, Chapter 14).
Comply with referral for psychological testing of your adolescent.	Provide referral for psychological testing of the adolescent to estimate acute and chronic event-related stress such as Trauma Symptom Inventory (TSI) or Beck Anxiety Disorder (BAD).
Agree to allow therapist to confer with your adolescent's school to help in development of a comprehensive psychoeducational treatment plan.	If appropriate, after interviewing the adolescent, and with adolescent's permission, request and receive parental permission to confer with his or her teachers and school administrators.

PARENTS' GOALS	THERAPIST'S INTERVENTIONS
Comply with referral for medical and psychiatric evaluations.	Provide referral for medical and psychiatric evaluations if appropriate.
Parents read to learn alternative ways to cope with the problem.	Assign parents to read *I Can't Get Over It* or *Life After Trauma: A Workbook for Healing* (see Bibliotherapy, Chapter 17).
Develop new coping strategies.	Coach parents in developing new strategies for coping with their adolescent's problem.
Parents develop new parenting skills and understand how to deal with their adolescent's anxiety.	Assign parents to read books on how to deal with their anxiety and increase parenting skills, such as *Making Families Work and What to Do When They Don't* (see Bibliotherapy Chapter 17).
Monitor your adolescent's medication schedule and report all reactions or failures to take meds.	If the adolescent is on meds, instruct parents on need for a regular schedule and feedback that may indicate need for revised dosage.
Meet with other parents who are experiencing similar difficulties, and share solutions for coping with the problem.	Refer parents to self-help group or group on parenting skills (see Self-Help Groups and 800 Numbers, Chapter 18, and Online Resources, Chapter 19).
Discuss a treatment termination plan and resolve related issues.	Develop a treatment termination plan and discuss issues of separation anxiety and dependency.

ADOLESCENT'S GOALS	THERAPIST'S INTERVENTIONS
Engage in non-threatening therapeutic interaction and build alliance to enhance treatment outcome.	Engage the adolescent in a therapeutic alliance to enhance outcome of treatment.
Learn about diagnosis and develop realistic expectations of self.	Educate the adolescent about the diagnosis and discuss symptomatology so he or she can adjust self-expectations.
Cooperate in evaluation of Post-traumatic Stress Disorder	Refer for or administer to the adolescent the Trauma Symptom Checklist for Children (TSCC) for adolescents up to age 16, or the Trauma Symptom Inventory (TSI) to evaluate symptomatology in older adolescents.
Identify sleep problems and undergo treatment if necessary.	Investigate for sleep disorder and treat if necessary. See appropriate treatment plan.
Read about various techniques for getting a good night's sleep.	Assign the adolescent to read *All I Want is a Good Night's Sleep* (see Bibliotherapy, Chapter 17).
Learn that you can control nightmares and other sleep problems.	If the adolescent has sleep problems, use technique called "Bad Dreams" (see Behavioral Techniques, Chapter 14).
Learn new methods for dealing with flashbacks.	Explore for flashbacks of traumatic event and systematically desensitize using relaxation technique (see Behavioral Techniques, Chapter 14).

ADOLESCENT'S GOALS	THERAPIST'S INTERVENTIONS
Understand how traumatic event was misinterpreted.	Investigate possible misinterpretation of traumatic event.
Learn new coping strategies and solutions.	Develop new coping strategies or alternate solutions.
Recognize underlying feelings of anger or depression and express appropriately.	Explore for underlying feelings of anger or depression.
Recognize physical cues and use appropriate cognitive strategies to deal more effectively with anxiety.	Teach the adolescent to recognize physical signs of anxious arousal to use as cues, and train in cognitive strategies to avoid flashbacks or panic attacks.
Identify irrational beliefs.	Explore irrational beliefs.
Reframe beliefs about stress.	Develop rational alternatives.
Learn from rolemodeling and shape new behaviors.	Role-play situations that create stress and role model new solutions for dealing with them (see "Role-playing," Behavioral Techniques, Chapter 14).
Use guided imagery and relaxation technique to master anxiety.	Use guided imagery and relaxation technique to gain mastery over anxieties (see Behavioral Techniques, Chapter 14).
Learn new ways to handle stressors.	Teach the adolescent relaxation technique to help deal with stress (see Behavioral Techniques, Chapter 14).

ADOLESCENT'S GOALS	THERAPIST'S INTERVENTIONS
Understand anxiety and realize that avoidance does not help	Teach the adolescent the laws of anxiety: anxiety is not dangerous or permanent; avoidance increases anxiety; confronting the problem can reduce anxiety; exposure can produce growth.
Communicate life story to therapist.	Have the adolescent relate the story of his or her life.
Express suppressed feelings in a non-threatening environment.	Play *The Talking, Feeling, Doing Game* to understand underlying processes in a non-threatening way (see Therapeutic Games, Chapter 15).
Discuss personal coping mechanisms developed to handle anxiety.	Investigate with the adolescent possible patterns of withdrawal used to avoid anxiety.
Recognize and relate how family impacts the problem.	Explore familial impact on the problem.
Learn positive self-talk.	Teach the adolescent positive self-talk to interrupt negative patterns.
Learn new technique for dealing with anxiety.	Teach diaphragmatic breathing to control anxiety (see Behavioral Techniques, Chapter 14).
Learn new relaxation techniques	Assign the adolescent to read *Everything You Need to Know About Stress* (see Bibliotherapy, Chapter 17).
Read assigned material and discuss with therapist	Assign the adolescent to read *The Anxiety and Phobia Workbook* and discuss with you (see Bibliotherapy, Chapter 17).

ADOLESCENT'S GOALS	THERAPIST'S INTERVENTIONS
Read about ways to avoid and work through fears.	Assign reading of *The Worry Control Workbook* (see Bibliotherapy, Chapter 17).
Shift focus of attention from problem to accomplishment.	Ask the adolescent to describe his or her accomplishments of past week.
Feel more confident as self esteem improves.	Compliment the adolescent to provide positive reinforcement whenever possible.
Communicate problematic feelings to develop new skills or options.	Recommend strenuous physical exercise to help the adolescent release frustrations.
Attempt to use new behavioral skills in school setting.	Urge the adolescent to test new behavioral skills in school environment.
Report results to therapist.	Provide positive reinforcement when client reports back that he or she has challenged anxiety-provoking situations. Praise attempt and reward success.
Learn new coping skills to deal with the trauma.	Assign to read *Feel the Fear and Do It Anyway* or *From Panic to Power* (see Bibliotherapy, Chapter 17).
Learn methods that can be used to advocate for yourself.	Instruct the adolescent in the techniques of self-advocacy.
Understand that you can deal with these issues and bring termination to an end successfully.	Develop termination plan and explain issues of separation anxiety and dependency.

FAMILY'S GOALS	THERAPIST'S INTERVENTIONS
Improve communications among family members to reduce familial anxiety.	Conduct family sessions or refer for family therapy to reduce anxiety and improve communication skills within the family.
Family members share their feelings surrounding the trauma and their responses to it. Work together to deal with the issues. The adolescent is less alienated.	Have family members explain their personal view of the trauma and its impact on each one of them. If other siblings were involved, see individually or refer for treatment.
Cooperate in amplifying family genogram.	Amplify family genogram created in first family session to help understand family history (see Behavioral Techniques, Chapter 14).
Discuss genogram openly to fully understand family history as it relates to anxiety.	Discuss genogram to reveal family history and possible family secrets dealing with trauma and anxiety.
Demonstrate boundaries, alliances, triangles, and emotional currents that may exacerbate the anxieties.	Explore family boundaries using sculpturing, a useful technique for understanding triangulation, alliances, and emotional currents (see "Family Sculpturing," Behavioral Techniques, Chapter 14).
Shift focus from problem to possible solutions.	If possible, have family imagine a future without the problem and suggest actions that can be taken now to make that future possible.

FAMILY'S GOALS	THERAPIST'S INTERVENTIONS
Think about what treatment outcome would look like. Explain what you would like to see change in other family members when treatment is completed.	Ask family members to think about what they might want to say about each other when treatment is completed.
Family realizes they have the power to make important changes even if they seem small.	Help family realize they have an opportunity to do some things differently.
Family members are empowered. They recognize that they can create positive change.	Ask family members to relate what they have accomplished in the past week.
Realize that major change is the result of small steps taken one at a time.	Help family identify and prioritize achievable goals.
Enhance understanding of condition and see how other families have handled similar problems.	Assign homework reading *Making Families Work and What to Do When They Don't* (see Bibliotherapy, Chapter 17).
Make use of available community resources.	Refer family to available resources in the community. (see Self-Help Groups and 800 Numbers, Chapter 18, and Online Resources, Chapter 19).
Reduce negative communication.	Develop a system of positive reinforcement with family to interact better with each other and reduce scapegoating.
Family works together to develop a treatment termination plan.	Discuss termination issues and develop plan to terminate treatment.

SEPARATION ANXIETY DISORDER—(309.21)

Separation Anxiety Disorder involves excessive anxiety about being separated from home or a major attachment figure. The anxiety is beyond that considered appropriate for the adolescent's developmental level. It must occur before age 18 and persist for at least four weeks to meet the requirements for this diagnosis.

Adolescents with this disorder are often uncomfortable traveling by themselves away from home or other familiar areas, and may be reluctant or refuse to go to school or camp, visit or sleep at the house of a friend, or go on errands alone. These children may be unable to stay in a room by themselves and may display clinging behavior or shadow a parent around the house. Their refusal to attend school leads to major academic difficulties as well as social withdrawal.

They typically have difficulty at bedtime and their nightmares usually focus on fear of destruction of the family by catastrophe. If separation is imminent, physical complaints usually include headaches or nausea, palpitations, dizziness, or feeling faint. Children with this disorder may be demanding, intrusive, and in need of constant attention. Their demands may lead to parental frustration as well as resentment and conflict in the family.

This diagnosis should not be made if the anxiety occurs exclusively during the course of a Pervasive Development Disorder, Schizophrenia, or other Psychotic Disorder in children or is better accounted for by Panic Disorder with Agoraphobia in adolescents.

Behavioral Symptoms
(severity index: 1–mild; 2–moderate; 3–intense)

		Severity
1.	Excessive and inappropriate anxiety when separated from home or major attachment figures	_____
2.	Persistent fear of losing major attachment figures or of harm coming to them	_____
3.	Persistent worry that a catastrophic event will result in separation from attachment figure	_____
4.	Reluctance or refusal to leave home or go to school due to fear of separation	_____
5.	Fear of being alone	_____
6.	Fear of going to sleep without closeness of an attachment figure	_____
7.	Repeated nightmares focused on separation by catastrophe	_____

8. Somatization in anticipation of imminent separation _____
9. Symptoms persist for four weeks or more _____
10. Symptoms cause significant distress in academic and social functioning _____

SEPARATION ANXIETY DISORDER TREATMENT PLAN

Patient: _____   Date: _____

I. OBJECTIVES OF TREATMENT
(select one or more)

1. Educate parents about disorder
2. Determine family history of the disorder
3. Help family develop better coping skills
4. Reduce pervasive anxiety and worry
5. Diminish symptoms of anxiety
6. Encourage compliance with educational programs and referrals
7. Reduce irrational beliefs, fears of loss and catastrophe
8. Reduce fear of being alone, promote socialization
9. Encourage school attendance, reduce alienation
10. Eliminate nightmares, establish normal bedtime routine
11. Restore adolescent and family to optimum level of functioning
12. Develop discharge plan for coping with everyday life

II. SHORT-TERM BEHAVIORAL GOALS AND INTERVENTIONS
(select goals and interventions appropriate for your patient)

NOTE: Separate goals and interventions are provided for Parents, Adolescent, and Family

PARENTS' GOALS	THERAPIST'S INTERVENTIONS
Parents collaborate with therapist in development of a treatment plan.	Establish therapeutic alliance with parents to enhance outcome of treatment.
Help therapist understand the development of your adolescent's anxiety problems.	Assess problem with parents and record a comprehensive history of the adolescent's development and separation anxiety problems.
Become aware of the diagnosis and what to appropriately expect from your adolescent.	Educate parents about the diagnosis.

PARENTS' GOALS	THERAPIST'S INTERVENTIONS
Cooperate in building a genogram to identify familial history and its relationship to separation anxiety problems.	Construct a genogram to better understand the family history and define how family deals with separation anxiety and its impact on the adolescent (see Behavioral Techniques, Chapter 14).
Enter treatment for Anxiety Disorder, if appropriate, to enhance outcome of your adolescent's therapy.	Evaluate parents for anxiety and social phobia problems and treat or refer for treatment as appropriate.
Develop awareness of how your personal theory influences cognition of the problem in your adolescent.	Explore parental theory of the problem.
Recognize fears and feelings of negative self-blame related to the problem.	Evaluate parents' fears and negative feelings of self-blame for the adolescent's problem.
Learn to reach beyond automatic cognitive reactions in viewing the problem.	Expand parental perspective beyond limited cognitive reactions.
Learn how to help your adolescent deal with stressors.	Teach parents the laws of anxiety: anxiety is not dangerous or permanent; avoidance increases anxiety; confronting the problem can reduce anxiety; exposure can produce growth.
Learn to deal with your adolescent's sleep disorder.	Investigate for sleep problems in the adolescent and teach parents how to deal with it.
Confront thoughts of exaggerated and unrealistic consequence—"what ifs?"	Guide parents in confronting distorted reactions to trigger situations.

PARENTS' GOALS	THERAPIST'S INTERVENTIONS
Identify cognitive distortions.	Weigh the reactions against evidence-based reality.
Restructure distortions with evidence-based consequences.	With parents, reframe distortions with reality-based reactions to stressors.
Learn diaphragmatic breathing as relaxation technique and teach your adolescent to help in relaxation.	Teach parents diaphragmatic breathing to assist the adolescent in relaxation (see Behavioral Techniques, Chapter 14).
Comply with referral for psychological testing of your adolescent.	Provide referral for psychological testing of the adolescent to evaluate intellectual capabilities and rule out other diagnostic considerations.
Provide permission for therapist to confer with school officials.	After interviewing the adolescent, if appropriate, request and receive parental permission to confer with his or her teachers and school administrators.
Comply with referral or medical and psychiatric evaluations.	Provide referral for medical and psychiatric evaluations if appropriate.
Develop new parenting skills.	Assign parents to read books on how to deal with their anxiety and increase parenting skills, such as *Making Families Work and What to Do When They Don't* and others (see Bibliotherapy, Chapter 17).
Monitor your adolescent's medication schedule and report all reactions or failures to take meds.	If the adolescent is on meds, instruct parents on need for a regular schedule and feedback that may indicate need for revised dosage.

PARENTS' GOALS	THERAPIST'S INTERVENTIONS
Meet with other parents who are experiencing similar difficulties, and share solutions for coping with the problem.	Refer parents to self-help group or group on parenting skills.
Read about anxiety disorders to better understand how to cope.	Assign books on anxiety disorders such as *Your Anxious Child* (see Bibliotherapy, Chapter 17).
Discuss a treatment termination plan and resolve related issues.	Develop a treatment termination plan and discuss issues of separation anxiety and dependency.

ADOLESCENT'S GOALS	THERAPIST'S INTERVENTIONS
Engage in non-threatening therapeutic interaction geared to appropriate developmental age.	Engage adolescent in age-appropriate therapeutic relationship.
Learn about diagnosis and develop realistic expectations of self.	Educate the adolescent about the diagnosis and discuss symptomatology so he or she can adjust self-expectations.
Understand underlying dynamics that lead to maladaptive behavior and stress.	Explore ways in which anxieties manifest themselves (e.g. fear of leaving home, catastrophe, being "too good").
Recognize underlying feelings of anger or depression and express appropriately.	Explore for underlying feelings of anger or depression (see appropriate treatment plan).
Realize that human beings are not perfect and reduce stressors imposed on self.	Teach the adolescent that human beings are not perfect.
Begin to see new role models deal with anxieties.	Use role-playing to reshape the adolescent's behavior (see Behavioral Techniques, Chapter 14).
Learn new ways to handle fears.	Role model successful ways to deal with fears.
Develop new techniques to deal with your separation anxiety.	Explore the fears or anxieties and develop techniques to empower the adolescent.
Identify feelings of low self-esteem related to anxieties.	Investigate for feelings of low esteem related to anxiety.
Begin to see possible solutions.	Discuss how to deal with negative feelings.
Identify irrational beliefs.	Explore irrational beliefs about fears and anxieties.

ADOLESCENT'S GOALS	THERAPIST'S INTERVENTIONS
Develop a plan to reduce anxieties.	Develop a S.M.A.R.T. action plan—Small, Measurable, Achievable, Realistic, Timelined goals (see "Change," Behavioral Techniques, Chapter 14).
Learn from role modeling and shape new behaviors.	Role model appropriate behavior.
Using relaxation techniques and guided imagery learn to gain control over feelings.	Teach relaxation techniques to master anxieties (see "Relaxation," Behavioral Techniques, Chapter 14).
Understand anxiety and realize that avoidance does not help.	Teach the adolescent the laws of anxiety: anxiety is not dangerous or permanent; avoidance increases anxiety; confronting the problem can reduce anxiety; exposure can produce growth.
Communicate your life story to therapist.	Have the adolescent relate the story of his or her life or play *Life Stories* (see Therapeutic Games, Chapter 15).
Express suppressed feelings in a non-threatening environment.	Play *The Talking, Feeling, Doing" Game* to understand underlying processes in a non-threatening way (see Therapeutic Games, Chapter 15).
Understand how trauma may have contributed to the existing disorder.	Explore the adolescent's background for trauma that may have exacerbated the disorder.

ADOLESCENT'S GOALS	THERAPIST'S INTERVENTIONS
Discuss personal coping mechanisms developed to avoid anxieties and stay at home or with parents.	Investigate with the adolescent possible patterns of withdrawal used to avoid anxieties and stay with his or her parents.
Recognize and relate how family impacts the problem.	Explore familial impact on the problem.
Somatization problems are treated.	Explore for somatization problems and treat (see appropriate treatment plan).
Learn positive self-talk.	Teach the adolescent positive self-talk to interrupt negative patterns.
Learn new technique for dealing with anxiety.	Teach diaphragmatic breathing to control anxiety (see Behavioral Techniques, Chapter 14).
Learn personal life skills such as insight, sense of humor, and persistence to better cope with problems.	Have the adolescent play *Bounce-Back* to develop resiliency (see Therapeutic Games, Chapter 15).
Shift focus of attention from problem to accomplishment.	Ask the adolescent to describe accomplishments for the past week.
Feel more confident as self-esteem improves.	Compliment the adolescent to provide positive reinforcement whenever possible.
Use exercise to deal with frustrations.	Show the adolescent that routine exercise helps release frustrations.
Report results to therapist.	Provide positive reinforcement when the adolescent reports back that he or she has challenged anxiety-provoking situations. Praise attempt and reward success.

ADOLESCENT'S GOALS	THERAPIST'S INTERVENTIONS
Learn techniques for turning fear into power.	Assign to read *Feel the Fear and Do It Anyway* (see Bibliotherapy, Chapter 17).
Learn ways to calm and conquer fears to get control of your life.	Assign to read *From Panic to Power* (see Bibliotherapy, Chapter 17).
Learn methods that can be used to advocate for yourself.	Instruct the adolescent in the techniques of self-advocacy.
Understand that you can deal with these issues and bring treatment to an end successfully.	Develop a treatment termination plan and explain issues of separation anxiety and dependency.

FAMILY'S GOALS	THERAPIST'S INTERVENTIONS
Improve communications among family members to reduce familial anxiety.	Conduct family sessions or refer for family therapy to reduce anger and/or alienation, and improve communication skills within the family.
Cooperate in amplifying family genogram.	Amplify family genogram created in first family session to help understand family history (see Behavioral Techniques, Chapter 14).
Discuss genogram openly to fully understand family history as it relates to anxiety.	Discuss genogram to reveal family history and possible family secrets dealing with anxiety.
Demonstrate boundaries, alliances, triangles, and emotional currents that may exacerbate the anxieties.	Explore family boundaries using sculpturing, a useful technique for understanding triangulation, alliances, and emotional currents (see "Family Sculpturing," Behavioral Techniques, Chapter 14).
Shift focus from problem to possible solutions.	Have family members imagine a future without the problem and suggest actions that can be taken now to make that future possible.
Think about what treatment outcome would look like. Explain what you would like to see change in other family members when treatment is completed.	Ask family members to think about what they might want to say about each other when treatment is completed.
Family members are empowered. They recognize that they can create positive change.	Ask family members to relate what they have accomplished in the past week.

FAMILY'S GOALS	THERAPIST'S INTERVENTIONS
Realize that major change is the result of small steps taken one at a time.	Help family identify and prioritize achievable goals.
Enhance understanding of condition and see how other families have handled similar problems.	Assign homework reading *Making Families Work and What to Do When They Don't* (see Bibliotherapy, Chapter 17).
Make use of available community resources.	Refer family to available resources in the community (see Self-Help Groups and 800 Numbers, Chapter 18, and Online Resources, Chapter 19).
Family works together to develop a treatment termination plan.	Discuss termination issues and develop a plan to terminate treatment.

SOCIAL PHOBIA—(300.23)

Social Phobia is marked by a persistent fear of social situations where evaluation by others is possible. The individual is afraid of acting in an embarrassing or humiliating manner, and often reacts to social interaction with panic attack. Usually, the individual recognizes the fear as excessive and unreasonable. Typically, the onset of this disorder is in the mid-teens after a childhood of shyness.

Children appear as excessively timid in unfamiliar settings and shrink away from contact with people they do not know. In extreme cases, mutism may be present. They typically do not participate in group play or other social activities, and cling to, or need to remain close to, a familiar adult. There must be evidence of the child's capacity to interact with familiar people and failure to interact in peer settings or with unfamiliar adults. Children with Social Phobia usually do poorly in school, may be school phobic, and avoid age-appropriate social activities.

When onset is in adolescence, social phobia leads to decreased ability to function academically. Despite contrary evidence in some clinical samples, the disorder is more prevalent in girls than in boys.

Behavioral Symptoms
(severity index: 1–mild; 2–moderate; 3–intense)

		Severity
1.	Persistent fear of social interactions where evaluation by others is possible	_____
2.	Fear of acting in social situations in an embarrassing or humiliating way	_____
3.	Exposure to social situations leads to panic attacks	_____
4.	Individual recognizes the fears as excessive and unreasonable	_____
5.	Feared social situations are avoided or endured under duress	_____
6.	The fear and duress interfere with the adolescent's activities of daily living	_____
7.	The fear or avoidance is not the result of drugs, medication, or a general medical condition	_____

NOTE: Behavioral symptoms for related panic attack and agoraphobia are listed below. These symptoms may occur with Social Phobia and other disorders, but are not DSM codable in themselves.

Panic Attack Symptoms

Panic attacks are characterized by intense fear in which four of the following develop quickly and increase to peak intensity within minutes:

1. Palpitations, pounding heart, increased pulse rate
2. Perspiration
3. Trembling, shaking
4. Feeling of choking or smothering
5. Chest pain
6. Nausea, dizziness
7. Derealization, depersonalization
8. Fear of losing control, going crazy, or dying
9. Numbness or tingling
10. Chills or hot flashes

Agoraphobia Symptoms

1. Anxiety of being in a situation or place where escape may be difficult or impossible
2. Anxiety over being in a place where a panic attack would be embarrassing
3. Anxiety over being in a place where help may not be available in case of a panic attack
4. The situation or place is avoided or endured with duress
5. The situation or place is endured with the help of a friend or companion

SOCIAL PHOBIA
TREATMENT PLAN

Patient: _____ Date: _____

I. OBJECTIVES OF TREATMENT *(select one or more)*

1. Educate parents about the disorder
2. Determine family history of the disorder
3. Help family develop better coping skills
4. Reduce pervasive anxiety and worry
5. Diminish symptoms of shyness
6. Diminish fear of social situations
7. Eliminate school phobia
8. Reduce and eliminate fear of embarrassment in social interactions
9. Control and eliminate panic attacks
10. Eliminate need for avoidance of social interactions
11. Encourage compliance with educational programs and referrals
12. Reduce irrational beliefs
13. Promote socialization
14. Reduce alienation
15. Restore the adolescent and family to optimum level of functioning
16. Develop discharge plan for coping with everyday life

II. SHORT-TERM BEHAVIORAL GOALS AND INTERVENTIONS
(select goals and interventions appropriate for your patient)

NOTE: Separate goals and interventions are provided for Parents, Adolescent, and Family

PARENTS' GOALS	THERAPIST'S INTERVENTIONS
Collaborate with therapist in development of a treatment plan.	Establish therapeutic alliance with parents to enhance outcome of the adolescent's treatment.

PARENTS' GOALS	THERAPIST'S INTERVENTIONS
Help therapist understand the development of your adolescent's anxiety problems.	Assess problem with parents and record a comprehensive history of the adolescent's development of excessive shyness or social phobias.
Become aware of the diagnosis and what to appropriately expect of your adolescent.	Educate parents about the diagnosis.
Cooperate in building a genogram to identify family history and its relationship to social phobias.	Construct a genogram to better understand the family history of social phobia or excessive shyness, and the methods the family has used to deal with it (see Behavioral Techniques, Chapter 14).
Enter treatment for anxiety or social phobias to support your adolescent's therapy.	Evaluate parents for anxiety problems or social phobia and refer for treatment.
Develop awareness of how your personal theory influences cognition of the problem in your adolescent.	Explore parental history of the problem.
Recognize situational triggers for your adolescent's avoidance behavior.	Have parents identify situational triggers for social avoidance behavior.
Recognize fears and self-blame related to the problem.	Evaluate parents' fears and negative feelings of self-blame for the adolescent's problem.
Learn to reach beyond automatic cognitive reactions in viewing the problem.	Expand parental perspective beyond cognitive reactions.

PARENTS' GOALS	THERAPIST'S INTERVENTIONS
Learn how to help your adolescent deal with stressors.	Teach parents the laws of anxiety: anxiety is not dangerous or permanent; avoidance increases anxiety; confronting the problem can reduce anxiety; exposure can produce growth.
Learn how to empower your adolescent rather than provide secondary gains for avoidance behavior.	Help parents realize and teach the adolescent that most people are afraid of something, but each time they face their fear they become stronger. Avoidance weakens.
Learn how to deal with your adolescent's sleep problems.	Investigate for sleep problems in adolescent and teach parents how to deal with them (see appropriate treatment plan).
Confront thoughts of exaggerated or unrealistic expectations in social situations.	Guide parents in confronting distorted reactions to social situations.
Identify cognitive distortions.	Weigh the reactions against evidence-based reality.
Restructure distortions with evidence-based consequences.	With parents, reframe distortions with reality-based reactions to stressors.
Learn diaphragmatic breathing and help your adolescent use this as a relaxation technique.	Teach parents diaphragmatic breathing to assist child in relaxation (see Behavioral Techniques, Chapter 14).
Agree to allow therapist to confer with school officials to help in development of a comprehensive psycho-educational program for your adolescent.	Get parental permission to confer with school officials.

PARENTS' GOALS	THERAPIST'S INTERVENTIONS
Comply with referrals for medical and psychiatric evaluation.	Provide referral for medical and psychiatric evaluations if appropriate.
Read assigned book to learn new coping skills.	Assign parents to read *Feel the Fear and Do It Anyway* or *The Worry Control Workshop* (see Bibliotherapy, Chapter 17).
Develop new parenting skills.	Assign parents to read *Making Families Work and What to Do When They Don't* or alternate to increase their parenting skills (see Bibliotherapy, Chapter 17).
Monitor your adolescent's medication schedule and report all reactions and failures to take meds.	If the adolescent is on medication, instruct parents on need for a regular schedule and feedback that might indicate a need for dosage adjustment.
Meet with other parents who are experiencing similar difficulties and share solutions for coping with the problem.	Refer parents to self-help group or group on parenting skills.
Read about anxiety disorders and further enhance your coping skills.	Assign parents to read *Your Anxious Child* (see Bibliotherapy, Chapter 17).
Discuss a treatment termination plan and resolve related issues.	Develop a treatment termination plan and discuss issues of separation anxiety and dependency.

ADOLESCENT'S GOALS	THERAPIST'S INTERVENTIONS
Enter non-threatening therapeutic interaction geared to appropriate developmental age.	Engage the adolescent in an age-appropriate therapeutic relationship.
Agree on treatment plan and problems to be addressed.	Develop a treatment plan and select target problems to work on.
Learn the symptoms and nature of Social Phobia.	Instruct the adolescent on the nature of Social Phobia.
Understand underlying dynamics that lead to Social Phobia.	Explore ways in which Social Phobia manifests itself.
Cooperate in building genogram and identify patterns of interaction.	Construct genogram to better understand family interrelationships.
Recognize Social Phobia history and how the family has dealt with social anxieties.	Investigate history of Social Phobia with the adolescent.
Become aware of situational triggers and avoidance behavior.	Identify situational triggers for phobia and resulting avoidance behavior.
Follow through with referral and maintain medication regimen if prescribed.	If appropriate, refer for psychiatric evaluation and possible medication. Rule out drug abuse.
Understand nature of anxiety.	Teach the adolescent the nature of anxiety: anxiety is not dangerous or permanent; avoidance increases anxiety; confronting the problem can reduce anxiety; exposure can produce growth.
Understand that anxiety is diminished by confrontation and increased by avoidance.	Instruct the adolescent to confront first signs of anxiety rather than run from them.

ADOLESCENT'S GOALS	THERAPIST'S INTERVENTIONS
Learn new technique to help control anxiety.	Teach the adolescent diaphragmatic breathing to help in relaxation (see Behavioral Techniques, Chapter 14).
Keep a daily journal to record feelings and reactions in different social situations.	Urge the adolescent to start and maintain a daily journal to record feelings and reactions in social situations.
Complete homework as assigned.	Assign homework in which the adolescent can identify irrational beliefs and negative consequences (see Homework Assignments, Chapter 16).
Identify irrational or exaggerated beliefs.	Discuss homework with the adolescent.
Examine beliefs for negative consequences and reframe.	Help the adolescent examine irrational and exaggerated beliefs and reframe them for positive consequences.
Realize that human beings are not perfect, and reduce stressors imposed on yourself.	Teach the adolescent that human beings are not perfect.
Recognize underlying feelings of anger or depression and express appropriately.	Probe for underlying feelings of anger or depression and treat (see appropriate treatment plan).
Adjust performance requirements from "perfect" to "good enough."	Help the adolescent to lower self-expectations.
Learn to focus on the task, not the audience.	Instruct the adolescent to ignore the audience in social situations and concentrate on the task at hand.

ADOLESCENT'S GOALS	THERAPIST'S INTERVENTIONS
Explore issues of shame, rejection, and abandonment as they may impact phobia.	Investigate history of shame, rejection, and abandonment that may foster phobias.
Replace destructive negative self-talk with positive self-affirmations.	Instruct the adolescent to recognize negative self-talk and replace it with positive self-talk.
Build and practice assertiveness skills	Explain principles of assertiveness – equal respect for self and other.
Use hypnosis to confront phobias and eliminate avoidance behaviors.	With parental permission, teach the adolescent self-hypnosis to cope with phobias. Provide audiotape for home use (see Behavioral Techniques, Chapter 14).
Challenge real social situations that were formerly troublesome, and provide feedback on feelings and reactions.	Have the adolescent gradually increase exposure to real-life social situations and provide feedback on reactions.
Practice anxiety control psychodramatically.	Conduct role-playing exercises that focus on phobias. Desensitize the adolescent to fearful social situations (see Behavioral Techniques, Chapter 14).
Overcome fears of certain places and situations, develop and expand confidence.	Urge the adolescent to externalize his or her role-playing skills and challenge fears of certain places and situations.
Learn new ways to handle fears.	Role model successful ways to deal with fears.
Realize that others also feel bad and overcome that feeling.	Investigate for feelings of low self-esteem related to anxiety.

ADOLESCENT'S GOALS	THERAPIST'S INTERVENTIONS
Begin to see possible solutions.	Discuss how to deal with negative feelings.
Communicate your life story to therapist.	Have the adolescent relate the story of his or her life.
Express suppressed feelings in a non-threatening environment.	Play *The Talking, Feeling, Doing Game* to understand underlying processes in a non-threatening way (see Therapeutic Games, Chapter 15).
Understand how trauma may have contributed to existing disorder.	Explore the adolescent's background for trauma that may have caused or contributed to the disorder.
Discuss personal coping mechanisms developed to handle the disorder.	Investigate with the adolescent possible patterns of withdrawal used to avoid anxieties.
Recognize and relate how family impacts the problem.	Explore familial impact on the problem.
Learn life skills such as insight, sense of humor, and resiliency to increase your ability to cope with problems	Use the *Bounce-Back* game to teach the adolescent specific resiliency skills (see Therapeutic Games, Chapter 15).
Shift focus of attention from problems to accomplishments.	Ask the adolescent to describe his or her accomplishments of the past week.
Feel more confident as self-esteem improves.	Compliment the adolescent whenever possible to provide positive reinforcement.
Use exercise to relieve tension.	Recommend routine exercise to help relieve tensions.

ADOLESCENT'S GOALS	THERAPIST'S INTERVENTIONS
Attempt to use new control skills in school.	Urge the adolescent to use new control skills in classroom setting.
Report results to therapist.	Provide positive reinforcement when he or she reports challenging anxiety-provoking situation. Praise attempt, reward success.
Read assigned book to learn new survival skills.	Assign the adolescent to read *The Teenage Survival Book* (see Bibliotherapy, Chapter 17).
Learn new strategy for moving from pain to power.	Assign the adolescent to read *Feel the Fear and Do It Anyway* or alternate (see Bibliotherapy, Chapter 17).
Learn methods that can be used to advocate for yourself.	Instruct the adolescent in technique of self-advocacy.
Understand you can deal with theses issues and bring therapy to an end successfully.	Develop a treatment termination plan and resolve problems of dependency and separation anxiety.

FAMILY'S GOALS	THERAPIST'S INTERVENTIONS
Improve communication among family members to reduce familial anxiety.	Conduct family sessions or refer for family therapy to reduce anger and/or alienation, and improve communication.
Cooperate in amplifying existing genogram.	Expand genogram created in parental session to determine personal views and understand family history of phobia.
Demonstrate family boundaries, alliances, triangles, and emotional currents that may exacerbate Social Phobia.	Using family sculpturing, explore family boundaries (see Behavioral Techniques, Chapter 14).
Identify secondary gains generated by the disorder.	Explore for secondary gains within family that reinforce the disorder.
Identify situational triggers.	Identify situational triggers that may cause episodes of Social Phobia.
Family clarifies feelings of shame or guilt.	Investigate familial feelings of shame or guilt over Social Phobia.
Negative hidden messages are exposed and reduced.	Explore for hidden messages family uses to create further problems for the adolescent.
Realize you have the power to make important changes even if they seem small.	Have family members realize they have an opportunity to do some things differently.
Think about what treatment outcome would look like. Explain what you would like to see change in other family members.	Ask family members what they want to say about each other when treatment is complete.

FAMILY'S GOALS	THERAPIST'S INTERVENTIONS
Imagine future without the problem.	Have family members imagine a future without the problem or with the problem controlled. Suggest actions that can be taken now to make that future possible.
Realize you can create positive change.	Empower family members to create positive change.
Realize that major change is the result of many small steps taken one at a time.	Help family identify and prioritize achievable goals.
Enhance understanding of Social Phobia and see how other families have handled similar problems.	Assign homework reading for family members *Making Families Work and What to Do When They Don't* (see Bibliotherapy, Chapter 17).
Make use of available community resources.	Refer family to available resources in the community (see Self-Help Groups and 800 Numbers, Chapter 18 and Online Resources, Chapter 19).
Reduce negative communication.	Develop system of positive reinforcement within family to improve interaction.
Work together to develop and implement a treatment termination plan.	Discuss termination issues and develop a viable plan to end treatment.

SPECIFIC PHOBIA—(300.29)

Specify:

Animal: cued by inserts or animals, usually begins in early childhood.

Natural Environment: cued by environment elements (i.e. hurricanes, storms, floods etc.), usually begins in childhood.

Blood Injection: cued by blood and injury, highly familial.

Situational: cued by specific situations (i.e. public transportation, tunnels, bridges, elevators etc.) highly familial and bimodal, onset in early childhood to mid-20s.

Other: cued by fear or avoidance of situations that might lead to choking, vomiting or contracting an illness, "space" phobia, and childhood fears of loud noises or costumed characters.

Specific Phobia involves the persistent, excessive, and unreasonable fear of objects or situations that provoke an immediate anxiety response characterized as a panic attack. In children, the anxiety may be expressed by crying, tantrums, freezing, or clinging. Fear of animals is common and usually transitory. Although adults and older adolescents may realize that the fear is excessive or unreasonable, younger adolescents clearly may not. Usually, the object or situation is avoided, but sometimes may be endured under duress. For children under 18 years of age, the situation must persist for more than six months to qualify for the diagnosis of Specific Phobia. The phobia must significantly interfere with the individual's daily scholastic or social activities. There are several types of Specific Phobia that should be specified with the diagnosis, including Animal, Natural Environment, Blood-Injection, Injury, Situational, and Other. Such fears are common in adolescents, but the level of impairment is usually insufficient to warrant a diagnosis.

Behavioral Symptoms
(severity index: 1–mild; 2–moderate; 3–intense)

		Severity
1.	Excessive and unreasonable fear of an object or situation	_____
2.	Immediate anxiety upon exposure to object or situation	_____
3.	Excessively clingy	_____
4.	Throws tantrums or cries a great deal	_____
5.	Freezes	_____
6.	Fails to recognize unreasonable nature of fear	_____
7.	The object or situational trigger is avoided or endured	_____
8.	The avoidance or distress significantly interferes with the adolescent's daily life	_____

NOTE: Agoraphobia and Panic Attack occur with several other disorders, but are not codable disorders in themselves. Behavioral symptoms for both of these conditions are included above under Social Phobia.

SPECIFIC PHOBIA TREATMENT PLAN

Patient: _____ Date _____

I. OBJECTIVES OF TREATMENT *(select one or more)*

1. Educate parents about the disorder
2. Determine family history of the disorder
3. Help family develop better coping skills
4. Reduce pervasive anxiety and worry
5. Diminish excessive fear of object or situation
6. Decrease anxiety when exposed to object or situation
7. Eliminate need to avoid or endure object or situation
8. Eliminate interference with activities of daily living
9. Encourage compliance with educational programs and referrals
10. Reduce irrational beliefs
11. Promote socialization and reduce alienation
12. Restore the adolescent to optimum level of functioning
13. Develop discharge plan for coping with everyday life

II. SHORT-TERM BEHAVIORAL GOALS AND INTERVENTIONS
(select goals and interventions appropriate for your patient)

NOTE: Separate goals and interventions are provided for the treatment of Parents, Adolescent, and Family

PARENTS' GOALS	THERAPIST'S INTERVENTIONS
Parents collaborate with therapist in development of a treatment plan.	Establish therapeutic alliance with parents to enhance outcome of treatment.
Help therapist understand development of your adolescent's specific phobia.	Assess problem with parents, identify specific phobia, and record a comprehensive history of the adolescent's disorder.
Explore and understand origin of your adolescent's fears.	Explore with parents the original source of fear in the adolescent.

PARENTS' GOALS	THERAPIST'S INTERVENTIONS
Cooperate in building a genogram to identify familial history and its relationship to phobias.	Construct a genogram to better understand the family history of phobias and define how family deals with them and their impact on the adolescent (see Behavioral Techniques, Chapter 14).
Reduce severity of fear.	Examine with parents both their fears and the adolescent's fears, and look at related reality issues.
Enter treatment for phobias or anxiety if appropriate to enhance outcome of your adolescent's therapy.	Evaluate parents for phobia or anxiety problems and treat or refer for treatment as appropriate.
Develop awareness of how your personal theory influences cognition of the problem in your adolescent.	Explore parental theory of the problem.
Recognize fears and feelings of negative self-blame related to the problem.	Evaluate parents' fears and negative feelings of self-blame for the adolescent's problem.
Learn to reach beyond automatic cognitive reactions in viewing the problem.	Expand parental perspective beyond limited cognitive reactions.
Learn how to help your adolescent deal with stressors.	Teach parents the laws of anxiety: anxiety is not dangerous or permanent; avoidance increases anxiety; confronting the problem can reduce anxiety; exposure can produce growth.
Identify cognitive distortions	Weigh the reactions against evidence-based reality.

PARENTS' GOALS	THERAPIST'S INTERVENTIONS
Restructure distortions with evidence- based consequences	With parents, reframe distortions with reality-based reactions to stressors.
Learn diaphragmatic breathing as a relaxation technique and teach your adolescent to help in relaxation.	Teach parents diaphragmatic breathing to assist the adolescent in relaxation (see Behavioral Techniques, Chapter 14).
Comply with referral for psychological testing of your adolescent.	After interviewing the adolescent and, if appropriate, provide referral for psychological testing to evaluate intellectual capabilities and rule out other diagnostic considerations.
Agree to allow therapist to confer with your adolescent's school to help in development of a comprehensive psycho-educational treatment plan.	After interviewing the adolescent, request and receive parental permission to confer with teachers and school administrators.
Comply with referral for medical and psychiatric evaluations.	Provide referral for medical and psychiatric evaluations if appropriate.
Parents develop new parenting skills.	Assign parents to read books on how to deal with their anxiety and increase parenting skills, such as *Making Families Work and What to Do When They Don't*, and *Mastering Your Special Phobia* and other selections (see Bibliotherapy, Chapter 17).
Monitor your adolescent's medication schedule and report all reactions or failures to take meds.	If the adolescent is on meds, instruct parents on need for a regular schedule and feedback that may indicate need for revised dosage.

PARENTS' GOALS	THERAPIST'S INTERVENTIONS
Meet with other parents who are experiencing similar difficulties, and share solutions for coping with the problem.	Refer parents to self-help group or group on parenting skills.
Read about anxiety disorders to better understand how to cope.	Assign books on anxiety disorders such as *Your Anxious Child* (see Bibliotherapy, Chapter 17).
Discuss a treatment termination plan and resolve related issues.	Develop a treatment termination plan and discuss issues of separation anxiety and dependency.

ADOLESCENT'S GOALS	THERAPIST'S INTERVENTIONS
Enter non-threatening therapeutic interaction geared to appropriate developmental age.	Engage the adolescent in an age-appropriate therapeutic relationship.
Understand cues that trigger phobias.	Explore ways in which phobias manifest themselves (e. g., cued by animals, environment, blood, situations, other).
Explore and understand origin of your fear.	Explore with adolescent the origins of his or her fear.
Learn about diagnosis and develop realistic expectations of self.	Educate the adolescent about the diagnosis and discuss symptomatology so he or she can adjust self-expectations.
Assist therapist in constructing genogram to better understand history of phobias in family of origin.	Construct genogram with the adolescent to improve understanding of family history of phobias (see Behavioral Techniques, Chapter 14).
Understand underlying dynamics that lead to maladaptive behavior and stress.	Explore ways in which anxieties manifest themselves and clarify underlying dynamics.
Recognize underlying feelings of anger or depression and express appropriately.	Explore for underlying feelings of anger or depression (see appropriate treatment plan).
Begin to see new role models deal with anxieties.	Shape the adolescent's behavior by role modeling new ways to deal with specific phobias (see Behavioral Techniques, Chapter 14).

ADOLESCENT'S GOALS	THERAPIST'S INTERVENTIONS
Maintain a daily journal to monitor triggers that induce fear and subsequent feelings and reactions.	If the adolescent is well motivated, instruct him or her to maintain a notebook to record feelings and reactions to objects or situations that trigger fear.
Recognize irrational fears.	Use feedback from homework notebook to identify irrational beliefs that lead to phobias.
Test irrational beliefs and replace them with rational evidence-based system.	Investigate the irrational beliefs and replace them with rational system based on available evidence.
Begin to see possible solutions.	Discuss how to deal with negative feelings.
Using relaxation techniques or hypnosis to help the adolescent gain control over feelings.	Teach relaxation techniques and guided imagery to master anxieties (see "Relaxation," or "Hypnosis," Behavioral Techniques, Chapter 14).
Understand anxiety and realize that avoidance does not help.	Teach the adolescent the laws of anxiety: anxiety is not dangerous or permanent; avoidance increases anxiety; confronting the problem can reduce anxiety; exposure can produce growth.
Communicate your life story to therapist.	Have the adolescent relate the story of his or her life.
Express suppressed feelings in a non-threatening environment.	Play *The Talking, Feeling, Doing Game* to understand underlying processes in a non-threatening way (see Therapeutic Games, Chapter 15).

ADOLESCENT'S GOALS	THERAPIST'S INTERVENTIONS
Understand how trauma may have contributed to existing disorder.	Explore the adolescent's background for trauma that may have exacerbated the disorder.
Discuss personal coping mechanisms developed to handle the disorder.	With the adolescent, investigate possible patterns of withdrawal used to avoid anxieties.
Confront and challenge identified triggers for phobia.	Urge the adolescent to challenge and confront the object or situation that triggers a fear response. Reward and repeat success.
Learn positive self-talk.	Teach the adolescent positive self-talk to interrupt negative patterns.
Learn new techniques to nurture yourself and deal with emotional difficulties.	Use the *Positive Thinking Game* or *The Ungame* to teach ways positive self-talk can help control emotional difficulties (see Therapeutic Games, Chapter 15).
Shift focus of attention from problem to accomplishment.	Ask the adolescent to describe his or her accomplishments for the past week.
Feel more confident as self-esteem improves.	Compliment the adolescent to provide positive reinforcement whenever possible.
Reduce stress and anxiety by exercise.	Recommend routine exercise to help the adolescent release frustrations.
Attempt to use new control skills in school.	If appropriate, urge the adolescent to use new control skills in classroom setting.

ADOLESCENT'S GOALS	THERAPIST'S INTERVENTIONS
Report results to therapist.	Provide positive reinforcement when the adolescent reports back that he or she has challenged anxiety-provoking situations. Praise attempt and reward success.
Read assigned book.	Assign to read *Everything You Need to Know About Stress* (see Bibliotherapy, Chapter 17).
Learn new strategies.	Assign to read *Feel the Fear and Do It Anyway*, and *From Panic to Power* (see Bibliotherapy, Chapter 17).
Learn methods that can be used to advocate for yourself.	Instruct the adolescent in the techniques of self-advocacy.
Understand that you can deal with these issues and bring treatment to an end successfully.	Develop a treatment termination plan and explain issues of separation anxiety and dependency.

FAMILY'S GOALS	THERAPIST'S INTERVENTIONS
Improve communications among family members to reduce familial anxiety.	Conduct family sessions or refer for family therapy to reduce anger and/or alienation, and improve communication skills.
Understand family history of phobias and your personal view of the family.	Amplify family genogram created in early parental session and compare with the adolescent's view of family history of phobias.
Discuss genograms openly to fully understand family history as it relates to anxiety.	Discuss genograms to reveal family history and possible family secrets dealing with anxiety.
Demonstrate boundaries, alliances, triangles, and emotional currents that may exacerbate the anxieties.	Explore family boundaries using sculpturing, a useful technique for understanding triangulation, alliances, and emotional currents (see "Family Sculpturing," Behavioral Techniques, Chapter 14).
Share coping styles and uncover irrational beliefs.	Explore with family members the ways they deal with their personal fears and explore for irrational beliefs.
Replace irrational reactions to triggers.	Replace irrational family belief system with rational beliefs.
Improve communication skills.	Teach family the principles of assertiveness—equal respect for self and others.
Recognize that avoidance increases anxiety and enhance your abilities to help "identified patient" cope.	Instruct family on laws of anxiety: anxiety is not dangerous or permanent; avoidance increases anxiety; confronting the problem can reduce anxiety; exposure can produce growth.

FAMILY'S GOALS	THERAPIST'S INTERVENTIONS
Shift focus from problem to possible solutions.	If possible, have family imagine a future without the problem and suggest actions that can be taken now to make that future possible.
Think about what treatment outcome would look like. Explain what you would like to see change in other family members when treatment is completed.	Ask family members to think about what they might want to say about each other when treatment is completed.
Family members realize they have the power to make important changes even if they seem small.	Help family members realize they have an opportunity to do some things differently.
Family members are empowered. They recognize that they can create positive change.	Ask family members to relate what they have accomplished in the past week.
Realize that major change is the result of small steps taken one at a time.	Help family identify and prioritize achievable goals.
Enhance understanding of condition and see how other families have handled similar problems. Discuss readings with therapist.	Assign homework reading *Making Families Work and What to Do When They Don't* or *Mastering Your Special Phobia* and discuss (see Bibliotherapy, Chapter 17).
Make use of available community resources.	Refer family to available resources in the community. (see Self-Help Groups and 800 Numbers, Chapter 18 and Online Resources, Chapter 19).
Reduce negative communication.	Develop a system of positive reinforcement with family to interact better with each other and reduce scapegoating.

FAMILY'S GOALS	THERAPIST'S INTERVENTIONS
Family works together to develop a treatment termination plan.	Discuss termination issues and develop a plan to terminate treatment.

5
BEHAVIOR DISORDERS

ATTENTION DEFICIT/HYPERACTIVITY DISORDER—(314.XX)

Specify: Combined Type: .01
Predominantly Inattentive Type: .00
Predominantly Hyperactive-Impulsive Type: .01

Attention deficit/hyperactivity disorder (AD/HD) is characterized by a persistent pattern of inattention, hyperactivity, or impulsivity that is more frequent or severe than expected given the child's level of development. Symptoms may appear singly or in combination, and are usually displayed before age seven. The diagnosis must be distinguished from age-appropriate behavior of normally active children. The disorder is substantially more frequent in males than females.

AD/HD deals with three behavioral characteristics: inattention, hyperactivity, and impulsivity that cause impairment and distress at home, at school, and in social situations. Inattention is marked by failure to pay close attention to details and the tendency to make careless mistakes in schoolwork or other tasks. Work is often messy and without considered thought. There is no follow-through and tasks are often left uncompleted. Hyperactivity is characterized by fidgeting or failure to remain seated in school, or excessive and inappropriate running or climbing. Hyperactivity varies with age and development level and should be diagnosed cautiously in younger children. Impulsivity is manifest by difficulty in delaying responses or taking turns, and often interrupting or intruding on others. Psychostimulants are the single most effective intervention in the treatment of AD/HD. Antidepressants are also used. Non-pharmacological interventions are critical for the treatment of low self-esteem and subsequent psychosocial problems associated with the disorder.

Behavioral Symptoms
(severity index: 1–mild; 2–moderate; 3–intense)

                                                                                                           Severity

Attention
1. Fails to pay close attention to details in school or social situations   _____
2. Does not seem to listen when spoken to directly   _____
3. Does not follow through on instructions   _____
4. Fails to finish tasks   _____
5. Has difficulty organizing tasks and activities   _____
6. Avoids or dislikes tasks that require sustained mental effort   _____
7. Loses things that are necessary for tasks and activities   _____
8. Is easily distracted by extraneous stimuli   _____
9. Forgetful in daily activities   _____

Hyperactivity-Impulsivity
1. Fidgets or squirms in seat   _____
2. Cannot remain in seat when expected   _____
3. Inappropriately overactive   _____
4. Subjective feelings of restlessness   _____
5. Has difficulty engaging appropriately in leisure activities   _____
6. Feels or acts as if "driven by a motor"   _____
7. Talks excessively   _____
8. Blurts out answers before questions are completed   _____
9. Has difficulty awaiting turn   _____
10. Interrupts or intrudes on conversations or activities of others   _____

ATTENTION DEFICIT/HYPERACTIVITY DISORDER TREATMENT PLAN

Patient: _____   Date: _____

I. OBJECTIVES OF TREATMENT *(select one or more)*

1. Educate parents about this disorder
2. Investigate family history of the disorder
3. Help family develop better coping skills
4. Increase frustration tolerance
5. Reduce aggression and anxiety
6. Encourage compliance with educational programs and referrals
7. Improve self-esteem
8. Reduce irrational beliefs
9. Promote socialization
10. Reduce alienation
11. Assure compliance with medical regimen
12. Focus concentration for increased time span
13. Develop a balanced life plan
14. Develop a discharge plan for coping with everyday life

II. SHORT-TERM BEHAVIORAL GOALS AND INTERVENTIONS
(select goals and interventions appropriate for your patient)

NOTE: Separate goals and interventions are provided for the treatment of Parents, Adolescent, and Family

PARENTS' GOALS	THERAPIST'S INTERVENTIONS
Collaborate with therapist in development of a treatment plan.	Establish therapeutic alliance with parents to enhance outcome of treatment.
Help therapist understand your adolescent's development to get a complete picture.	Assess problem with parents and record a comprehensive history of the adolescent's development in order to accurately assess problems.

PARENTS' GOALS	THERAPIST'S INTERVENTIONS
Become aware of the diagnosis and what to appropriately expect from your adolescent.	Educate parents about the diagnosis.
Cooperate in building a genogram to identify familial history and its relationship to AD/HD.	Construct a genogram to better understand the family history and its impact on the adolescent (see Behavioral Techniques, Chapter 14).
Develop awareness of how your personal theory influences cognition of the problem.	Explore parental theory of the problem.
Recognize fears and feelings of negative self-blame related to the problem.	Evaluate parents' fears and negative feelings of self-blame for the adolescent's problem.
Learn to reach beyond automatic cognitive reactions in viewing the problem.	Expand parental perspective beyond limited cognitive reactions.
Undergo treatment for underlying problems that may exacerbate your adolescent's condition.	Explore for underlying problems in parents, (e.g. anxiety, depression) and treat or refer for therapy (see appropriate treatment plan).
Agree to allow therapist to confer with your adolescent's school to help in development of a comprehensive psychoeducational treatment plan.	After interviewing the adolescent, request and receive parental permission to confer with teachers and school administrators.
Comply with referral for medical and psychological testing of your adolescent.	Provide referral for psychological testing of the adolescent to evaluate intellectual capabilities and rule out other diagnostic considerations.

PARENTS' GOALS	THERAPIST'S INTERVENTIONS
Comply with referral for medical and psychiatric evaluations.	Provide referral for medical and psychiatric evaluations if appropriate.
Buy or rent *Captain's Log* to use at home to help your adolescent reduce learning problems and improve self-esteem.	Educate parents who can afford *Captain's Log* (see Therapeutic Games, Chapter 15) on how to intervene with the computerized cognitive training system at home to improve frustration tolerance, reinforce focus, and improve self-esteem. Note: *Captain's Log* must also be available in therapist's office.
As alternative to *Captain's Log*, acquire *Personal Trainer*, or *Smart Driver* computer software programs for cognitive training at home.	As alternative to *Captain's Log* system, assign parents to use *Personal Trainer*, or *Smart Driver* software programs at home to improve the adolescent's cognitive skills such as sustained attention, visual tracking, rule following, and planning (see Therapeutic Games, Chapter 15).
Help increase your adolescent's cognitive skills by introducing him or her to these games and participating to improve communication.	Other alternatives for expanding the adolescent's cognitive skills are *Bop It*, and *Simon* (see Therapeutic Games, Chapter 15).
Meet with other parents who are experiencing similar difficulties and share solutions for coping with the problem.	Refer parents to self-help group (see Self-Help Groups and 800 Numbers, Chapter 18, and Online Resources, Chapter 19).

PARENTS' GOALS	THERAPIST'S INTERVENTIONS
Read about AD/HD to better understand how to cope with the problem.	Assign reading of *Taking Charge of ADHD* or *Living with ADD* (see Bibliotherapy, Chapter 17).
Make use of community resources.	Educate parents about available community resources (see Self-Help Groups and 800 Numbers, Chapter 18, and Online Resources, Chapter 19).
Discuss and approve a treatment termination plan and resolve termination issues.	Develop a treatment termination plan and discuss issues of separation including anxiety and dependency.

ADOLESCENT'S GOALS	THERAPIST'S INTERVENTIONS
Engage in therapeutic relationship.	Engage the adolescent in an age-appropriate therapeutic relationship.
Learn about diagnosis and develop alternate problem-solving strategies.	Educate client about the diagnosis and discuss symptomatology so he or she may develop alternate problem-solving strategies.
Develop a better understanding of your relationships while improving communications.	Role-play stressful situations to help the adolescent work out problems in a safe environment (see Behavioral Techniques, Chapter 14).
Learn self-regulatory self-talk.	Model self-regulatory statements.
Mimic self-regulatory behavior.	Perform self-regulatory tasks with adolescent.
Perform self-regulatory talk.	Guide the adolescent in self-regulatory talk.
Generate alternative solutions.	Brainstorm alternative solutions.
Learn to self-monitor behavior.	Teach the adolescent to self-monitor behavior.
Observe acceptable expression of feelings	Discuss socially acceptable expression of feelings.
Learn that it is okay to express feelings.	Praise or reward the adolescent for expressing feelings appropriately.
Recognize underlying feelings of anger or depression and express appropriately.	Explore for underlying feelings of anger or depression (see appropriate treatment plan).

ADOLESCENT'S GOALS	THERAPIST'S INTERVENTIONS
Realize others also feel bad and effectively overcome the feeling. Begin to see possible solutions.	Investigate for feelings of low esteem related to AD/HD. Discuss negative feelings and what to do about them.
Identify irrational beliefs.	Explore irrational beliefs about AD/HD.
Reframe beliefs about AD/HD.	Discuss the beliefs and develop rational alternatives.
Use *Captain's Log* in office to improve cognitive skills.	Assign the adolescent to play *Captain's Log* if available (see Therapeutic Games, Chapter 15) to improve frustration tolerance, reinforce focused attention, improve self-esteem, and engage in brainstorming problem-solving techniques.) Note: Computer must be available in therapist's office to play these games.
Use *Personal Trainer* or *Smart Driver* software at home to improve cognitive skills.	As alternative to *Captain's Log*, assign client to use *Personal Trainer* or *Smart Driver* computer software if the adolescent has a computer at home (see Therapeutic Games, Chapter 15).
Using hypnosis, guided imagery or relaxation techniques, learn to gain control over feelings.	Use relaxation techniques hypnosis, or guided imagery to gain mastery over anxieties (see Behavioral Techniques, Chapter 14).
Understand anxiety and realize that avoidance does not help.	Teach the adolescent the laws of anxiety: anxiety is not permanent or dangerous; avoidance increases anxiety; confronting the problem can reduce anxiety; exposure can produce growth.

ADOLESCENT'S GOALS	THERAPIST'S INTERVENTIONS
Communicate your life story to therapist.	Have the adolescent relate the story of his or her life, or use *The Storytelling Game* (see Therapeutic Games, Chapter 15).
Express suppressed feelings in a non-threatening environment.	Have the adolescent play *The Talking, Feeling, Doing Game* to understand underlying processes in a non-threatening way (see Therapeutic Games, Chapter 15).
Understand how trauma may have contributed to existing disorder.	Explore the adolescent's background for trauma that may have exacerbated the disorder.
Discuss personal coping mechanisms developed to handle the disorder.	With the adolescent, investigate possible patterns of withdrawal used to avoid AD/HD problems.
Recognize and relate how family impacts the problem.	Explore familial impact on the problem.
Understand your learning modality i.e. visual, auditory, or kinesthetic) and learn how to learn.	Help the adolescent become a better learner by reviewing the Swassing-Barbe checklist of Observable Modality Strengths with him or her (see "Learning," Behavioral Techniques, Chapter 14).
Significantly improve behavior.	Build the adolescent's confidence to level to where he or she understands that unfocused behavior can be controlled.
Develop and use an organizational system to complete tasks at hand.	Help the adolescent develop and implement an organizational system to help complete tasks.

ADOLESCENT'S GOALS	THERAPIST'S INTERVENTIONS
Learn to prioritize tasks to assure completion of a project.	Teach the adolescent how to prioritize tasks.
Recognize triggers of impulsive behavior and learn to think before acting.	Urge the adolescent to recognize and confront triggers of impulsive behavior.
Learn more about AD/HD and how to cope with it.	Assign the adolescent to read *Coping With ADD/ADHD* or *AD/HD—A Teenager's Guide* (see Bibliotherapy, Chapter 17).
Participate in self-help group to increase understanding and control, get feedback from peers,	Refer the adolescent to self-help group (see Self-Help Groups and 800 Numbers, Chapter 18, and Online Resources, Chapter 19).
Understand that you can deal with these issues and bring treatment to an end successfully.	Develop a treatment termination plan and explain issues of separation anxiety and dependency.

FAMILY'S GOALS	THERAPIST'S INTERVENTIONS
Improve communications among family members.	Conduct family sessions or refer for family therapy to reduce anger and/or alienation, and improve communication skills within the family.
Cooperate in amplifying family genogram.	Amplify family genogram created in first family session to help understand family history.
Discuss genogram openly to fully understand family history as it relates to AD/HD.	Discuss genogram to reveal family history and possible family secrets dealing with AD/HD.
Demonstrate boundaries, alliances, triangles, and emotional currents that may exacerbate the problem.	Explore family boundaries using sculpturing, a useful technique for understanding triangulation, alliances, and emotional currents (see "Family Sculpturing," Behavioral Techniques, Chapter 14).
Shift focus from problem to possible solutions.	If appropriate, have family imagine a future without the problem and suggest actions that can be taken now to make that future possible.
Think about what treatment outcome would look like. Explain what you would like to see change in other family members when treatment is completed.	Ask family members to think about what they might want to say about each other when treatment is completed.
Family members realize they have the power to make important changes even if they seem small.	Help family members realize they have an opportunity to do some things differently.

FAMILY'S GOALS	THERAPIST'S INTERVENTIONS
Family members are empowered. They recognize that they can create positive change.	Ask family members to relate what they have accomplished in the past week.
Gain insights into learning modalities and become better learners.	Review the Swassing-Barbe checklist to help family members understand their learning modality strengths (see Behavioral Techniques, Chapter 14).
Realize that major change is the result of small steps taken one at a time.	Help family identify and prioritize achievable goals.
Enhance understanding of condition and see how other families have handled similar problems.	Assign homework reading *Success Stories: A Guide to Fulfillment with Attention Deficit Disorder* or *Healing ADD: Simple Exercises That Will Change Your Daily Life* (see Bibliotherapy, Chapter 17).
Make use of available community resources.	Refer family to available resources in the community (see Self-Help Groups and 800 Numbers, Chapter 18, and Online Resources, Chapter 19).
Reduce negative communication.	Develop a system of positive reinforcement with family to interact better with each other and reduce scapegoating.
Family works together to develop a treatment termination plan.	Discuss termination issues and develop plan to terminate treatment.

CONDUCT DISORDER—(312.8)

Specify: Childhood-onset type
            Adolescent-onset type

Conduct Disorder is marked by the repeated and persistent violation of the basic rights of others or accepted age-appropriate societal norms or rules. This behavior takes four forms: (1) aggressive conduct that causes or threatens physical harm to others or animals; (2) non-aggressive conduct that causes property loss or damage; (3) deceitfulness or theft; and (4) serious violations of rules. In order to meet the criteria for this diagnosis, three of the four behaviors must be present for twelve months and one behavior for the past six months. The behaviors are usually found in various settings, including home, school, and community. Children and adolescents with this disorder often initiate aggression and react aggressively toward others. They may bully, threaten, or intimidate others; initiate frequent fights; use a weapon that can cause serious harm, (e.g. brick, bottle, knife, gun); act physically cruel to people or animals; confront a victim (e.g. mugging, purse snatching, extortion, armed robbery); force someone into sexual activity (rape); or commit assault or homicide. The destruction of others' property may include deliberate fire setting with the intention of causing serious damage, or deliberately destroying property in other ways (e.g. school or church vandalism, smashing car windows, slashing tires). Deceitfulness and theft may include breaking into someone else's house, building, or car; lying or breaking promises to obtain goods or favors or to avoid debts or obligations; or stealing without confronting the victim (e.g., shoplifting, forgery). Children with this disorder may also violate school and parental rules. They frequently develop a pattern before age 13 of staying out late at night despite parental objections. There may also be a pattern of running away from home overnight or a history of truancy from school.

There are two subtypes of conduct disorder. Childhood-onset type includes at least one characteristic of the disorder before age 10. These individuals, usually male, are frequently aggressive toward others and have disturbed peer relations. Adolescent-onset type does not show characteristics of the disorder before age 10, and these individuals are less likely to display aggressive behavior or have disturbed peer relations. The ratio of males to females in this type is lower than the childhood-onset type.

Conduct Disorder is considered more serious than Oppositional Defiant Disorder, and the prognosis is not as good. Parents may tend to reinforce non-compliant behavior and ignore or punish positive behavior. They may also display anti-social behaviors. There appears to be some relation to marital discord and criticism, conflict, or inconsistency in dealing with the child or adolescent.

Behavioral Symptoms
(severity index: 1–mild; 2–moderate; 3–intense)

To qualify for this diagnosis, at least three of the following must be present for twelve months and one for the past six months.

                                                                                          Severity

Aggression
1. Bullies, threatens, or intimidates others   _____
2. Initiates fights   _____
3. Has used a dangerous weapon   _____
4. Has been physically cruel to people   _____
5. Has been physically cruel to animals   _____
6. Has stolen while confronting victim   _____
7. Has forced someone into sexual activity   _____
8. Has committed assault or homicide   _____

Destruction of property
9. Has deliberately engaged in fire-setting with intention to do harm to others or cause serious damage   _____
10. Has deliberately destroyed the property of others   _____

Deceitfulness/Theft
11. Has broken into someone else's house, building, or car   _____
12. Often lies to obtain goods or favors or to avoid obligations   _____
13. Has stolen items without confronting victims (shoplifting)   _____

Rule Violation
14. Beginning before age 13, often stays out at night despite parents' objections   _____
15. Has run away from home twice overnight or once for longer period   _____
16. Starting before age 13, is often truant from school   _____

OPPOSITIONAL DEFIANT DISORDER—(313.81)

Oppositional Defiant Disorder is marked by recurrent negative, defiant, disobedient, and hostile behavior toward authority figures that lasts at least six months and is characterized by four of the following: losing temper, arguing with adults, defying adult rules or requests, deliberately doing things to annoy others, blaming others for his or her mistakes or behavior, being easily annoyed by others, being angry and resentful, and being spiteful and vindictive. This diagnosis requires that the stated behaviors occur more often than is typical of others of the same age and developmental level, and must result in impairment in functioning at home and in school. Late onset in adolescence may be the result of normal attempts at individuation. The characteristic defiance may appear as stubbornness, resistance to directions, and unwillingness to give in, compromise, or negotiate with adults or peers. Hostility usually involves verbal aggression without the physical aggression found in the more serious Conduct Disorder. Typical behaviors are almost always present in the home setting, but may not be evident at school or in the community. Adolescents with this disorder tend to justify their behavior as a response to unreasonable demands or circumstances.

Behavioral Symptoms
(severity index: 1–mild; 2–moderate; 3–intense)

To qualify for this diagnosis, the adolescent must exhibit a pattern of hostile and defiant behavior lasting six months and including at least four of the following:

		Severity
1.	Often loses temper	_____
2.	Often argues with adults	_____
3.	Often defies adult requests or rules	_____
4.	Often deliberately annoys others	_____
5.	Often blames others for his or her mistakes or behaviors	_____
6.	Is often easily annoyed by others	_____
7.	Is often angry and resentful	_____
8.	Is often spiteful and vindictive	_____

DISRUPTIVE BEHAVIOR DISORDER NOS—(312.9)

This category is reserved for disorders with characteristics of Conduct or Oppositional Defiant Disorder that do not fully meet the diagnostic requirements for either Conduct Disorder or Oppositional Defiant Disorder, but involve significant impairment.

CONDUCT DISORDER
OPPOSITIONAL DEFIANT DISORDER
DISRUPTIVE BEHAVIOR DISORDER NOS
TREATMENT PLAN

Patient: _____ Date: _____

I. OBJECTIVES OF TREATMENT *(select one or more)*

1. Educate parents about the disorder
2. Investigate family history of the disorder
3. Determine any parental psychopathology
4. Help family develop better parenting and coping skills
5. Reduce anxiety, anger, and depression related to the disorder
6. Encourage compliance with educational programs and referrals
7. Reduce parental antisocial behavior
8. Reduce irrational beliefs
9. Improve disruptive environment
10. Promote socialization
11. Reduce the adolescent's antisocial behaviors
12. Reduce alienation
13. Develop discharge plan for coping with everyday life

II. SHORT-TERM BEHAVIORAL GOALS AND INTERVENTIONS
(select goals and interventions appropriate for your patient)

NOTE: Separate goals and interventions are provided for the treatment of Parents, Adolescent, and Family

PARENTS' GOALS	THERAPIST'S INTERVENTIONS
Parents collaborate with therapist in development of a treatment plan.	Attempt to establish a therapeutic alliance with parents to enhance outcome of treatment.
Help therapist understand the adolescent's development and disorder.	Assess problem with parents and record a comprehensive history of the adolescent's development and the disorder.

PARENTS' GOALS	THERAPIST'S INTERVENTIONS
Become aware of the diagnosis and what to generally expect from your adolescent.	Educate parents about the diagnosis.
Undergo treatment for individual problems, which, in turn, enhances the outcome of your adolescent's therapy.	Explore for parental psychopathology (e.g. antisocial behaviors, marital discord etc.) and refer for treatment or treat.
Undergo testing and evaluation for psychiatric medication.	If appropriate, refer parents for psychological testing and psychiatric evaluation.
Become aware of maladaptive messages you are sending to your adolescent.	Identify if and how parents model antisocial behaviors that the adolescent translates as permission to defy authority.
Recognize your ineffective or inconsistent disciplinary practices.	Assess ineffective or inconsistent practices of discipline.
Develop awareness of how your personal theory influences cognition of the problem.	Explore parental theory of the problem.
Recognize fears and negative self-blame related to the problem.	Evaluate parents' fears and negative self-blame for the adolescent's problem.
Learn to reach beyond automatic cognitive reactions in viewing the problem.	Expand parental perspective beyond limited cognitive reactions.
Agree to allow therapist to confer with your adolescent's school to help in development of a comprehensive psycho-educational treatment plan.	After interviewing the adolescent, if appropriate, request and receive parental permission to confer with teachers and school administrators.

PARENTS' GOALS	THERAPIST'S INTERVENTIONS
Attend self-help group to improve parenting skills.	Evaluate parenting skills and, if necessary, refer to parenting skills group (see Self-Help Groups and 800 Numbers, Chapter 18, and Online Resources, Chapter 19).
Read about and improve parenting skills.	Assign reading of books on positive parenting (see *Making Families Work and What to Do When They Don't* or *Parents Do Make a Difference: How to Raise Kids with Solid Character, Strong Minds, and Caring Hearts*, Bibliotherapy, Chapter 17).
Learn the warning signs of violence and strategies to deal with them.	Assign parents to read *Lost Boys* or *Violence-Proof Your Kids Now* (see Bibliotherapy, Chapter 17).
Discuss a treatment termination plan and resolve termination issues.	Develop a treatment termination plan and discuss issues of separation and dependency with parents.

ADOLESCENT'S GOALS	THERAPIST'S INTERVENTIONS
Enter non-threatening therapeutic interaction geared to appropriate development level.	Attempt to engage the adolescent in an age-appropriate therapeutic relationship.
Learn about diagnosis and develop realistic expectations of self.	Educate the adolescent about the diagnosis and discuss symptomatology so he or she can adjust self-expectations.
Recognize underlying feelings of anger or depression and express appropriately.	Explore for underlying feelings of anger or depression.
Realize others also feel bad and overcome the feelings.	Investigate for feelings of low esteem related to conduct problems. Discuss how the adolescent feels and what to do about it.
Identify irrational beliefs.	Explore for irrational beliefs about Conduct Disorder.
Reframe beliefs about Conduct Disorder.	Discuss the beliefs and develop rational alternatives.
Learn by role modeling and shape new behaviors.	Role model appropriate behavior for the adolescent.
Using relaxation techniques hypnosis, or guided imagery, learn to gain control over feelings.	If the adolescent is well motivated and cooperative, use relaxation techniques, hypnosis, or guided imagery to master anger and anxiety (see Behavioral Techniques, Chapter 14).
Understand anxiety and realize that avoidance does not help.	Teach client the dynamics of anxiety: anxiety is not dangerous or permanent; avoidance increases anxiety; confronting the problem can reduce anxiety; exposure can produce growth.

ADOLESCENT'S GOALS	THERAPIST'S INTERVENTIONS
Tell therapist your life's story.	Have the adolescent relate the story of his or her life.
Understand process that gets you into trouble in order to control acting out.	Teach the adolescent about aggressive behavior: (1) Oversensitive to hostile cues and (2) attribute hostile intentions to others; therefore, (3) solve problems with aggressive actions, and (4) become rejected by others, which, in turn, contributes to (5) low self-esteem.
Enter treatment for anxiety, depression, or low self-esteem.	Explore for low self-esteem, anxiety, or depression and treat appropriately (see appropriate treatment plan).
Learn the difference between right and wrong while exploring the issues of crime, violence, character, and charity.	Play *The Conscience Game* to provide a lecture-free forum for moral development (see Therapeutic Games, Chapter 15).
Understand how trauma may have contributed to existing disorder.	Explore the adolescent's background for trauma that may have exacerbated the disorder.
Discuss personal coping mechanisms developed to handle the disorder.	With the adolescent, investigate possible patterns that trigger acting out.
Psychodynamically discover new ways to deal with problematic situations.	Role-play with the adolescent situations that get him or her into trouble and help develop new solutions in a safe environment (see Behavioral Techniques, Chapter 14).
Recognize and relate how family impacts the problem.	Explore familial impact on the problem.

ADOLESCENT'S GOALS	THERAPIST'S INTERVENTIONS
Learn positive self-talk.	Teach the adolescent positive self-talk to interrupt negative patterns.
Learn new technique for dealing with anxiety.	Teach diaphragmatic breathing to control anxiety (see Behavioral Techniques, Chapter 14).
Learn new techniques for dealing with emotional difficulties.	Use the *Positive Thinking Game* to teach how positive self-talk helps control emotional difficulties (see Therapeutic Games, Chapter 15.)
Shift focus of attention from problem to accomplishment.	Ask the adolescent to describe his or her accomplishments for the past week.
Feel more confident as self-esteem improves.	Compliment the adolescent to provide positive reinforcement whenever possible.
Develop an exercise schedule to reduce frustrations and the need to act out.	Recommend routine exercise to help the adolescent release frustrations.
Attempt to use new control skills in school.	Urge the adolescent to use new control skills in the classroom setting.
Report results to therapist.	Provide positive reinforcement when the adolescent reports back that he or she has acted appropriately in school. Praise attempt and reward success.
Read assigned book.	Assign to read *Ending the Struggle Against Yourself* or *Thoughts and Feelings: Taking Control of Your Moods and Your Life* (see Bibliotherapy, Chapter 17).

ADOLESCENT'S GOALS	THERAPIST'S INTERVENTIONS
Learn new strategies for dealing with aggressive behaviors.	Teach the adolescent new ways to reach others, simple strategies to reduce acting out, and new behaviors.
Learn methods that can be used to advocate for yourself.	Instruct the adolescent in the techniques of self-advocacy.
Understand that he or she can deal with these issues and bring treatment to an end successfully.	Develop a treatment termination plan and explain issues of separation anxiety and dependency.

FAMILY'S GOALS	THERAPIST'S INTERVENTIONS
Improve communications among family members.	Conduct family sessions or refer for family therapy to reduce anger and/or alienation, and improve communication skills within the family.
Cooperate in amplifying family genogram.	Amplify family genogram created in first family session to help understand family history.
Discuss genogram openly to fully understand family history as it relates to aggression.	Discuss genogram to reveal family history and possible family secrets dealing with aggression.
Demonstrate boundaries, alliances, triangles, and emotional currents that may exacerbate the problem.	Explore boundaries of family members using sculpturing, a useful technique for understanding triangulation, alliances, and emotional current, (see Behavioral Techniques, Chapter 14).
Family communicates how they handle aggression at home.	Explore sibling rivalry and the ways aggression is handled at home.
Learn new ways to deal with your aggressive behaviors.	Explore how parents manage their own anger and encourage prosocial behaviors to develop family cohesiveness.
Assume responsibility for changing your behavior.	Target problematic behaviors in the family and set realistic goals so family can take responsibility for changing their behaviors.

FAMILY'S GOALS	THERAPIST'S INTERVENTIONS
Realize that major change is the result of small steps taken one at a time.	Help family identify and prioritize achievable goals.
Shift focus from problem to possible solutions.	Have family imagine a future without the problem and suggest actions that can be taken now to make that future possible.
Reduce negative communication.	Develop a system of positive reinforcement with family to interact better with each other and reduce scapegoating.
Think about what treatment outcome would look like. Explain what you would like to see change in other family members when treatment is completed.	Ask family members to think about what they might want to say about each other when treatment is completed.
Family members realize they have the power to make important changes even if they seem small.	Help family members realize they have an opportunity to do some things differently.
Members are empowered. They recognize that they can create positive change.	Ask family members to relate what they have accomplished in the past week.
Make use of available community resources.	Refer family to available resources in the community (see Self-Help Groups and 800 Numbers, Chapter 18, and Online Resources, Chapter 19).
Family works together to develop a treatment termination plan.	Discuss termination issues and develop plan to terminate treatment.

6
BIPOLAR DISORDERS

Bipolar Disorders include recurrent mood disorders in which episodes of mania occur with or without major depression. Included in this category are Bipolar I Disorder, Bipolar II Disorder, Bipolar Disorder NOS, and Cyclothymia.

BIPOLAR I DISORDER—(296.XX)

Specify most recent episode: Single manic episode—(296.0x)
Hypomanic—(296.40)
Manic—(296.4x)
Mixed—(296.0x)
Depressed—(296.5)
Unspecified—(296.7)

Bipolar I Disorder is characterized by one or more Manic Episodes, or Mixed (Manic-Depressive) Episodes. Often patients have had one or more major Depressive Episodes as well. There are six subsets of Bipolar I Disorder depending on whether the individual is experiencing a first episode characterized as a Single Manic Episode, or a recurrence. Recurrence may be marked by a shift in polarity (Major Depressive Episode to a Manic or Mixed Episode, or a Manic Episode into a Depressive or Mixed Episode). Compared with adults, adolescents more often present with mixed episodes that cycle more rapidly. However, a Hypomanic Episode that evolves into a Manic or Mixed Episode, or vice versa, is considered a single episode. Fifty-nine percent of all cases of Bipolar I start in adolescence. Recurrent Bipolar I Disorders are specified by the current or most recent episode as follows:

Single Manic Episode—characterized by Manic symptoms for one week or requiring hospitalization, with no past Depressive Episodes—marked impairment in functioning.

Hypomanic—characterized by manic symptoms for at least four days without significant impairment in social or academic functioning—at least one previous Manic or Hypomanic Episode.

Manic—characterized by manic symptoms for one week or requiring hospitalization; at least one previous Manic, Major Depressive, or Mixed Episode—marked impairment in functioning. The first episode in males is more likely to be manic.

Depressed—characterized by depressive symptoms for a two-week period with at least one previous manic or mixed episode. Impairment is clinically significant. The first episode in females is usually Depressive.

Mixed—characterized by both Manic and Depressive symptoms nearly every day for one week, with significant impairment in functioning or requiring hospitalization. Mixed Episodes are more likely to appear in adolescents than adults.

Unspecified—characterized by Manic, Hypomanic, Mixed, or Depressive symptoms but not meeting the duration criteria listed above—at least one previous Manic or Mixed Episode and impairment is clinically significant.

Genetics and gender contribute to the incidence and severity of bipolar symptoms. The incidence of Bipolar I Disorder or Major Depressive Disorder among first-degree biological relatives of individuals with Bipolar I Disorder may be as high as 24%. More than 90% of individuals who have experienced a single Manic Episode will go on to have future episodes. More than 60% of Manic Episodes occur immediately before or after a Major Depressive Episode. Completed suicides occur in 10–15% of individuals with Bipolar I Disorder.

Mixed Episodes appear more frequently in adolescents and young adults than in older adults. Associated problems for adolescents include school failure, truancy, and episodic antisocial behavior. About 10–15% of adolescents with recurrent Major Depressive Episodes will go on to develop Bipolar I Disorder.

Most individuals with Bipolar I Disorder return to a functional level. However, some 20–30% continue to exhibit interpersonal and occupational difficulties. While medication is the primary treatment modality for Bipolar Disorders, a biopsychosocial approach that incorporates therapy, medication, and psychoeducation is most productive and effective. The therapeutic alliance among the adolescent, family, and clinician is important in managing the disorder. Mood swings may alter an adolescent's willingness to comply with a treatment plan (including medication). An assessment of the adolescent's risk to themselves or others must determine the appropriate level of care. Patients experiencing a severe Manic Episode are often hospitalized. After hospitalization, regular outpatient sessions are necessary to fine-tune medication.

MANIC AND DEPRESSIVE EPISODES DEFINED

Manic Episode

A Manic Episode is marked by an abnormal and persistent elevated or irritable mood including at least three of the following symptoms and lasting for one week or requiring hospitalization. In the case of irritable mood, four of the following are necessary to meet the criteria. Social or academic functioning is impaired. There are psychotic features. Hospitalization may be required to preclude harm to self or others.

1. Abnormally talkative, pressured speech
2. Flight of ideas or racing thoughts
3. Marked increase in goal-directed activity
4. Psychomotor agitation
5. Easily distracted by external stimuli
6. Excessive involvement in pleasurable activities with a high potential for negative consequences
7. Decreased need for sleep
8. Inflated self-esteem or grandiosity

Depressive Episodes

A Major Depressive Episode is marked by five or more of the following symptoms in a two-week period that mark a change in usual functioning. The symptoms must include depressed mood (or irritable mood in adolescents or children) or loss of interest.

1. Depressed mood most of the day
2. Decreased pleasure or interest in activities
3. Significant weight change (+/– 5%) in past 30 days
4. Insomnia or hypersomnia
5. Retardation or psychomotor agitation
6. Fatigue or loss of energy

7. Feelings of worthlessness or excessive guilt
8. Diminished ability to think or concentrate
9. Recurrent thoughts of death
10. Recurrent suicidal ideations with or without a specific plan
11. Suicide attempt

BIPOLAR DISORDER NOS—(296.XX)

Bipolar Disorder NOS includes disorders with bipolar features that do not meet any of the criteria for any of the specific disorders listed. These may include rapid alternation of Manic and Depressive symptoms (over days) that does not meet the duration criteria specified for Manic or Major Depressive Episodes, or recurrent Hypomanic Episodes without Depressive symptoms. Refer to the Manic and Depressive Episode descriptions above.

Behavioral Symptoms
Single Manic Episode, Hypomanic, Mixed, and NOS
(severity index: 1–mild; 2–moderate; 3–intense)

Abnormal, persistent elevated, expansive or irritable mood lasting for one week, including three of the following, and causing significant impairment in social or academic functioning or the need for hospitalization. There are psychotic features.

		Severity
1.	Abnormally talkative, pressured speech	_____
2.	Flight of ideas or racing thoughts	_____
3.	Marked increase in goal-directed activity	_____
4.	Psychomotor agitation	_____
5.	Easily distracted by external stimuli	_____
6.	Excessive involvement in pleasurable activities with a high potential for negative consequences	_____
7.	Decreased need for sleep	_____
8.	Inflated self-esteem or grandiosity	_____

BIPOLAR I DISORDER
SINGLE MANIC EPISODE, HYPOMANIC, MIXED, AND NOS
TREATMENT PLAN

Patient: _____ Date: _____

I. OBJECTIVES OF TREATMENT—Bipolar I Disorder, Single Manic Episode (*select one or more*)

1. Educate parents about disorder
2. Determine family history of the disorder
3. Help family develop better coping skills
4. Reduce pervasive anxiety and worry
5. Instruct parents about stress management
6. Control pressurized speech
7. Reduce psychomotor agitation
8. Increase ability to maintain concentration
9. Control potentially destructive activities
10. Restore normal sleep pattern
11. Reduce grandiosity
12. Increase ability to focus on a single thought or task
13. Encourage compliance with educational programs and referrals
14. Work with educators to facilitate learning
15. Reduce irrational beliefs
16. Promote socialization, reduce alienation
17. Restore adolescent and family to optimum level of functioning
18. Develop discharge plan for coping with everyday life

BIPOLAR II DISORDER—(296.89)

Specify: Hypomanic
Depressed

Bipolar II Disorder is characterized by one or more Major Depressive Episodes (defined above) in conjunction with at least one Hypomanic Episode. (Hypomanic Episodes are distinguished from Manic Episodes by the level of impairment. Social and educational functioning are *not* impaired in Hypomanic Episodes.) The most recent episode should be specified as Hypomanic or Depressed. The existence of a Manic or Mixed Episode would preclude the diagnosis of Bipolar II Disorder. The symptoms must cause significant distress or impairment in social, occupational or other areas of functioning. Completed suicide occurs in 10–15% of cases of Bipolar II Disorder.

Behavioral Symptoms
(severity index: 1–mild; 2–moderate; 3–intense)

	Severity
1. Depressed mood most of the day	_____
2. Decreased pleasure or interest in activities	_____
3. Significant weight change (+/– 5%) in past 30 days	_____
4. Insomnia or hypersomnia	_____
5. Retardation or psychomotor agitation	_____
6. Fatigue or loss of energy	_____
7. Feelings of worthlessness or excessive guilt	_____
8. Diminished ability to think or concentrate	_____
9. Recurrent thoughts of death	_____
10. Recurrent suicidal ideations with or without a specific plan	_____
11. Suicide attempt	_____

BIPOLAR II DISORDER
TREATMENT PLAN

Patient: _____   Date: _____

I. OBJECTIVES OF TREATMENT—Bipolar II Disorder
(select one or more)

1. Educate parents about disorder
2. Determine family history of the disorder
3. Help family develop better coping skills
4. Reduce pervasive anxiety and worry
5. Instruct parents about stress management
6. Reduce persistent depression
7. Restore interest in former pleasurable activities
8. Restore normal eating pattern
9. Restore normal sleep pattern
10. Eliminate feelings of worthlessness, guilt
11. Improve energy level
12. Eliminate or control suicidal ideations
13. Encourage compliance with educational programs and referrals
14. Work with educators to promote learning
15. Reduce irrational beliefs
16. Promote socialization, reduce alienation
17. Restore the adolescent and family to optimum level of functioning
18. Develop discharge plan for coping with everyday life

CYCLOTHYMIC DISORDER—(301.13)

Cyclothymic Disorder is a chronic, fluctuating mood disturbance characterized by periods of hypomanic and depressive symptoms. In order to meet the qualifications for this disorder, the symptoms must persist for two years in adults or one year in children and adolescents. Individuals with this disorder are not without symptoms for more than two months. The symptoms cause significant impairment in academic and social functioning. Hypomanic symptoms are insufficient to meet the criteria for a Manic Episode, while the Depressive symptoms are insufficient to meet those for a Major Depressive Episode. The diagnosis is contingent upon the absence of Major Depressive, Manic, or Mixed Episodes over the initial period. After the initial period, Manic or Mixed Episodes (Bipolar I Disorder) or Major Depressive Episodes (Bipolar II Disorder) may be superimposed on Cyclothymic Disorder in a dual diagnosis.

Behavioral Symptoms
(severity index: 1–mild; 2–moderate; 3–intense)

NOTE: Cyclothymic Disorder should **not** fully meet the criteria sets for hyomanic or depressive symptoms.

Hypomanic Symptoms

In order to meet the qualifications for this disorder, three of the following symptoms must be present, but not severe enough to cause impairment in educational/or social functioning, or to require hospitalization. Psychotic features are absent.

		Severity
1.	Grandiosity, inflated or insecure self-esteem	_____
2.	Hyposomnia alternating with hypersomnia	_____
3.	Talkative, pressurized speech	_____
4.	Flight of ideas, racing thoughts	_____
5.	Easily distracted by external stimuli	_____
6.	Psychomotor agitation	_____
7.	Increase in goal-directed activity	_____
8.	Excessive involvement in pleasurable, high-risk activities	_____
9.	Depressive period alternating with Manic	_____
10.	Apathy or mental confusion alternating with creativity	_____

Depressive Symptoms

In order to meet the qualifications for this disorder, the patient must exhibit five or more of the following symptoms in a two-week period, one of which must be depressed mood or loss of interest.

		Severity
1.	Depressed mood	_____
2.	Diminished pleasure or interest in almost all activities	_____
3.	Significant weight change (+/– 5%)	_____
4.	Insomnia or Hypersomnia	_____
5.	Psychomotor agitation or retardation	_____
6.	Fatigue or loss of energy	_____
7.	Feelings of worthlessness or excessive guilt	_____
8.	Indecisiveness, inability to concentrate	_____
9.	Recurrent thoughts of death	_____
10.	Suicidal ideations with or without a plan	_____
11.	Suicide attempt	_____
12.	Major impairment in academic or social functioning	_____

CYCLOTHYMIC DISORDER TREATMENT PLAN

Patient: _____   Date: _____

I. OBJECTIVES OF TREATMENT *(select one or more)*

1. Diminish grandiosity
2. Restore normal sleep pattern
3. Reduce pressurized speech
4. Control flight of ideas
5. Increase ability to concentrate
6. Ease psychomotor agitation
7. Eliminate pleasurable activities with negative consequences
8. Ease depression
9. Restore interest in usual activities
10. Reduce fatigue
11. Increase self-esteem
12. Diminish guilt feelings
13. Control suicidal ideations
14. Prevent suicide
15. Prevent relapse

II. SHORT-TERM BEHAVIORAL GOALS AND INTERVENTIONS
(Select goals and interventions appropriate for your patient)

NOTE: Separate goals and interventions are provided for Parents, Adolescent, and Family

PARENTS' GOALS	THERAPIST'S INTERVENTIONS
Parents collaborate with therapist in development of a treatment plan.	Establish therapeutic alliance with parents to enhance outcome of treatment.
Help therapist understand the development of your adolescent's anxiety problems.	Assess problem with parents and record a comprehensive history of the adolescent's development and anxiety problems.

PARENTS' GOALS	THERAPIST'S INTERVENTIONS
Identify your adolescent's symptoms and learn parenting skills to deal with them.	Explore with parents the symptoms they are dealing with and the techniques they use to help the adolescent.
Become aware of the diagnosis and what to appropriately expect from your adolescent.	Educate parents about the diagnosis.
Cooperate in building a genogram to identify familial history and its methods for dealing with the adolescent.	Construct a genogram to (1) better understand the family history since there is a high likelihood that biological relatives share the disorder and (2) to determine how the family has dealt with the disorder in the past. (see Behavioral Techniques, Chapter 14).
Understand possible need for hospitalization.	Explain to parents the possible need for hospitalization of the adolescent and attempt to decrease their anxiety.
Agree with need for immediate hospitalization.	If parents believe the adolescent is actively suicidal, refer the adolescent for immediate hospitalization.
Comply with referral for psychological testing of your adolescent.	If not actively suicidal, provide referral for psychological testing of the adolescent or get parental permission to administer appropriate tests to confirm existence of disorder and severity of the symptoms.
Comply with medical referral.	Refer adolescent for medical evaluation to rule out symptoms that mimic the disorder.

PARENTS' GOALS	THERAPIST'S INTERVENTIONS
Have your adolescent treated for medical problem.	Confirm or revise diagnosis. Rule out Disorder Due to a General Medical Condition.
Follow through with psychiatric evaluation to assess need for medication and possible anti-suicide measures.	Provide referral for psychiatric evaluation and follow up to confirm the appointment was kept.
Maintain regular medication schedule and report urges to ignore or discontinue meds.	If mediation is prescribed, confirm that prescription is filled and meds are taken on schedule.
Undergo evaluation of sexual abuse and, if necessary, enter treatment.	Evaluate for or rule out sexual abuse. If necessary, have parents treated.
Learn new strategies for dealing with stress interpersonally and intrapersonally.	Teach parents about stress management to reduce potential precipitants to negative events.
Allow therapist to confer with the adolescent's school teachers and school administrators to develop a comprehensive psychoeducational treatment plan.	Request and receive parental permission to confer with the adolescent's teachers and school administrators.
Identify sleep problems and receive treatment.	Investigate with parents for sleep disorder or nightmares and see that the adolescent gets treatment as required (see appropriate treatment plan).
Enter treatment for anxiety, if appropriate, to enhance outcome of your adolescent's therapy.	Evaluate parents for psychological disorders and refer for treatment if appropriate.

PARENTS' GOALS	THERAPIST'S INTERVENTIONS
Become aware of how your personal theory influences cognition of the problem in your adolescent.	Explore parental theory of the problem.
Recognize fears and feelings of self-blame related to your adolescent's disorder.	Evaluate parents' fears and negative feelings of self-blame for the adolescent's problem.
Learn to reach beyond automatic cognitive reactions in viewing the problem.	Expand parental perspective beyond limited cognitive reactions.
Learn how to help the adolescent deal with stressors.	Instruct parents in laws of anxiety: anxiety is not dangerous or permanent; avoidance increases anxiety; confronting the problem can reduce anxiety; exposure can produce growth.
Confront thoughts of exaggerated and unrealistic consequences—"what ifs?"	Guide parents in confronting distorted reactions.
Identify cognitive distortions.	Weigh the reactions against evidence-based reality.
Restructure distortions with evidence-based consequences.	With parents, reframe distortions with reality-based reactions to stressors.
Learn innovative techniques for helping the adolescent.	Assign parents to read *Survival Strategies for Parenting Children with Bipolar Disorder* (see Bibliotherapy, Chapter 17).
Learn diaphragmatic breathing as relaxation technique and teach your adolescent to help in relaxation.	Teach parents diaphragmatic breathing to assist the adolescent in relaxation (see Behavioral Techniques, Chapter 14).

PARENTS' GOALS	THERAPIST'S INTERVENTIONS
Develop new parenting skills.	Assign parents to read books on how to deal with their anxiety about the adolescent's disorder and increase parenting skills, such as *Making Families Work and What to Do When They Don't* or *Wonderful Ways to Love a Child* or *Try and Make Me: A Revolutionary Program for Raising Your Defiant Child Without Losing Your Cool* (see Bibliotherapy, Chapter 17).
Meet with other parents who are experiencing similar difficulties and share solutions for coping with the problem.	Refer parents to self-help group or group on parenting skills.
Discuss a treatment termination plan and resolve related issues.	Develop a treatment termination plan and discuss issues of separation anxiety and depression.

ADOLESCENT'S GOALS	THERAPIST'S INTERVENTIONS
Enter non-threatening therapeutic interaction geared to appropriate developmental age.	Engage the adolescent in appropriate therapeutic relationship.
Learn about diagnosis and develop realistic expectations of self.	Educate the adolescent about the diagnosis and discuss symptomatology so he or she can adjust self-expectations.
Understand underlying dynamics that lead to maladaptive behavior and stress.	Explore ways in which the disorder manifests itself (e.g. pressurized speech, flight of ideas, psychomotor agitation, easily distracted, excessive activity, decreased need for sleep, grandiosity, sexual acting out, risky behaviors) and clarify underlying dynamics.
Report to therapist all destructive self-talk and thoughts of harm to self or others.	Explain self-talk to adolescent. Closely monitor destructive thoughts and urges.
Understand possible need for hospitalization.	Explain to the adolescent possible need for hospitalization and resolve related anxieties.
Accept hospitalization as necessary to protect self or others.	Hospitalize the adolescent when advisable to prevent suicide or harm to others.
Enter into "suicide pact" with therapist to report all suicidal ideations and active plans.	If the adolescent is not actively suicidal, suggest and implement a "suicide pact" in which he or she agrees to inform you of any active plans and to talk to you before taking action. Have adolescent understand how serious this is, and that parents need to be informed, informed, even if it is considered a breach of confidentiality.

ADOLESCENT'S GOALS	THERAPIST'S INTERVENTIONS
Undergo medical evaluation.	Refer the adolescent for medical evaluation to rule out other disorders that mimic the disorder.
If necessary, be treated for physical condition.	Confirm or revise diagnosis. Rule out Disorder Due to a General Medical Condition.
Undergo evaluation for substance abuse and, if required, enter 12-step program.	Investigate and rule out substance abuse. If positive, revise diagnosis and treat (see appropriate treatment plan).
Follow through with referral for psychiatric evaluation to assess possible medication or other anti-suicide measures.	Discuss referral for psychiatric evaluation with adolescent. Follow up to confirm appointment was kept.
Maintain regular medication schedule and report urges to ignore or discontinue meds.	If medication is prescribed, confirm that prescription is filled and that medication is taken on schedule.
Provide prompt feedback on the effectiveness of the medication and possible side effects.	Instruct the adolescent on the need for feedback. Refer for adjustment of dosage as required.
Adolescent's depression is confirmed.	Refer for or administer the Beck Depression Inventory—II (BDI-1-11) to confirm existence of the disorder and intensity of the depression.
Intent is clinically assessed.	Refer for or administer Beck Scale for Suicidal Ideation (BSSI) to evaluate adolescent's intent.
Confirm or rule out sexual abuse.	Evaluate for sexual abuse and treat if necessary (see appropriate treatment plan).

ADOLESCENT'S GOALS	THERAPIST'S INTERVENTIONS
Replace destructive self-talk with positive affirmations of self-worth and the ability to cope successfully with the activities of daily living.	Replace destructive self-talk with positive affirmations drawing on past success with ADL.
Cooperate in building genogram and explain family history related to the disorder.	Construct genogram with adolescent to determine the adolescent's personal view of family history and ways the family deals with the disorder.
Understand feelings that result in acting out, and learn to think before acting.	Clarify underlying feelings that lead to pathological behavior.
Accept idea that you have a chronic disorder.	Educate the adolescent about the chronic nature of the disorder to reduce anger and denial.
Learn technique to help slow down when manic.	Teach the adolescent diaphragmatic breathing and relaxation techniques to slow down pressured speech or flight of ideas (see Behavioral Techniques, Chapter 14).
Learn to better handle everyday stress.	Assign the adolescent to read *Everything You Need to Know About Stress* (see Bibliotherapy, Chapter 17).
Build new assertiveness skills.	Teach the adolescent the principles of assertiveness—equal respect for self and others.
Replace negative thoughts with feelings of self-worth based on past experience.	Discuss positive past experience with ADL and feelings of self-worth. Provide trigger to reframe negative thoughts and feelings.

ADOLESCENT'S GOALS	THERAPIST'S INTERVENTIONS
Diminish need to "hide out" because of guilt or anger over having this disorder.	Gradually build the adolescent's confidence to a level where avoidance behavior is no longer a rational response.
Realize that you are more than the disorder and use unique skills to deal with problems.	Reinforce adolescent's new skills and strengths.
Recognize your grandiosity and reframe your thinking and behavior.	Investigate the adolescent's grandiose thinking and behavior.
Become more aware of behavioral triggers and how to control them.	Discuss psychomotor agitation and its triggers.
Develop awareness of grandiose behaviors and how to reduce them.	Confront grandiose behaviors and explore underlying dynamics that precipitate them.
Gradually become aware of the possible negative consequences of acting out.	Explore excessive involvement in pleasurable activities that have potentially negative consequences.
Participate in recreational activities with others.	Review the adolescent's past interest in recreational activities (sports, exercise, chess, cards etc.) and urge him or her to join external exercise or recreational group to renew pattern of contact and communication with others.
Keep a daily journal to record continuing depressive feelings and situations that trigger them. Record success in overcoming these feelings. Discuss with therapist.	Assign the adolescent to maintain a daily journal to record feelings of depression and success in overcoming these feelings (see Homework Assignments, Chapter 16).

ADOLESCENT'S GOALS	THERAPIST'S INTERVENTIONS
Pressurized speech eases.	Teach the adolescent active listening skills.
Sleep pattern improves.	Investigate for sleep problems and see that the adolescent is treated if necessary (see appropriate treatment plan).
Identify triggers for dreams or nightmares.	Explore dreams or nightmares that interrupt sleep.
Read assigned book and learn new techniques for soothing yourself to sleep.	Assign the adolescent with sleep problem to read *Can't You Sleep, Little Bear?* (see Bibliotherapy, Chapter 17).
Realize that others also feel bad, but overcome that feeling.	Investigate for low self-esteem related to the disorder.
Begin to see possible solutions.	Discuss how to deal with negative feelings.
Identify irrational beliefs.	Explore irrational beliefs about manic episodes.
Reframe beliefs about fears and anxieties.	Change irrational beliefs by exploring rational alternatives.
Understand anxiety and realize that avoidance does not help.	Teach the adolescent the laws of anxiety: anxiety is not dangerous or permanent; avoidance increases anxiety; confronting the problem can reduce anxiety; exposure can produce growth.
Communicate life story to therapist.	Have the adolescent relate his or her life story.
Express suppressed feelings in a non-threatening environment.	Play *The Talking, Feeling, Doing Game* to understand underlying processes in a non-threatening way (see Therapeutic Games, Chapter 15).

ADOLESCENT'S GOALS	THERAPIST'S INTERVENTIONS
Understand how trauma may have contributed to the existing disorder.	Explore the adolescent's background for trauma that resulted in or exacerbated the disorder.
Learn new skills to deal with your world.	Play *The Odyssey Islands Game* to reinforce morality, improve social skills, and increase problem solving (see Therapeutic Games, Chapter 15).
Discuss personal coping mechanisms developed to deal with manic behavior.	Investigate with adolescent possible patterns of excessive behaviors used to deal with mania.
Recognize and relate how family impacts the problem.	Explore familial impact on the problem.
Learn positive self-talk.	Teach the adolescent positive self-talk to interrupt negative patterns.
Learn new techniques to nurture yourself and deal with emotional difficulties.	Use the *Positive Thinking Game*, or *The Ungame* to teach ways positive self-talk can help control emotional difficulties (see Therapeutic Games, Chapter 15).
Shift focus of attention from problem to accomplishment.	Ask the adolescent to describe his or her accomplishments for the past week.
Develop new ways to release excessive energy.	Recommend routine exercise to help release frustrations.
Attempt to use new control skills in school.	If appropriate, urge the adolescent to use new control skills in the classroom setting.

ADOLESCENT'S GOALS	THERAPIST'S INTERVENTIONS
Report results to therapist.	Provide positive reinforcement when the adolescent reports back that he or she has challenged anxiety-provoking situations. Praise attempt and reward success.
Read assigned book and learn new skills and insights in changing destructive behavior.	Assign the adolescent to read *The Teens' Solutions Workbook* (see Bibliotherapy, Chapter 17).
Learn new strategies for managing problem behaviors.	Assign to read *SOS Help for Emotions* or alternate selection (see Bibliotherapy, Chapter 17).
Learn methods that can be used to advocate for yourself.	Instruct the adolescent in the techniques of self-advocacy.
Understand that you can deal with these issues and bring treatment to an end successfully.	Develop a treatment termination plan and explain issues of separation anxiety and dependency.

FAMILY'S GOALS	THERAPIST'S INTERVENTIONS
Improve communications among family members to reduce familial anxiety.	Conduct family sessions or refer for family therapy to reduce anger and/or alienation, and improve communication skills.
Accept the fact that a family member has a chronic disorder.	Educate family about the chronic nature of the disorder to reduce denial, anger, and blame.
Build family genogram and compare it with adolescent's genogram.	Amplify family genogram created in parent session and compare with adolescent genogram to understand family idea of the problem versus the adolescent's view.
Discuss genogram openly to fully understand family history as it relates to the disorder.	Discuss genogram to reveal family history and possible family secrets dealing with the disorder.
Demonstrate boundaries, alliances, triangles, and emotional currents that may exacerbate the anxieties.	Explore family boundaries using sculpturing, a useful technique for understanding triangulation, alliances, and emotional currents (see "Family Sculpturing," Behavioral Techniques, Chapter 14).
Improve communications among family members.	Identify interpersonal problems among family members and work toward promoting healthier interactions and reducing stress.
Shift focus from problem to possible solutions.	Have family imagine solutions to the problem that can be implemented to deal with the disorder when it manifests itself.

FAMILY'S GOALS	THERAPIST'S INTERVENTIONS
Think about what treatment outcome would look like. Explain what you would like to see change in other family members when treatment is completed.	Ask family members to think about what they might want to say about each other when treatment is completed.
Learn problem-solving techniques and begin working as a team.	Assign family reading *13 Steps to Help Families Stop Fighting* (see Bibliotherapy, Chapter 17).
Family realizes they have the power to make important changes even if they seem small.	Help family realize they have an opportunity to do some things differently.
Family members are empowered. They recognize that they can create positive change.	Ask family members to relate what they have accomplished in the past week.
Realize that major change is the result of small steps taken one at a time.	Help family identify and prioritize achievable goals.
Enhance understanding of condition and see how other families have handled similar problems.	Assign homework reading *Making Families Work and What to Do When They Don't* (see Bibliotherapy, Chapter 17).
Plan and take trips together to become more adhesive.	Encourage family to plan and go on outings to reduce alienation (i.e. museums, picnics etc.).
Make use of available community resources.	Refer family to available resources in the community (see Self-Help Groups and 800 Numbers, Chapter 18, and Online Resources, Chapter 19).
Reduce negative communication.	Develop a system of positive reinforcement within family to interact better with each other and reduce scapegoating.

FAMILY'S GOALS	THERAPIST'S INTERVENTIONS
Family works together to develop a treatment termination plan.	Discuss treatment termination issues and develop plan to terminate treatment.

7
DEPRESSIVE DISORDERS

MAJOR DEPRESSIVE DISORDER—(296.XX)

Specify: Single Episode—(296.2x)
Recurrent Episode—(296.3x)

Specifiers coded in the sixth digit:
1—Mild
2—Moderate
3—Severe without Psychotic Features
4—Severe with Psychotic Features
5—In Partial Remission
6—In Full Remission

Major Depressive Disorder is characterized by one or more Major Depressive Episodes without a history of Manic, Mixed, or Hypomanic episodes. If Manic, Mixed, or Hypomanic Episodes occur, the diagnosis should be revised to Bipolar Disorder. Although a substantial percentage of individuals diagnosed with severe Major Depressive Disorder die by suicide, the figure is much lower for children and adolescents. The disorder occurs twice as frequently in girls as in boys. Major Depressive Disorder may be preceded by Dysthymic Disorder and may coexist with other disorders.

Behavioral Symptoms
(severity index: 1–mild; 2–moderate; 3–intense)

Single Episode specifier requires five or more of the following symptoms occurring in a two-week period. Symptoms occur most all day, almost every day.

Recurrent Episodes specifier requires two consecutive months between episodes.

		Severity
1.	Depressed mood (as observed by parents or others)	_____
2.	Diminished interest or pleasure in almost all activities, socially withdrawn	_____
3.	Significant weight loss or gain, increase or decrease in appetite	_____
4.	Insomnia or hypersomnia	_____
5.	Psychomotor agitation or retardation	_____
6.	Irritable	_____
7.	Somatic complaints	_____
8.	Fatigue, loss of energy	_____
9.	Feelings of worthlessness, excessive guilt	_____
10.	Diminished ability to think or concentrate	_____
11.	Recurrent thoughts of death	_____
12.	Recurrent suicidal ideations, with or without a plan	_____
13.	Attempted suicide	_____

DYSTHYMIC DISORDER—(300.4)

Specify: Early onset: before age 21
Late onset: after age 21

Between 5 and 10% of all Americans suffer from Major Depression or Dysthymia every year. Dysthymia has fewer symptoms and is less severe than Major Depression. It is differentiated from a normal non-clinically depressed mood by the intensity and pervasiveness of the symptoms that are in excess of those considered normal reactions to the difficulties of life. The adolescent must have experienced depressed mood and at least two of the symptoms listed below for a period of two years to meet the requirements for this diagnosis.

Dysthymic Disorder occurs equally in boys and girls and usually impairs school performance and interpersonal relations. Adolescents with this disorder typically display low self-esteem, are cranky and irritable, and tend to be pessimistic. Patients with Dysthymia are vulnerable to Major Depression. Studies have shown that psychotherapy is an effective treatment. If no progress is apparent, the adolescent should be reevaluated and the treatment plan adjusted to include viable alternatives.

Behavioral Symptoms
(severity index: 1–mild; 2–moderate; 3–intense)

		Severity
1.	Pervasive depressed mood	_____
2.	Generalized loss of interest	_____
3.	Feelings of helplessness or hopelessness	_____
4.	Fatigue	_____
5.	Irritability, excessive anger	_____
6.	Decreased activity, productivity, or effectiveness	_____
7.	Poor concentration	_____
8.	Low self-esteem	_____
9.	Insomnia, hypersomnia	_____
10.	Difficulty making decisions	_____
11.	Excessive or inappropriate guilt	_____
12.	Poor appetite	_____
13.	Overeating	_____
14.	Thoughts of suicide or death	_____

DEPRESSIVE DISORDER NOS—(311)

Included in this category are disorders with depressive features that do not meet the requirements for Major Depressive Disorder, Dysthymic Disorder, or related mood disorders. Examples include Premenstrual Dysmorphic Disorder, Minor Depressive Disorder, Recurrent Brief Depressive Disorder, Postpsychotic Depressive Disorder, and a Major Depressive Episode superimposed on Delusional or Psychotic Disorder.

MAJOR DEPRESSIVE DISORDER
DYSTHYMIC DISORDER
DEPRESSIVE DISORDER NOS
TREATMENT PLAN

Patient: _____ Date: _____

I. OBJECTIVES OF TREATMENT *(select one or more)*

1. Educate parents about the disorder
2. Determine family history of the disorder
3. Help family develop better coping skills
4. Reduce persistent depression, diminish symptoms
5. Reduce pervasive anxiety and worry
6. Eliminate suicide plans, control suicidal ideations
7. Eliminate feelings of worthlessness, guilt
8. Restore normal eating patterns
9. Encourage compliance with educational programs and referrals
10. Improve energy level
11. Reduce irrational beliefs
12. Restore interest in former pleasurable activities
13. Promote socialization, reduce alienation
14. Restore adolescent and family to optimum level of functioning

II. SHORT-TERM BEHAVIORAL GOALS AND INTERVENTIONS
(select goals and interventions appropriate for your patient)

NOTE: Separate goals and interventions are provided for Parents, Adolescent, and Family

PARENTS' GOALS	THERAPIST'S INTERVENTIONS
Collaborate with therapist in development of a treatment plan.	Establish therapeutic alliance with parents to enhance outcome of treatment.
Help therapist understand your adolescent's development of major depression.	Assess problem with parents and record a comprehensive history of the adolescent's development of major depression.

PARENTS' GOALS	THERAPIST'S INTERVENTIONS
If actively suicidal, hospitalize your adolescent immediately to preclude harm to self.	If the adolescent is actively suicidal, have parents hospitalize him or her immediately.
Undergo immediate evaluation to determine possible need for hospitalization.	If parents report that the adolescent has suicidal ideations, evaluate immediately to determine need for hospitalization.
Develop a plan in case your adolescent goes into crisis.	Teach parents to recognize when the adolescent is in crisis and develop strategies for dealing with the situation (i.e. suicide pact, hospitalization etc.).
Become aware of the diagnosis and what to appropriately expect.	Educate parents about the diagnosis. Explain chronicity of the disorder and contagion of depression.
Realize that anger is a pitfall.	Inform parents that family members often become angry with the depressed adolescent.
Cooperate in building a genogram to identify familial history and its relationship to depression.	Construct a genogram to better understand the family history and define how family deals with depression and its impact on the adolescent (see Behavioral Techniques, Chapter 14).
Enter treatment for depression or other existing disorders to enhance the adolescent's treatment.	Evaluate parents for depression or other psychiatric problems and treat or refer for treatment.

PARENTS' GOALS	THERAPIST'S INTERVENTIONS
Develop awareness of how your personal theory influences cognition of the problem in adolescent.	Explore parental theory of the problem.
Identify other problems associated with Major Depressive Disorder.	Investigate other problems that may be associated with Major Depressive Disorder (i.e. sleep disorders, somatization, eating disorders, guilt, worthlessness, fatigue).
Recognize fears and feelings of negative self-blame related to the problem.	Evaluate parents' fears and negative feelings of self-blame for the adolescent's problem.
Have your adolescent tested to confirm diagnosis and determine level of intensity of depression.	Refer the adolescent for psychological testing or test him or her in individual session using Beck's Depression Inventory (BDI-1-11) to confirm diagnosis and determine level of intensity of depression.
Learn to reach beyond automatic cognitive reactions in viewing the problem.	Expand parental perspective beyond limited cognitive reactions.
Parents learn to deal with sleep disorder of your adolescent.	Investigate for sleep problems in the adolescent and teach parents how to deal with problem.
Have your adolescent evaluated for medical problems and treated if necessary.	Refer the adolescent for medical evaluation to rule out Disorder Due to a General Medical Condition.
If sexual abuse is confirmed, have your adolescent placed in protected environment and treated.	Evaluate and rule out sexual abuse. If suspected that parents are abusers, refer for treatment and notify appropriate authorities.

PARENTS' GOALS	THERAPIST'S INTERVENTIONS
Identify existing triggers that may cause depression.	Investigate with parents underlying feelings and identify issue that may cause or contribute to depression.
Become aware of possible resentment toward your adolescent for being depressed.	Assess possible anger and resentment parents or other family members may have toward the adolescent because of the depression.
Recognize your anger and control your acting on it.	Understand that depressed people are often the targets of anger by those around them.
Learn diaphragmatic breathing as relaxation technique and teach your adolescent to help in relaxation.	Teach parents diaphragmatic breathing to assist the adolescent in relaxation (see Behavioral Techniques, Chapter 14).
Agree to allow therapist to confer with your adolescent's school to help in development of a comprehensive psychoeducational treatment plan.	After interviewing the adolescent, and with his or her permission, request and receive parental permission to confer with the adolescent's teachers and school administrators.
Develop new parenting skills to deal with depression and eliminate guilt and anxiety.	Assign parents to read *Making Families Work and What to Do When They Don't* and *Feeling Good* (see Bibliotherapy, Chapter 17).
Learn creative options for building self-esteem in your family.	Assign parents to read *Self-Esteem: A Family Affair* (see Bibliotherapy, Chapter 17).
Monitor your adolescent's medication schedule and report all reactions or failures to take meds.	If the adolescent is on meds, instruct parents on need for a regular schedule and feedback that may indicate need for revised dosage.

PARENTS' GOALS	THERAPIST'S INTERVENTIONS
Meet with other parents who are experiencing similar difficulties, and share solutions for coping with the problem.	Refer parents to self-help group or group on parenting skills (see Self-Help Groups and 800 Numbers, Chapter 18, and Online Resources, Chapter 19).
Read about depressive disorders and suicide to better understand how to cope.	Assign parents to read *A Parent's Guide for Suicidal and Depressed Teens* (see Bibliotherapy, Chapter 17).
Discuss a treatment termination plan and resolve related issues.	Develop a treatment termination plan and discuss issues of separation anxiety and dependency.

ADOLESCENT'S GOALS	THERAPIST'S INTERVENTIONS
Engage in therapy.	Engage the adolescent in a therapeutic relationship.
Learn about diagnosis and develop realistic expectations of self.	Educate the adolescent about the diagnosis and discuss symptomatology so he or she can adjust self-expectations.
Undergo treatment for sleep disorder.	Investigate for sleep disorder and treat if necessary. See appropriate treatment plan.
Identify symptoms related to the disorder.	Explore ways in which depression manifests itself (irritability, somatization, guilt, feelings of worthlessness, fatigue etc.)
Have medical exam. If necessary, be treated medically.	Refer for medical exam to rule out Disorder Due to a General Medical Condition. If positive, change diagnosis and refer the adolescent for medical treatment.
Follow up with referral.	Refer for psychiatric evaluation and possible medication.
Maintain medication regimen.	Encourage the adolescent to maintain a regular medication schedule and warn against mixing medication with street drugs or alcohol.
Discuss with therapist your reactions to psychiatric evaluation and meds.	Discuss the adolescent's reaction to evaluation and medication if prescribed.
Realize that human beings are not perfect, and reduce stressors imposed on self.	Teach the adolescent that human beings are not perfect.

ADOLESCENT'S GOALS	THERAPIST'S INTERVENTIONS
Willingly enter into "suicide pact" with therapist and agree to inform therapist before taking any action.	If the adolescent is clearly not suicidal, but has ideations, implement a "suicidal pact."
Recognize and clarify underlying feelings of depression.	Explore and clarify underlying feelings of depression.
Your depression is confirmed and intensity defined.	Refer for or administer Beck's Depression Inventory (BDI-1-11) to confirm existence of the disorder and the level of intensity.
Recognize family climate and identify where to turn for support.	Explore adolescent's perceptions of his or her family climate (i.e., closeness, distance, supportive or not).
Realize others also feel bad and overcome those feelings. Discuss how you feel with therapist and what you can do about it.	Investigate for feelings of low esteem related to depression.
Understand how trauma may have contributed to existing disorder.	Explore the adolescent's background for trauma that may have exacerbated the depression.
Undergo treatment for sexual abuse. Be relocated to safe environment if parents are abusers.	Investigate for sexual abuse. If the adolescent is being abused, notify authorities and treat (see appropriate treatment plan). If parents are abusers, have the adolescent removed to safe environment.
Spell out the characteristics of your family (i.e. physical and emotional boundaries, cut-offs, and toxic issues.)	Construct a genogram to understand adolescent's perception of how his or her family of origin has dealt with depression and uncover toxic issues.

ADOLESCENT'S GOALS	THERAPIST'S INTERVENTIONS
Recognize existing triggers that cause depression.	Explore issues and feelings that lead to depression.
Recognize and express feelings of self-rage and anger.	Probe for possible feelings of anger and self-rage.
Through role-playing, better understand your relationships with others and develop better style of communications.	Use role-playing to clarify the adolescent's relationships and style of communications.
Replace negative self-talk.	Explain self-talk and encourage the adolescent to replace negative self-talk with positive affirmations.
Understand anxiety and realize that avoidance does not help.	Teach the adolescent the laws of anxiety: anxiety is not dangerous or permanent; avoidance increases anxiety; confronting the problem can reduce anxiety; exposure can produce growth.
Communicate your life story to therapist.	Have the adolescent relate the story of his or her life, or play *Life Stories* (see Therapeutic Games, Chapter 15).
Express suppressed feelings in a non-threatening environment.	Play *The Talking, Feeling, Doing Game* to understand underlying processes in a non-threatening way (see Therapeutic Games, Chapter 15).
Discuss personal coping mechanisms developed to handle the disorder.	Investigate with the adolescent possible patterns of withdrawal used to avoid anxieties.
Recognize and relate how family impacts the problem.	Explore familial impact on the problem.

ADOLESCENT'S GOALS	THERAPIST'S INTERVENTIONS
Learn new technique for dealing with anxiety.	Teach diaphragmatic breathing to control anxiety (see Behavioral Techniques, Chapter 14).
Use art to help express feelings about your past, present, and future.	Help the adolescent comprehend past, present, and future and express feelings about major life events.
Shift focus of attention from problem to accomplishment.	Ask the adolescent to describe his or her accomplishments for the past week.
Develop a realistic plan to reduce depression.	Help adolescent develop S.M.A.R.T. action plan—Small, Measurable, Achievable, Realistic, Timelined goals—to help focus on solutions and begin to see a future without depression.
Build new assertiveness skills.	Teach the adolescent the principles of assertiveness—equal respect for self and others.
Report results to therapist.	Provide positive reinforcement when the adolescent reports back that he or she has challenged anxiety or depression-provoking situations. Praise attempt and reward success.
Learn new techniques for dealing with depression.	With parents' permission, use hypnosis, visualization, or relaxation techniques to coach the adolescent to handle triggers of depression. Provide audiotape for home use (see Behavioral Techniques, Chapter 14).

ADOLESCENT'S GOALS	THERAPIST'S INTERVENTIONS
Learn the secret of optimistic thinking to change attitudes and behavior.	Assign to read *Feeling Good* (see Bibliotherapy, Chapter 17).
Learn simple ways to change your life.	Assign to read *When Living Hurts: For Teenagers and Young Adults* or *Do One Thing Different* (see Bibliotherapy, Chapter 17).
Learn methods that can be used to advocate for yourself.	Instruct the adolescent in the techniques of self-advocacy.
Diminish need to "hide out" because of guilt and/or shame over being depressed.	Gradually build the adolescent's self-confidence to a point where avoidance behavior is no longer a rational response.
Realize that it is important to ask for what you want.	Encourage the adolescent to reach out and ask for what he or she wants with the caveat that he or she might not get it.
Realize that you are more than just a disorder and can use your unique skills to deal with problems.	Empower the adolescent by reinforcing skills and strengths.
Understand that you can deal with these issues and bring treatment to an end successfully.	Develop a treatment termination plan and explain issues of separation anxiety and dependency.

FAMILY'S GOALS	THERAPIST'S INTERVENTIONS
Improve communications among family members to reduce familial anxiety.	Conduct family sessions or refer for family therapy to reduce anger and/or alienation, and improve communication skills.
Cooperate in amplifying existing genogram.	Amplify genograms created in parental and adolescent sessions to clarify family history.
Discuss genogram to understand family members' views of the problem and how depression has been handled.	Have family discuss expanded genogram to understand history associated with depression and family members' views of the problem.
Demonstrate boundaries, alliances, triangles, and emotional currents that may exacerbate the anxieties.	Explore family boundaries using sculpturing, a useful technique for understanding triangulation, alliances, and emotional currents (see Behavioral Techniques, Chapter 14).
Explain how depression impacts your life and suggest strategies for dealing with it.	Explore with each family member how depression affects them and possible strategies for dealing with it.
Shift focus from problem to possible solutions.	Have family members imagine a future without the problem and suggest actions that can be taken now to make that future possible.
Other family members are treated.	Determine if other family members have Major Depressive Disorder and treat or refer for treatment.

FAMILY'S GOALS	THERAPIST'S INTERVENTIONS
Understand that it is normal, but counterproductive to get angry with a depressed family member.	Explain dynamics of depression cycle. Depression triggers anger in others, which, in turn, exacerbates the depression.
Family members realize they have the power to make important changes even if they seem small.	Help family members realize they have an opportunity to do some things differently.
Learn new ways to deal with unpleasant feelings.	Encourage prosocial behaviors to develop family cohesiveness.
Family members are empowered. They recognize that they can create positive change.	Ask family members to relate what they have accomplished in the past week.
Realize that major change is the result of small steps taken one at a time.	Help family develop S.M.A.R.T. action plan—Small, Measurable, Achievable, Realistic, Timelined goals (see Behavioral Techniques, Chapter 14).
Focus on strengths rather than weaknesses.	Have each family member identify strengths they see in the other members.
Enhance understanding of depression and learn how other families have dealt with this disorder.	Assign homework reading of *Making Families Work and What to Do When They Don't* or *Self-Esteem: A Family Affair* (see Bibliotherapy, Chapter 17).
Make use of available community resources.	Refer family to available resources in the community (see Self-Help Groups and 800 Numbers, Chapter 18, and Online Resources, Chapter 19).

FAMILY'S GOALS	THERAPIST'S INTERVENTIONS
Plan and hold outings together to build family cohesiveness.	Encourage family outings and other activities (trips, museums, picnics, beach, ballgames etc.) to reduce alienation.
Reduce negative communication.	Develop a system of positive reinforcement with family to interact better with each other and reduce scapegoating.

BEREAVEMENT—(V62.82)

Bereavement is a reaction to the death of a loved one. Some grieving people react with symptoms typical of Major Depressive Disorder (e.g. sadness, insomnia, poor appetite, weight loss). Typically, they regard the depressed mood as normal. The duration of the Bereavement and how it is expressed may vary widely among different cultural groups. However, the diagnosis of Major Depressive Disorder is not usually given unless the symptoms persist for more than two months. Certain symptoms may be helpful in differentiating Major Depression and Bereavement. Bereavement may include guilt about actions or lack of action at the time of death, thinking he or she, too, should have died, and auditory and visual hallucinations of the deceased. Depression may include other unrelated guilt and thoughts of death, preoccupation with feelings of worthlessness, marked psychomotor retardation, prolonged functional impairment, and other hallucinatory experiences. V-codes, such as that for Bereavement, should be entered on Axis IV of the *DSM-IV* Multiaxial Assessment System with the associated impairment coded on Axis I.

Behavioral Symptoms
(severity index: 1–mild; 2–moderate; 3–intense)

		Severity
1.	Denial or numbness	_____
2.	Major persistent depression	_____
3.	Inability to fall asleep or stay asleep	_____
4.	Nightmares or night terrors	_____
5.	Loss of appetite	_____
6.	Separation anxiety	_____
7.	Adjustment disorders	_____
8.	Serious impairment of school activities	_____
9.	Helplessness or hopelessness	_____
10.	Hyperactivity	_____
11.	Persistent anger	_____
12.	Guilt over being a survivor	_____
13.	Constant anxiety or panic attacks	_____
14.	Hears voice of or sees transitory images of deceased	_____
15.	Difficulties in interpersonal relationships	_____
16.	Somatization	_____
17.	Acts out in various ways	_____

BEREAVEMENT TREATMENT PLAN

Patient: _____ Date: _____

I. OBJECTIVES OF TREATMENT *(select one or more)*

1. Educate parent(s) or caregivers about the stages of death
2. Determine whether the death was sudden or after a long illness
3. Help family develop better coping skills
4. Help the mourners through the grieving process
5. Reduce pervasive anxiety and worry
6. Diminish symptoms of anxiety and guilt
7. Resolve feelings of despair and hopelessness
8. Eliminate sleep disturbances and nightmares
9. Restore appetite, stop weight loss
10. Encourage compliance with educational programs and referrals
11. Reframe irrational beliefs
12. Promote socialization, reduce alienation
13. Develop discharge plan for coping with everyday life

II. SHORT-TERM BEHAVIORAL GOALS AND INTERVENTIONS
(select goals and interventions appropriate for your patient)

NOTE: Separate goals and interventions are provided for Parents, Adolescent, and Family

PARENTS' GOALS	THERAPIST'S INTERVENTIONS
Collaborate with therapist in the development of a treatment plan	Attempt to establish a therapeutic alliance with parents or caregiver to enhance outcome of treatment.
Identify the circumstances of the death and the adolescent's reaction to it.	Explore nature of the death and how the adolescent has reacted.
Parents are treated for grief reactions to death in order for them to be more available.	If parents exhibit post-traumatic symptoms or separation anxiety treat them individually from the adolescent.

PARENTS' GOALS	THERAPIST'S INTERVENTIONS
Parents identify their style of dealing with death.	Explore how parents dealt with the death. Did they respond overtly to the loss and talk about it, or did they go underground emotionally, acting as if it never happened?
Parents are treated to help them through the process of mourning. reaction	If death was of a sibling, investigate the parent's and treat or refer for treatment.
Parents identify underlying death anxieties.	Explore parents underlying death anxieties.
Identify religious beliefs and what the parents have told the adolescent about death.	Explore parents' religious beliefs about death and what they have told the adolescent.
Learn the stages of death and understand that mourning is a normal and important act.	Educate the family about the stages of mourning (denial, anger, bargaining, depression, and accommodation) to help them understand normal grieving.
Parents understand that it is okay to express their reactions and encourage their family to talk about it.	Encourage parents to express pain and grief reactions to their loss in order to help them act as role models for their family.
Parents realize that death anxiety is a universal problem and that its denial can lead to other problems.	Educate the parents to realize that death anxiety is universal and if we deny death, or don't talk about it with our children, it can cause further problems.
Develop awareness of how your personal theory influences cognition of the problem in your adolescent.	Explore parental theory of the problem.

PARENTS' GOALS	THERAPIST'S INTERVENTIONS
Recognize fears and feelings of negative self-blame.	Evaluate parent's fears and negative feelings of self-blame related to the death.
Learn to reach beyond automatic cognitive reactions in dealing with death.	Expand parental perspective beyond limited cognitive reactions.
Parents learn how to help themselves and their family deal with anxiety.	Teach parents the dynamics of anxiety: anxiety is not permanent or dangerous; avoidance increases anxiety; confronting the problem can reduce anxiety; exposure can produce growth.
Family understands that certain tasks need to be accomplished so they can continue to live.	Teach parents to understand that the experience of grief is not a passive state. To move beyond it involves adaptation to be in the world without the dead person.
Parents learn to deal with the adolescent's sleep disorder.	Investigate for sleep problems or nightmares in the adolescent, and teach parents how to deal with it.
Confront thoughts of exaggerated and unrealistic consequences—"what ifs?"	Guide parents in confronting distorted reactions to trigger situations.
Identify cognitive distortions.	Weigh the actions against evidence-based reality.
Parents understand that going through a transitional period of grief can lead to greater development.	Educate parents to understand the Phoenix Model: (1) Impact, (2) Chaos, (3) Adaptation, (4) Equilibrium, (5) Transformation (see *The Phoenix Phenomenon: Rising From the Ashes of Grief* in Bibliotherapy, Chapter 17).

PARENTS' GOALS	THERAPIST'S INTERVENTIONS
Parents attend bereavement group, get support from others, and share coping solutions.	Refer parents to a bereavement group in order to help them connect with others who are also experiencing grief (see Self-Help Groups and 800 Numbers, Chapter 18, and Online Resources, Chapter 19).
Parents develop new parenting skills and learn how to help their family cope with death.	Assign parents books to read on how to deal with death and increase parenting skills, such as *Making Families Work and What to Do When They Don't* (see Bibliotherapy, Chapter 17).
Discuss a treatment termination plan and resolve related issues.	Develop a treatment termination plan and discuss issues of separation anxiety and dependency.

ADOLESCENT'S GOALS	THERAPIST'S INTERVENTIONS
Develop a therapeutic relationship in order to help you through the loss of a loved one.	Engage the adolescent in a therapeutic relationship in order to enhance the outcome of treatment.
Identify the way you are attempting to deal with the death.	Investigate how the adolescent is dealing with the death.
Express the way the loss has affected you	Explore the crisis. What effect has the loss had on the family and ultimately on the adolescent?
Realize that you can look to others for support.	Identify and explore the availability of support systems. Are there aunts, uncles, or friends available to help the family adjust to the "emotional shock wave."
Understand the necessary stages of grief and be reassured that you will be able to get through the grieving process.	Educate the child about the stages of grief: (1) shock or denial and disbelief; (2) anger about the loss, a yearning for the lost person, or "Why did it happen to me?"; (3) chaos and despair: "How can it ever get better?"; and (4) bargaining, "If I behave better or if I am a better person, things will improve." Help the adolescent to see new ways to reorganize and create a new life, while reassuring the adolescent that he or she will be able to get through the grieving process.
Identify your feelings about the death of the sibling.	If it was a sibling who died, explore how the surviving adolescent is dealing with the loss. Does the survivor blame self or feel guilty?

ADOLESCENT'S GOALS	THERAPIST'S INTERVENTIONS
Identify your feelings about the death in order to work through the pain of grief.	Determine which stage of grief the survivor is experiencing.
Understand that there can also be physical responses to loss.	Investigate for any physical responses such as hyperactivity, or somatization (i.e. tightness in the chest, stomach pains, fatigue etc.).
Undergo treatment for sleep disorder.	Investigate for symptoms of a sleep disorder, nightmares, insomnia etc. (see appropriate treatment plan).
Realize that human beings are not perfect, and reduce stressors imposed on the self.	Teach the adolescent that human beings are not perfect.
Identify the impact of the loss on schoolwork.	Explore for any manifestations of academic problems related to the death and treat accordingly (see appropriate treatment plan).
Realize that others also feel bad when a loved one dies and that talking about it helps.	Investigate for feelings of low self-esteem related to the loss.
Cooperate in building a genogram to identify familial history and typical cultural and emotional responses to death.	Construct a genogram to better understand the family history and define how they historically deal with death (i.e., culturally, religiously, and emotionally). What familial support systems are available? (See Behavioral Techniques, Chapter 14.)
Identify irrational beliefs.	Explore irrational beliefs about death.

ADOLESCENT'S GOALS	THERAPIST'S INTERVENTIONS
Parent states whether the adolescent was included or excluded in the mourning process.	Investigate how the funeral was handled. Was the adolescent excluded to avoid upsetting him or her or included to realistically involve him or her in mourning the death.
Reframe beliefs about fears and anxieties	Discuss the beliefs and develop rational alternatives.
Express your feelings psychodramatically to complete his or her business with the deceased.	If appropriate for the stage of grieving, role-play (using an empty chair to represent the deceased). Have the adolescent express what he or she would like to have said to the deceased while he or she was still alive (see Behavioral Techniques, Chapter 14).
Using guided imagery learn to gain control over feelings.	With parents' permission, teach adolescent relaxation techniques and guided imagery to master anxieties (see Behavioral Techniques, Chapter 14).
Understand anxiety and realize that avoidance doe not help.	Teach adolescent the dynamics of anxiety: anxiety is not permanent or dangerous; avoidance increases anxiety; confronting the problem can reduce anxiety; exposure can produce growth.
Communicate your life story to the therapist.	Have the adolescent relate the story of his or her life.

ADOLESCENT'S GOALS	THERAPIST'S INTERVENTIONS
Express suppressed feelings about saying goodbye to a loved one.	Play *The Goodbye Game* to dispel myths and false ideas regarding death (see Therapeutic Games, Chapter 15).
Discuss personal coping mechanisms developed to handle death.	With the adolescent, investigate possible patterns of social withdrawal or becoming overly active as a way of dealing with feelings about the deceased.
Recognize and discuss how the family affects the problem.	Explore the family's impact on the problem. Are they supportive; do they talk about the death or pretend that it never happened? Remind the adolescent that anxiety and uncertainty are normal parts of grief.
Learn positive self-talk.	Teach the adolescent positive self-talk to interrupt negative patterns.
Learn new techniques for relaxing and dealing with anxieties.	Teach diaphragmatic breathing to help the adolescent relax and reduce stress (see Behavioral Techniques, Chapter 14).
Identify the ways that you have changed.	Investigate ways that the adolescent has changed in an attempt to create meaning for what he or she has gone through.
Shift focus of attention from problem to accomplishments.	Ask the adolescent to describe his or her accomplishments for the past week

ADOLESCENT'S GOALS	THERAPIST'S INTERVENTIONS
Feel more confident as self-esteem improves.	Compliment the adolescent to provide positive reinforcement whenever possible.
Learn to cope with losses.	Assign to read *Grief's Courageous Journey* or *Necessary Losses* (see Bibliotherapy, Chapter 17).
Learn how to avoid hazards and grow through the experience of Bereavement.	Assign an older adolescent to read *The Phoenix Phenomenon: Rising From the Ashes of Grief* (see Bibliotherapy, Chapter 17).
Learn methods that you can use to advocate for yourself.	Instruct the adolescent in the techniques of self-advocacy.
Understand that you can deal with these issues and bring treatment to a successful end.	Develop a treatment termination plan and explain issues of separation anxiety and dependency.

FAMILY'S GOALS	THERAPIST'S INTERVENTIONS
Improve communications among family members to reduce familial anxiety.	Conduct family sessions or refer for family therapy to reduce alienation, improve communication skills, and enhance understanding of the impact of the loss on the family.
Drawings offer help in communicating alliances and feelings and may also allow members to express toxic issues.	Ask family members (especially the children) to draw pictures of the family before and after the death.
Cooperate in amplifying family genogram.	Amplify genogram created in first parental session to help understand how the family has historically dealt with death culturally, religiously, and emotionally.
Discuss genogram openly to fully understand family history as it relates to the issue of death.	Discuss genogram to reveal family history and possible family secrets about death (see Behavioral Techniques, Chapter 14).
Demonstrate boundaries, alliances, triangles, and emotional currents that may exacerbate the problem.	Explore boundaries using family sculpturing, a useful technique for understanding triangulation, alliances, and emotional currents (see Behavioral Techniques, Chapter 14).
Identify outside sources who can lend support and help the grieving process.	Determine if there are members of the extended family (aunts, uncles, cousins) who can provide additional support.

FAMILY'S GOALS	THERAPIST'S INTERVENTIONS
Each family member identifies his or her reaction to the loss.	Explore individual reactions to the death. See how each member felt before and after the loss.
Family understands the normal stages of grieving and what to expect from each other.	If the rest of the family doesn't know about the stages of grief, explain it using both the Kubler-Ross Model: Denial, Anger, Bargaining, Depression, and Acceptance (Kubler-Ross, 1997), or the Phoenix Model: Impact, Chaos Adaptation, Equilibrium, and Transformation.
Each member shares his or her view, which encourages bonding and reduces stress.	Have each member explore their feelings about the person and the death in order to give their sorrow words, which can be cathartic. Discuss each member's adaptations.
Identify methods of coping.	Discuss methods of coping.
Identify ways family can grow out of loss.	Have the family members imagine a future without their loved one and suggest actions that can be taken now which can help them grow even in the middle of a loss.
Identify irrational thoughts related to the death.	Explore irrational methods of coping in parents, children, and adolescents. Do they feel guilty for the death, blame each other etc.?
Each member identifies their unfinished business with the deceased and psychodynamically works through relevant issues that are unresolved.	Use role-playing with an empty chair (the chair representing the person who died). Ask family members to express what they would like to relate

FAMILY'S GOALS	THERAPIST'S INTERVENTIONS
	to the dead person. Include any unfinished business they would like to complete (see Behavioral Techniques, Chapter 14).
Identify hidden blame in order to work it out.	Explore for hidden blame among family members.
Each member identifies if and how he or she experiences survivor's guilt.	Investigate for survivor's guilt and educate family that it is a normal part of the grieving process.
Family identifies the changes created by the loss and their impact.	Explore the crisis the loss has produced in the family (i.e. financial, housing, single parenting etc.).
Family realizes that through growth and adaptation they can find hope.	Educate family about the phases of adaptation and help them realize their old life has ended. Help them to let go and see that this process can be the birthplace of hope.
Family becomes empowered by realizing that through trial and error they can take on new roles and grow.	Assist family to establish equilibrium by taking on new roles and by planning a life without the deceased person.
Each family member strengthens himself or herself by developing new and productive roles.	Help each family member build self-confidence through realistic, actual achievements.
Each member individually develops S.M.A.R.T. action plan.	Develop a S.M.A.R.T. action plan—Small, Measurable, Achievable, Realistic, Timelined goals (see "Change," Behavioral Techniques, Chapter 14).

FAMILY'S GOALS	THERAPIST'S INTERVENTIONS
Family members realize they have the power to make important changes, even if they seem small.	Help family realize they have an opportunity to do some things differently.
Family members are empowered. They recognize that they can create positive change.	Ask family members to relate what they have accomplished in the past week.
Realize that major change is the result of small changes taken one at a time	Help family identify and prioritize achievable goals.
Identify individual transformation.	Have each member identify ways he or she has transformed since the death of the loved one.
Discuss the assigned books to enhance understanding of grief.	Assign homework reading *The Phoenix Phenomenon: Rising From the Ashes of Grief*, and *Living Beyond Loss: Death in the Family* (see Bibliotherapy, Chapter 17).
Make use of available community resources.	Refer family to available bereavement groups in the community (see Self-Help Groups and 800 Numbers, Chapter 18, and Online Resources, Chapter 19).
Reduce negative communication.	Develop a system of positive reinforcement with family to help them interact better with each other and reduce scapegoating.
Family works together to develop a treatment termination plan.	Discuss termination issues and develop plan to terminate treatment.

8
EATING DISORDERS

This category includes Anorexia Nervosa and Bulimia Nervosa.

ANOREXIA NERVOSA—(307.1)

Anorexia Nervosa is characterized by an abnormal drive toward thinness and perfection, an intense fear of gaining weight or becoming fat, and a refusal to maintain a normal body weight. The onset usually begins in adolescence with a disturbance in the way individuals think about the size and weight of their bodies. Females are twice as likely as males to be affected by this disorder. The norms of Western society, cognitive distortions, and family obsessions have been identified as contributing factors. Anorexia is increasingly found in younger children mainly because of cultural pressures that extol thinness (i.e. fashion models, TV actresses, Barbie). The disorder can be related to certain athletic activities such as ballet dancing, gymnastics, and ice-skating.

There are two subtypes of this disorder: Restricting and Purging. The restricting type reduces body weight by controlling calories, and these patients are usually obsessed with food intake and feelings of superiority because of their food control. The binge-eating, purging type patient controls weight by vomiting and using laxatives and/or diuretics. Unlike bulimic patients, they do not regularly overeat, but will purge even small amounts of food.

Behavioral Symptoms
(severity index: 1–mild; 2–moderate; 3–intense)

		Severity
1.	Body weight is significantly (85%) below normal	_____
2.	Intense fear of gaining weight or becoming fat	_____
3.	Clings to the shelter of childhood	_____
4.	Amenorrhea–absence of three consecutive menstrual cycles	_____
5.	Denies seriousness of low body weight	_____
6.	Restricts calorie intake; obsessed with low calorie, low-fat foods	_____
7.	Overeats and purges by vomiting, or by use of laxatives, enemas, or diuretics	_____
8.	Uses excessive exercise to control weight	_____
9.	Feels superior to others because of food control	_____
10.	Extremely self-critical; needs to be perfect	_____

BULIMIA NERVOSA—(307.51)

Bulimia Nervosa is marked by binge eating followed by inappropriate compensatory methods to prevent weight gain such as purging, excessive exercise, and use of laxatives, enemas, or diuretics. Body size and weight excessively influence self-esteem. The disorder typically begins in adolescence or early adulthood, predominantly in females. Binge eating usually occurs in secrecy and is accompanied by a feeling of lack of control. Binge eating is usually triggered by dysmorphic mood, interpersonal stressors, or intense hunger following a prolonged period of dieting. Patients are typically reluctant to discuss symptoms as the result of embarrassment or ambivalence toward binging. Some evidence of pathology in the family of origin exists, and it is possible that the disorder is linked to sexual abuse. There are two subtypes of Bulimia Nervosa: Purging and Non-Purging. The latter relies on fasting and over-exercising to control weight.

Behavioral Symptoms
(severity index: 1–mild; 2–moderate; 3–intense)

		Severity
1.	Recurrent binge eating	_____
2.	Feeling of loss of control during binge	_____
3.	Inappropriate use of vomiting, laxatives, enemas, or diuretics	_____
4.	Over-exercising	_____
5.	Exhibits low self-esteem	_____
6.	Over-concern with body weight and fatness	_____
7.	Extremely self-critical	_____
8.	Depressed and/or anxious	_____
9.	Difficulties with family of origin	_____
10.	Poor interpersonal skills	_____

ANOREXIA NERVOSA
BULIMIA NERVOSA
TREATMENT PLAN

Patient: _____ Date: _____

I. OBJECTIVES OF TREATMENT *(select one or more)*

1. Educate parents about the disorder
2. Determine family history of the disorder
3. Evaluate and reduce idiosyncratic beliefs related to food and weight
4. If appropriate, identify sexual abuse
5. Help family develop better coping skills
6. Reduce preoccupation with food, promote weight gain
7. Establish healthy eating patterns, promote weight gain
8. Reduce stressors that cause adolescent to under eat
9. Reduce irrational fears of becoming fat
10. Eliminate purging by self-induced vomiting or laxative abuse
11. Eliminate compulsive exercise
12. Develop healthy coping styles, restore normal eating patterns
13. Mitigate need for perfection
14. Decrease need to control environment and be superior
15. Reduce alienation, promote socialization
16. Restore adolescent and family to optimum level of functioning
17. Make full use of available community resources
18. Develop discharge plan for coping with everyday life

II. SHORT-TERM BEHAVIORAL GOALS AND INTERVENTIONS
(select goals and interventions appropriate for your patient)

NOTE: Separate goals and interventions are provided for Parents, Adolescent, and Family

PARENTS' GOALS	THERAPIST'S INTERVENTIONS
Collaborate with therapist in development of a treatment plan.	Establish therapeutic alliance with parents to enhance outcome of treatment.

PARENTS' GOALS	THERAPIST'S INTERVENTIONS
Help therapist understand development of your adolescent's eating disorder.	Assess problem with parents and record a comprehensive history of the adolescent's development of eating problems.
Comply with referral for psychiatric and/or medical evaluation.	Provide referral for psychiatric and/or medical evaluation as appropriate.
Comply with referral for dental evaluation.	If the adolescent is vomiting to control weight, refer for dental evaluation to assess and treat damage to teeth.
Become aware of the diagnosis and what to appropriately expect from your adolescent.	Educate parents about the diagnosis.
Understand seriousness your adolescent's condition and comply with immediate hospitalization.	If the adolescent is significantly underweight, refer for immediate hospitalization.
Identify dysfunctional attitudes or cognitive distortions within family system	Explore for maladaptive assumptions, expectations, tacit beliefs, or cognitive distortions related to eating.
Identify maladaptive ways you role model weight control.	Discuss methods used by parents to control weight (i.e. diet pills, laxatives etc.).
Cooperate in building a genogram to identify familial history and its relationship to eating disorder.	Construct a genogram to better understand the family history and define how family deals with food and its impact on the adolescent's eating patterns (see Behavioral Techniques, Chapter 14).

PARENTS' GOALS	THERAPIST'S INTERVENTIONS
Enter treatment for identified problems to enhance outcome of your adolescent's therapy.	Evaluate parents for anxiety, depression, eating problems, or marital discord and treat or refer for treatment as appropriate
Develop awareness of how your personal attitudes influence cognition of the problem in your adolescent.	Explore parental theory of the problem and impact it has on the adolescent's problem (i.e. need for perfection, negative reaction to obesity etc.).
Identify and discuss societal and family obsession with thinness.	Investigate parental issues that reinforce pathological eating patterns.
Learn to reach beyond automatic cognitive reactions in viewing the problem.	Expand parental perspective beyond limited cognitive reactions.
Recognize your expectations of your adolescent and pressures you exert for compliance with them.	Explore parental expectations of their adolescent and pressures they exert for perfection or compliance.
Mitigate pressures on your adolescent.	Guide parents in alleviating identified pressures on the adolescent.
Explore fears of allowing your adolescent to grow up and move through a healthy separation-individuation process.	Explore parental need to maintain the adolescent in childlike state and tacit induction of fear of growing up.
Confront and clarify mixed messages given to your adolescent.	Help parents confront distorted reactions and clarify mixed messages given to the adolescent.
Replace irrational ideas concerning weight with more rational goals.	Explore for irrational expectations about weight.

PARENTS' GOALS	THERAPIST'S INTERVENTIONS
Learn not to reinforce secondary gains of the adolescent's disorder.	Discuss secondary gains of eating disorder (i.e. feelings of superiority, admiration for control etc.).
Agree to allow therapist to confer with school to help in development of a comprehensive psychoeducational treatment plan for their adolescent.	If appropriate, after meeting with the adolescent and with his or her permission, request and receive parental permission to consult with teachers and school officials.
Identify others who exacerbate the disorder and reduce their impact.	Explore outside pressures that may exacerbate the disorder (i.e., pressure from coach, instructor, parents) and discuss ways to reduce negative forces in the adolescent's life.
Expand parenting skills and develop new techniques for coping with your adolescent's disorder.	Assign parents to read books on dealing with anxiety and increasing parenting skills such as *Making Families Work and What to Do When They Don't*, *The Deadly Diet*, *The Eating Illness Workbook*, and other selections (see Bibliotherapy, Chapter 17).
Monitor your adolescent's medication schedule and report all reactions or failures to take meds.	If the adolescent is on meds, instruct parents on the need for a regular schedule and feedback that may indicate need for revised dosage.
Meet with other parents who are experiencing similar difficulties, and share solutions for coping with the problem.	Refer parents to self-help group or group on parenting skills.
Discuss a treatment termination plan and resolve related issues.	Develop a treatment termination plan and discuss issues of separation anxiety and dependency.

ADOLESCENT'S GOALS	THERAPIST'S INTERVENTIONS
Agree with therapist on target problems.	Create treatment plan and agree with the adolescent on target problems.
Join in therapeutic alliance or collaborative treatment relationship.	Cultivate a therapeutic alliance or collaborative relationship to build trust and enhance treatment outcome.
Discuss underlying dynamics and possible causes of the disorder.	Encourage the adolescent to discuss feelings about self and clarify underlying dynamics that have created or contributed to eating disorder.
Follow-up with referrals and comply with recommendations.	Refer the adolescent for psychiatric, medical, and dental evaluations.
Discuss and resolve fear of hospitalization.	Explain need for hospitalization and refer the adolescent for in-patient treatment if necessary.
Explore possible mood disorders that may contribute to anorexia and bulimia.	Evaluate possible mood disorders that may contribute significantly to Anorexia, and treat (see appropriate treatment plan).
Identify means used to control weight besides limited food intake.	Explore use of diet pills, laxatives, diuretics or excessive exercise to control weight.
Communicate your life story to therapist.	Have the adolescent relate his or her life's story.
Maintain daily journal of eating patterns, feelings, triggers, and reactions. Discuss with therapist.	Assign the adolescent to keep daily journal of eating patterns and reactions and discuss with you.

ADOLESCENT'S GOALS	THERAPIST'S INTERVENTIONS
Explore irrational beliefs about becoming fat.	Examine the adolescent's beliefs about fatness and its consequences.
Cooperate in constructing genogram to identify familial eating problems (see Behavioral Techniques, Chapter 14).	Construct genogram to identify family eating problems from the adolescent's viewpoint.
Investigate societal and family obsessions with thinness.	Investigate family issues and attitudes that reinforce pathological eating pattern.
Realize that human beings are not perfect and reduce stressors imposed on self.	Teach the adolescent that human beings are not perfect.
Recognize underlying feelings of anger or depression and express appropriately.	Explore for underlying feelings of anger or depression and treat (see appropriate treatment plan).
Identify fear of becoming sexual.	Explore for sexual fears or fears of becoming an adult.
Understand that you use disorder to avoid separation-individuation and delay the move into adulthood.	Discuss fears of becoming an adult or the need to hide behind the shelter of childhood and avoid separation-individuation.
Replace distortions with rational thoughts about body.	Explore the adolescent's cognitive distortions about his or her body (i.e. "I'm too fat," "My thighs are ugly" etc.).
Replace abnormal weight goals with realistic goals.	Investigate the adolescent's need to have unrealistic goals for weight and replace with more realistic ones.

ADOLESCENT'S GOALS	THERAPIST'S INTERVENTIONS
Recognize the underlying need for perfection and how it started.	Address with the adolescent the need for perfection and its origins.
Accept lower expectations of self as "good enough." Live more comfortably within self.	Teach the adolescent that "good enough" is acceptable.
Recognize "secondary gains" (control, attention, feelings of superiority, avoidance of adulthood) and replace them with new coping skills.	Point out to the adolescent the secondary gains of food control and replace them with new coping skills.
Diminish and eliminate purging behavior.	Evaluate purging behavior and replace with new coping skills.
The adolescent builds confidence in relating to others, reduces pathological interactions.	Teach the adolescent more appropriate ways of interacting with others at home and school.
Confront and eliminate need to control family and others by passive-aggressive behavior (i.e. refusing to eat).	Point out any passive-aggressive need to use food to control family and others.
Learn new ways to handle fears.	Role model successful ways to deal with fears of getting fat.
Realize that others also feel bad and overcome the feeling.	Investigate for feelings of low esteem related to anxiety.
Begin to see possible solutions.	Discuss how to deal with negative feelings.
Understand how trauma may have contributed to this disorder.	Explore the adolescent's background for trauma that may have exacerbated the eating disorder.

ADOLESCENT'S GOALS	THERAPIST'S INTERVENTIONS
Discuss personal coping mechanisms developed to handle the disorder.	With the adolescent, investigate possible patterns of withdrawal and isolation caused by the disorder.
Recognize and relate how family impacts the problem.	Explore familial impact on the problem.
Express underlying feelings in a non-threatening environment.	Play *The Talking, Feeling, Doing Game* to understand underlying processes in a non-threatening way (see Therapeutic Games, Chapter 15).
Learn positive self-talk.	Teach the adolescent positive self-talk to interrupt negative eating patterns.
Learn new technique for dealing with anxiety.	Teach diaphragmatic breathing to control anxiety (see Behavioral Techniques, Chapter 14).
Learn to differentiate, identify and label levels of feeling and recognize that thoughts about circumstances cause feelings. Identify cognitive errors and replace with positive thinking.	Use the *Positive Thinking Game* and *The Talking, Feeling, Doing Game* to identify feelings and realize that perceptions cause feelings. Replace irrational negative thinking with positive thoughts (see Therapeutic Games, Chapter 15).
Read assigned books and discuss in session.	Assign the adolescent to read books on eating disorders, *The Deadly Diet* or *The Eating Illness Workbook* (see Bibliotherapy, Chapter 17).
Shift focus of attention from problem to accomplishment.	Ask the adolescent to describe his or her accomplishments for the past week.

ADOLESCENT'S GOALS	THERAPIST'S INTERVENTIONS
Use audiotape to increase self-esteem and develop better eating behavior.	With parental permission, use hypnosis or relaxation techniques to reduce stress and increase self-esteem while developing healthy eating patterns. Provide audiotape for home use (see Behavioral Techniques, Chapter 14).
Report results to therapist.	Assign the adolescent to challenge anxieties by eating a complete meal. Provide reinforcement by praising attempt and rewarding success.
Learn methods that can be used to advocate for yourself.	Instruct the adolescent in the techniques of self-advocacy.
Understand that you can deal with these issues and bring treatment to an end successfully.	Develop a treatment termination plan and explain issues of separation anxiety and dependency.

FAMILY'S GOALS	THERAPIST'S INTERVENTIONS
Improve communications among family members to reduce familial anxiety.	Conduct family sessions or refer for family therapy to reduce anger and/or alienation, and improve communication skills.
Understand family history and relate personal views of the disorder.	Amplify family genogram created in parental and adolescent sessions and compare personal views of eating disorders in the family.
Discuss genogram openly to fully understand family history.	Discuss genogram to reveal family history and possible family secrets related to the disorder.
Demonstrate boundaries, alliances, triangles, and emotional currents that may exacerbate the anxieties.	Explore family boundaries using sculpturing, a useful technique for understanding triangulation, alliances, and emotional currents (see "Family Sculpturing," Behavioral Techniques, Chapter 14).
Clarify and share your feelings about the problem.	Explore family members' views of the problem and identify feelings toward the adolescent.
Pathological behaviors are identified to correct poor eating habits.	Explore how family eats together and identify pathology that contributes to anorexia.
Understand how food is used to control family.	Discuss control issues associated with food in family.
Other family members with eating problems are treated.	Identify other family members who may have eating disorder(s) and immediately treat or refer for treatment (see appropriate treatment plan).

FAMILY'S GOALS	THERAPIST'S INTERVENTIONS
Explain your personal theory of the problem.	Ask family members to share their theories of why the eating problems exist.
Reduce any pathological eating in family that may contribute to the adolescent's eating disorder.	Explore family eating patterns, (i.e. Are they over involved with food? Sneaky eaters? Obsessed with weight issues? Do they eat alone or share meals?)
Identify sibling rivalries and their impact on perfectionism in the family.	Discuss sibling rivalry issues and how they impact on the need for perfection.
Shift focus from problem to possible solutions.	Have family imagine a future without the problem and suggest actions that can be taken now to make that future possible.
Think about what treatment outcome would look like. Explain what you would like to see change in other family members when treatment is completed.	Ask family members to think about what they might want to say about each other when treatment is completed.
Family members realize they have the power to make important changes even if they seem small.	Help family realize they have an opportunity to do some things differently.
Family members are empowered. They recognize that they can create positive change.	Ask family members to relate what they have accomplished in the past week.
Realize that major change is the result of small steps taken one at a time.	Help family identify and prioritize achievable goals.

FAMILY'S GOALS	THERAPIST'S INTERVENTIONS
Enhance understanding of condition and see how other families have handled similar problems.	Assign homework reading *Making Families Work and What to Do When They Don't*, *The Eating Illness Workbook*, or other selections (see Bibliotherapy, Chapter 17).
Make use of available community resources.	Refer family to available resources in the community (see Self-Help Groups and 800 Numbers, Chapter 18, and Online Resources, Chapter 19).
Reduce negative communication.	Develop a system of positive reinforcement with family to interact better with each other and reduce scapegoating.
Family works together to develop a treatment termination plan.	Discuss termination issues and develop a plan to terminate treatment.

9
GENERAL MEDICAL CONDITIONS

Mental disorders are often associated with comorbid medical conditions and vice versa. For the purposes of this book, General Medical Conditions include Personality Change Due to a General Medical Condition—(310.1), Mental Disorder Not Otherwise Specified Due to a General Medical Condition—(293.9), and Psychological Factor Affecting Medical Condition—(316). The medical condition is coded on Axis III of the *DSM-IV* Muliaxial Assessment System with an appropriate ICD-9 number. However, the name of the psychological condition should be included on Axis I.

PERSONALITY CHANGE DUE TO A GENERAL MEDICAL CONDITION—(310.1)

The essential feature of this diagnosis is a persistent personality disturbance that is due to a medical problem. There is a change in the adolescent's previous personality patterns. Common manifestations include instability, aggression out of proportion to the associated stressors, apathy, or paranoid ideations. The adolescent is usually regarded as "not himself or herself." The diagnosis is coded on Axis I and the general medical condition, in ICD-9 notation on Axis III.

Behavioral Symptoms
(severity index: 1–mild; 2–moderate; 3–intense)

Specify:
- Labile
- Disinhibited
- Aggressive
- Apathetic
- Paranoid
- Other
- Combined

		Severity
1.	Persistent change in personality not considered normal development and lasting for one year	_____
2.	Personality disturbance is related to medical condition	_____
3.	Causes problems or impairments in school and/or in other important areas of functioning	_____

MENTAL DISORDER NOT OTHERWISE SPECIFIED DUE TO A GENERAL MEDICAL CONDITION—(293.9)

This category is used when the disturbance does not fully meet the criteria (i.e. dissociative symptoms due to complex partial seizures).

PSYCHOLOGICAL FACTORS AFFECTING MEDICAL CONDITION—(316)

Included here are behavioral or psychological factors that adversely affect a medical condition and constitute a significant risk to health. Such factors may be founded in *DSM-IV* Axis I and II disorders, personality traits that do not fully meet the criteria for these disorders, and social and environmental stressors. This disorder, too, is coded on *DSM-IV* Axis III. (Note: Pain is not diagnosed as a psychological factor causing medical symptoms, but as Pain Disorder with psychological factors or medical conditions.)

Behavioral Symptoms
(severity index: 1–mild; 2–moderate; 3–intense)

NOTE: A General Medical Condition (Axis III) exists

		Severity
1.	Substance use/dependence interferes with medical treatment	_____
2.	Mental disorder affects general medical condition	_____
3.	Psychological factor affects, exacerbates, or delays recovery from general medical condition	_____
4.	Personality or coping style affects general medical condition	_____
5.	Negative health behavior affects general medical condition	_____
6.	Stress-related responses exacerbate medical symptoms	_____
7.	Psychological factor increases health risk	_____
8.	Major impairment in educational, social, or other areas of functioning	_____

MENTAL DISORDER OR PERSONALITY CHANGE DUE TO A GENERAL MEDICAL CONDITION

PSYCHOLOGICAL FACTORS AFFECTING GENERAL MEDICAL CONDITION

TREATMENT PLAN

Patient: _____ Date: _____

I. OBJECTIVES OF TREATMENT *(select one or more)*

1. Educate parents about the disorder
2. Determine family history of the disorder
3. Help family develop better coping skills
4. Reduce pervasive anxiety and worry
5. Control stressors that affect medical problem
6. Identify medical problems that impact psychological problems and refer for treatment
7. Increase awareness of medical-psychological interaction
8. Replace problem behavior with new coping skills
9. Reduce impact of medical and psychological problems on family
10. Reduce irrational beliefs
11. Promote socialization, reduce alienation
12. Optimize treatment and stabilize medical and/or psychological condition
13. Restore child/adolescent and family to optimum level of functioning

II. SHORT-TERM BEHAVIORAL GOALS AND INTERVENTIONS
(select goals and interventions appropriate for your patient)

NOTE: Separate goals and interventions are provided for Parents, Adolescent, and Family

PARENTS' GOALS	THERAPIST'S INTERVENTIONS
Collaborate with therapist in development of a treatment plan.	Establish therapeutic alliance with parents to enhance outcome of treatment.

PARENTS' GOALS	THERAPIST'S INTERVENTIONS
Help therapist understand the development of your adolescent's medical and psychological problems.	Assess problem with parents and record a comprehensive history of the adolescent's development and medical/psychological problems.
Increase your understanding of the medical problem.	Explore parents' limited understanding and clarify the medical problem.
Become aware of the diagnosis and what to appropriately expect from your adolescent.	Educate parents about the diagnosis.
Cooperate in revealing past patterns of sickness behavior.	Explore history of hospitalizations, treatments, and physicians.
Comply with referral and assure your adolescent receives appropriate care.	Assess severity of the problem and refer for appropriate level of care.
Recognize secondary gains your adolescent derives from the illness.	Identify secondary gains derived from illness.
Assure your adolescent gets help with pain management.	Investigate pain associated with illness and refer to pain clinic if appropriate.
Have your adolescent evaluated for both medical and psychiatric problems.	After interviewing the adolescent, provide with referrals for both medical and psychopharmacological evaluations.
Cooperate in building a genogram to identify familial history and its relationship to medical or psychological problems.	Construct a genogram to better understand the family history and define how family historically deals with illness (see Behavioral Techniques, Chapter 14).

PARENTS' GOALS	THERAPIST'S INTERVENTIONS
Enter treatment for pathology, if appropriate, to enhance outcome of child/adolescent therapy.	Evaluate parents for pathology and refer for treatment if appropriate.
Identify personality or behavioral changes related to illness.	Explore parental view of personality or behavioral changes due to illness.
Understand that is it normal to have a range of feelings with chronic life-threatening illness.	If illness is lifethreatening or chronic, encourage parents to ventilate feelings in order to release guilt, fear, anger, and blame.
Identify systemic stressors that affect psychosocial adjustment.	Investigate systemic stressors that may impede psychosocial adjustment.
Develop awareness of how your personal theory influences cognition of the problem in your adolescent.	Explore parental theory of the problem.
Understand that the problem is being addressed both medically and psychologically.	Collaborate with medical doctor to establish a team approach to treatment.
Be informed about your adolescent and his or her illness.	Educate parents about the illness to reduce distorted perceptions and help them understand what to expect from the adolescent and his or her illness.
Confront thoughts of exaggerated and unrealistic consequences—"what ifs?"	Guide parents in confronting distorted reactions to trigger situations.
Identify impact of illness on family life.	Explore impact of illness on family life and how it has affected caregivers.

PARENTS' GOALS	THERAPIST'S INTERVENTIONS
Understand how to help your adolescent live with pain (see "Relaxation" and "Hypnosis," Behavioral Techniques, Chapter 14).	If the adolescent is in pain, teach methods of pain management or refer to pain management clinic.
Agree to allow therapist to confer with your adolescent's school to develop a comprehensive psychoeducational treatment plan.	If appropriate, after interviewing the adolescent and with his or her permission, request and receive parental permission to confer with teachers and school administrators.
Restructure distortions with evidence-based consequences	With parents, reframe distortions with reality-based reactions to stressors.
Realize your adolescent is a whole person with an illness.	Help parents see their adolescent as a whole person and not just a disorder.
Develop new parenting skills.	Assign parents to read books on how to deal with their anxiety and increase parenting skills, such as *Making Families Work and What to Do When They Don't* or *Living with Life-Threatening Illness: A Guide for Patients, Their Families, and Caregivers* or *Full Catastrophe Living: Using the Wisdom of Your Body and Mind to Face Stress, Pain, and Illness* (see Bibliotherapy, Chapter 17).
Monitor your adolescent's medication schedule and report all reactions or failures to take meds.	If the adolescent is on meds, instruct parents on need for a regular schedule and feedback that may indicate need for revised dosage.

PARENTS' GOALS	THERAPIST'S INTERVENTIONS
Meet with other parents who are experiencing similar difficulties, and share solutions for coping with the problem.	Refer parents to self-help group or group on parenting skills.
Discuss a treatment termination plan and resolve related issues.	Develop a treatment termination plan and discuss issues of separation anxiety and dependency.

ADOLESCENT'S GOALS	THERAPIST'S INTERVENTIONS
Enter therapeutic relationship.	Engage the adolescent in therapeutic or collaborative working relationship to build trust and enhance treatment outcome.
Improve treatment outlook. Diminish feelings of fear and isolation	Cultivate alliance.
Discuss treatment plan and agree on target problems.	Confirm diagnosis; assess impairments and formulate treatment plan. Discuss target problems with the adolescent.
Recognize underlying feelings of anger or depression and express appropriately.	Explore for underlying feelings of anger or depression.
Realistically understand what to expect in dealing with the disorder.	Educate the adolescent about the disorder so he or she knows what to expect.
Identify whether problems are acute or chronic.	Determine whether the medical condition is chronic or acute in order to help the adolescent make the necessary life adaptations.
Realize that others also feel bad and overcome those feelings.	Investigate for feelings of low esteem related to medical and/or psychological problems. Discuss how the adolescent feels and what to do about it.
Accept hospitalization as necessary for your own safety.	Explore for suicidal ideations and, if active plan exists, refer the adolescent for immediate hospitalization.

ADOLESCENT'S GOALS	THERAPIST'S INTERVENTIONS
Adolescent agrees to "suicide pact."	If the adolescent has suicidal ideations, but no active plan, enter into "suicide pact" in which the adolescent agrees not to act without notifying you first. Inform parents if necessary.
Identify irrational beliefs.	Explore for irrational beliefs.
Reframe beliefs based on rational evidence.	Discuss the beliefs and develop rational alternatives.
Understand underlying dynamic that may lead to maladaptive solutions and somatization.	Explore ways fears are related to illness and clarify how they manifest themselves.
Diminish self-loathing or self-recriminations and perceived imperfections.	Teach the adolescent that perfection is not required or necessary.
Recognize feelings of anger or depression and express appropriately.	Probe for underlying feelings of depression or anger and treat (see appropriate treatment plan).
Recognize secondary gains related to illness and abandon them.	Explore for secondary gains associated with illness.
Adolescent learns methods of coping with pain.	Explore for pain and teach adolescent how to live with pain rather than live in pain.
Become aware of impact of illness on moods and feelings.	Determine possible personality changes related to illness.
Recognize past trauma and enhance personal coping mechanisms developed to handle this disorder.	Determine history of physical or psychological trauma that may have exacerbated this disorder.

ADOLESCENT'S GOALS	THERAPIST'S INTERVENTIONS
Explain how family dynamics impact the problem both positively and negatively	Encourage the adolescent to recognize and explain the impact of family dynamics on the problem.
Understand anxiety and realize that avoidance does not help.	Teach the adolescent the laws of anxiety: anxiety is not permanent or dangerous; avoidance increases anxiety; confronting the problem can reduce anxiety; exposure can produce growth.
Tell therapist your life's story.	Have the adolescent relate the story of his or her life or play *Life Stories*, (see Therapeutic Games, Chapter 15).
Adolescent learns self-hypnosis or relaxation techniques to reduce pain and ways mind can affect body.	With parents' permission, use hypnosis or relaxation techniques to help reduce effects of pain. Provide audiotape for home use.
Realize you are whole person with a disorder.	Help the adolescent see that he or she is a whole person and not just a disorder.
Understand how trauma may have contributed to existing disorder.	Explore the adolescent's background for trauma that may have exacerbated the disorder.
Identify and understand ways you are scapegoated by friends and family.	Explore for scapegoating by friends and family because of illness.
Understand how to be more assertive and reduce scapegoating.	Teach the adolescent principles of assertiveness to reduce scapegoating.

ADOLESCENT'S GOALS	THERAPIST'S INTERVENTIONS
Learn positive self-talk.	Teach the adolescent positive self-talk to interrupt negative patterns.
Learn new technique for dealing with anxiety.	Teach diaphragmatic breathing to control anxiety (see Behavioral Techniques, Chapter 14).
Identify how illness impedes peer relations. Recognize that these relationships can empower you.	Explore ways illness impedes peer relations. Help the adolescent recognize the power of peer relationships.
Learn problem solving.	Teach client the principles of problem solving: (1) stay calm, take a deep breath; (2) think about what is bothering you; (3) create S.M.A.R.T. action plan—Small, Measurable, Achievable, Realistic, Timelined goals; (4) select three different solutions, pick the best one, do the best you can, if it doesn't work, stay calm and try again. Remember perseverance works; don't give up (see "Change," Behavioral Techniques, Chapter 14).
Shift focus of attention from problem to accomplishment.	Ask the adolescent to describe his or her accomplishments for the past week.
Feel more confident as self-esteem improves.	Compliment the adolescent to provide positive reinforcement whenever possible.
Develop an exercise regimen to help release frustration.	If the adolescent is capable, recommend routine exercise to help release frustrations.

ADOLESCENT'S GOALS	THERAPIST'S INTERVENTIONS
Meet with others who have similar problems and develop a support network.	Refer to self-help groups where the adolescent can meet and talk to peers with similar problems (see Self-Help Groups and 800 Numbers, Chapter 18, and Online Resources, Chapter 19).
Read assigned book and learn strategies for dealing with stress, illness, and pain.	Assign the adolescent to read *Living with Chronic Illness* or *Full Catastrophe Living: Using the Wisdom of Your Body and Mind to Face Stress, Pain, and Illness* (see Bibliotherapy, Chapter 17).
Read assigned book and learn necessary technique to succeed.	Assign the adolescent to read *What Teens Need to Succeed* (see Bibliotherapy, Chapter 17).
Read assigned book and earn how to use self-hypnosis for healing.	Assign to read *Discovering the Power of Self-Hypnosis: A New Approach for Enabling Change and Promoting Healing* (see Bibliotherapy, Chapter 17).
Learn methods that can be used to advocate for yourself.	Instruct the adolescent in the techniques of self-advocacy.
Understand that you can deal with these issues and bring therapy to an end successfully.	Develop a treatment termination plan and explain issues of separation anxiety and dependency.

FAMILY'S GOALS	THERAPIST'S INTERVENTIONS
Improve communications among family members to reduce levels of anger and alienation.	Conduct family sessions or refer for family therapy to reduce anger and/or alienation, and improve communication skills within the family.
Cooperate in amplifying family genogram.	Augment genogram created in parental session to help understand structure of family and spell out physical and emotional boundaries including toxic issues (see Behavioral Techniques, Chapter 14).
Discuss genogram openly to fully understand family history as it relates to anxiety over medical issues.	Discuss genogram to reveal family history and possible family secrets and defenses surrounding illness.
Demonstrate boundaries, alliances, triangles, and emotional currents that may exacerbate the anxieties.	Explore family boundaries using sculpturing, a useful technique for understanding triangulation, alliances, and emotional currents (see "Family Sculpturing," Behavioral Techniques, Chapter 14).
Negative interactions (i.e., jealousy, competition, enmity) are reduced to establish homeostasis.	Investigate sibling rivalries and reduce negative interactions.
Understand the disorder and what to expect.	Educate family members about the disorder and the expected outcomes of treatment.
Family interactions are improved.	Ease family anxiety and teach new skills for interacting with the adolescent.

FAMILY'S GOALS	THERAPIST'S INTERVENTIONS
Think about what treatment outcome would look like. Explain what you would like to see change in other family members when treatment is completed.	Ask family members to think about what they might want to say about each other when treatment is completed.
Recognize irrational beliefs and reframe them based on rational evidence.	Identify irrational beliefs and reframe them for new outcomes.
Family members realize they have the power to make important changes even if they seem small.	Help family realize they have an opportunity to do some things differently.
Identify stressors that impede the adolescent's psychosocial adjustment.	Investigate how family sees stressors that impede the psychological adjustment of the adolescent.
Realize that major change is the result of small steps taken one at a time.	Help family identify and prioritize achievable goals.
Identify how illness impedes relations. Recognize that these relationships can empower you.	Explore ways illness impedes peer relations. Help family recognize the power of relationships and connectedness.
Learn problem solving.	Teach family the principles of problem solving: (1) stay calm, take a deep breath; (2) think about what is bothering you; (3) create a S.M.A.R.T. action plan—Small, Measurable, Achievable, Realistic, Timelined goals; (4) select three different solutions, pick the best one, do the best you can, if it doesn't work, stay calm and try again. Remember perseverance works; don't give up (see "Change," Behavioral Techniques, Chapter 14).

FAMILY'S GOALS	THERAPIST'S INTERVENTIONS
Recognize the need for peer relations.	Teach family to recognize how the power of peer relations helps the adolescent.
Make use of available community resources.	Refer family to available resources in the community (see Self-Help Groups and 800 Numbers, Chapter 18, and Online Resources, Chapter 19).
Reduce negative communication.	Develop a system of positive reinforcement with family to interact better with each other and reduce scapegoating
Family works together to develop treatment termination plan.	Discuss treatment termination issues and develop a plan to terminate treatment.

10
IMPULSE CONTROL DISORDERS

Impulse Control Disorders involve the failure to resist an urge, drive, or temptation that can be harmful to oneself or others. The adolescent feels mounting tension or arousal before the act, and pleasure, relief, or gratification after the act. There may or may not be subsequent feelings of regret, guilt, or self-reproach.

INTERMITTENT EXPLOSIVE DISORDER—(312.34)

This disorder is marked by the recurrent failure to resist aggressive impulses that result in assault or property destruction. The act is usually out of proportion to any provocation and usually follows the classic tension-relief sequence. Regret or remorse may follow.

The disorder is more prevalent in males than females. Onset appears to be in late adolescence and is usually abrupt. Indications of general impulsivity or aggressiveness may exist between explosive incidents, especially among adolescents with narcissistic, obsessive, paranoid, or schizoid traits who are prone to outbursts of anger under stress. The disorder may result in school suspension, troubled personal relationships, accidents, hospitalization, or jail.

Behavioral Symptoms
(severity index: 1–mild; 2–moderate; 3–intense

		Severity
1.	Failure to resist urge to commit aggressive acts of assault or property damage	_____
2.	The degree of aggression is out of proportion to any provocation	_____
3.	General impulsivity or aggression may exist between explosive incidents	_____
4.	Subsequent feelings of guilt, remorse, or self-reproach may or may not be present	_____

INTERMITTENT EXPLOSIVE DISORDER TREATMENT PLAN

Patient: _____ Date: _____

I. OBJECTIVES OF TREATMENT *(select one or more)*

1. Develop ability to resist aggressive impulses
2. Reduce general impulsivity and/or aggression
3. Understand underlying stressors that lead to assaultive or destructive acts
4. Eliminate danger to self and others
5. Enhance ability to act appropriately toward others
6. Develop better response to underlying stressors
7. Encourage strategies that enable improved coping skills
7. Help parents to establish and maintain firm boundaries and consistent limits when adolescent acts out
8, Educate parents about disorder
9. Explore family history of disorder
10. Help parents develop better parenting styles
11. Promote socialization
12. Restore family and adolescent to optimum levels of functioning
13. Develop discharge plan for everyday life

II. SHORT-TERM BEHAVIORAL GOALS AND INTERVENTIONS
(select goals and interventions appropriate for your patient)

NOTE: Separate goals and interventions are provided for Parents, Adolescent, and Family

PARENTS' GOALS	THERAPIST'S INTERVENTIONS
Collaborate with therapist in development of a treatment plan.	Attempt to establish a therapeutic alliance with parents to enhance outcome of treatment.
Help therapist understand your adolescent's development and disorder.	Assess problem with parents and record a comprehensive history of the adolescent's development and the disorder.

PARENTS' GOALS	THERAPIST'S INTERVENTIONS
Cooperate in building genogram to better understand family patterns.	Construct a genogram to better understand family history and define family behavioral patterns. Explore repetition over generations (see Behavioral Techniques, Chapter 14).
Become aware of the diagnosis and what to generally expect from your adolescent.	Educate parents about the diagnosis.
Undergo treatment for individual problems, which, in turn, enhances outcome of your adolescent's therapy and reduces tension in the home.	Explore for parental psychopathology (e.g. antisocial behaviors, marital discord etc.) and refer for treatment or treat.
Undergo testing and evaluation for psychiatric medication.	If appropriate, refer parents for psychological testing and psychiatric evaluation.
Become aware of maladaptive messages you are sending to your adolescent.	Identify if and how parents model antisocial behaviors that the adolescent translates as permission to act out.
Recognize your ineffective or inconsistent disciplinary practices.	Assess ineffective or inconsistent practices of discipline.
Develop awareness of how your personal theory influences cognition of the problem.	Explore parental theory of the problem.
Follow-up on referral for psychiatric and medical evaluations	After interviewing the adolescent, if necessary, provide parents with referral for psychiatric and medical evaluations.

PARENTS' GOALS	THERAPIST'S INTERVENTIONS
Monitor your adolescent's medication schedule and report all reactions and failure to take meds.	If the adolescent is prescribed medication, instruct parents of the need for regular schedule and feedback that may indicate need for dosage adjustment.
Recognize fears and negative self-blame related to the problem.	Evaluate parents' fears and negative self-blame for the adolescent's problem.
Identify how the disorder disrupts family life.	Explore effects of disorder on the family.
Learn to reach beyond automatic cognitive reactions in viewing the problem.	Expand parental perspective beyond limited cognitive reactions.
Confront thoughts of exaggerated and unrealistic consequences—"what ifs?"	Guide parents in confronting distorted reactions to trigger situations.
Identify cognitive distortions	Weigh the reactions against evidence-based reality.
Restructure distortions with evidence-based consequences	With parents, reframe distortions with reality-based reactions to stressors.
Learn diaphragmatic breathing as relaxation technique and teach your adolescent to help in relaxation.	Teach parents diaphragmatic breathing to assist the adolescent in relaxation (see Behavioral Techniques, Chapter 14).
Agree to allow therapist to confer with your adolescent's school to help in development of a comprehensive psychoeducational treatment plan.	If appropriate, and with adolescent's permission, request and receive parental permission to confer with teachers and school officials.

PARENTS' GOALS	THERAPIST'S INTERVENTIONS
Attend self-help group to improve parenting skills.	Evaluate parenting skills and, if necessary, refer to parenting skills group (see Self-Help Groups and 800 Numbers, Chapter 18, and Online Resources Chapter 19).
Read about and improve parenting skills.	Assign reading of books on positive parenting (see *Making Families Work and What to Do When They Don't* or *Parents Do Make a Difference: How to Raise Kids with Solid Character, Strong Minds, and Caring Hearts*, Bibliotherapy, Chapter 17).
Read about techniques to help identify and address problem behaviors.	Assign parents to read books on adolescent behavior problems (see *How to Handle a Hard-to-Handle Kid*, Bibliotherapy, Chapter 17).
Learn effective, effective, calm disciplinary strategies.	Teach parents effective discipline strategies. Assign to read *Try and Make Me: A Revolutionary Program for Raising Your Defiant Child Without Losing Your Cool* (see Bibliotherapy, Chapter 17).
Make positive use of community resources.	Educate parents about available community resources (see Self-Help Groups and 800 Numbers, Chapter 18, and Online Resources, Chapter 19).
Discuss a treatment termination plan and resolve termination issues.	Develop a treatment termination plan and discuss issues of separation and dependency with parents.

ADOLESCENT'S GOALS	THERAPIST'S INTERVENTIONS
Enter non-threatening therapeutic interaction geared to appropriate development level.	Engage the adolescent in an age-appropriate therapeutic relationship.
Learn about diagnosis and develop realistic expectations of self.	Educate the adolescent about the diagnosis and discuss symptomatology.
Identify familial impact on the problem.	With the adolescent, discuss the familial impact on the problem.
Understand the triggers that result in acting out.	Identify the triggers that create the urge to act out.
Learn new techniques for dealing with anger.	Develop strategies that enable improved coping skills.
Learn to think about the consequences before exploding.	Teach the adolescent to insert thought between urge and action.
Recognize underlying feelings of anger or depression and express appropriately.	Explore for underlying feelings of anger or depression.
Identify triggers and learn to avoid them.	Explore for stimuli that may trigger an episode.
Realize that when he or she acts out, they end up feeling bad about themselves.	Discuss the connection between acting out, guilt, remorse, and self-rapprochement.
Be treated for substance abuse.	Investigate for substance abuse and treat if positive (see appropriate treatment plan).
Identify irrational beliefs.	Explore for irrational beliefs about self.
Reframe beliefs.	Discuss the beliefs and develop rational alternatives.

ADOLESCENT'S GOALS	THERAPIST'S INTERVENTIONS
Learn ways to problem solve and resist destructive urges to act out.	Develop problem-solving methods that can be used to interrupt aggressive impulses.
Using relaxation techniques and guided imagery learn to gain control over feelings.	With parents' permission, use hypnosis, relaxation techniques and guided imagery to master anxieties (see Behavioral Techniques, Chapter 14).
Understand anxiety and realize that avoidance does not help.	Teach client the laws of anxiety: anxiety is not permanent or dangerous; avoidance increases anxiety; confronting the problem can reduce anxiety; exposure can produce growth.
Tell therapist your life's story.	Have the adolescent relate the story of his or her life.
Understand process that gets you into trouble in order to control acting out.	Teach the adolescent about aggressive behavior: (1) Over-sensitive to hostile cues; (2) attribute hostile intentions to others; therefore (3) solve problems with aggressive actions; and (4) become rejected by others; contributing to (5) low self-esteem.
Enter treatment for anxiety, depression, or low self-esteem.	Explore for low self-esteem, anxiety, or depression and treat appropriately (see appropriate treatment plan).
Understand how trauma may have contributed to existing disorder.	Explore the adolescent's background for trauma that may have exacerbated the disorder.

ADOLESCENT'S GOALS	THERAPIST'S INTERVENTIONS
Discuss personal coping mechanisms developed to handle the disorder.	With the adolescent, investigate possible patterns that trigger acting out.
Recognize and relate how family impacts the problem.	Explore familial impact on the problem.
Learn positive self-talk.	Teach the adolescent positive self-talk to interrupt negative patterns.
Learn problem-solving methods to put thought between thought of stealing and action.	Teach the adolescent the principles of problem solving: (1) stay calm, take a deep breath; (2) think about what is bothering you; (3) create S.M.A.R.T. action plan—Small, Measurable, Achievable, Realistic, Timelined goals; (4) select three different solutions, pick the best one, do the best you can, if it doesn't work, stay calm and try again. Remember, perseverance works; don't give up (see "Change," Behavioral Techniques, Chapter 14).
Recognize regression as a chance to work harder and assume more responsibility	Reframe relapse as an opportunity rather than a failure.
Learn to self-monitor to prevent relapse.	Help the adolescent develop the ability to monitor self and prevent relapses.
Visualize how the power of the mind can reduce stress and provide tools to reduce acting out behavior.	With parents permission, use hypnosis, relaxation techniques, or guided imagery to control acting out behavior (see Behavioral Techniques, Chapter 14).

ADOLESCENT'S GOALS	THERAPIST'S INTERVENTIONS
Learn new techniques for dealing with emotional difficulties.	Use the *Positive Thinking Game* or *Bounce-Back* to teach how positive self-talk helps control emotional difficulties (see Therapeutic Games, Chapter 15).
Shift focus of attention from problem to accomplishment.	Ask the adolescent to describe his or her accomplishments for the past week.
Feel more confident as self-esteem improves.	Compliment the adolescent to provide positive reinforcement whenever possible.
Communicate problematic feelings to develop new skills or options.	Recommend routine exercise to help the adolescent release frustrations.
Attempt to use new control skills in school.	Urge the adolescent to use new control skills in the classroom setting.
Report results to therapist.	Provide positive reinforcement when client reports back that he or she has spoken up in school. Praise attempt and reward success.
Read assigned book.	Assign to read *What Do You Stand For?* in order to build better coping skills and build character (see Bibliotherapy, Chapter 17).
Learn new strategies for dealing with aggressive behaviors.	Assign handouts from S.E.A.L.S. books or *Life Management Skills* to teach positive ways to relate to others, simple strategies to reduce acting out, and new behaviors.

ADOLESCENT'S GOALS	THERAPIST'S INTERVENTIONS
Learn methods that you can use to advocate for yourself.	Instruct the adolescent in the techniques of self-advocacy.
Understand that he or she can deal with these issues and bring therapy to an end successfully.	Develop a treatment termination plan and explain issues of separation anxiety and dependency.

FAMILY'S GOALS	THERAPIST'S INTERVENTIONS
Improve communications among family members.	Conduct family sessions or refer for family therapy to reduce anger and/or alienation, and improve communication skills within the family.
Cooperate in amplifying family genogram.	Amplify family genogram created in first family session to help understand family history.
Discuss genogram openly to fully understand family history as it relates to aggression and stealing.	Discuss genogram to reveal family history and possible family secrets dealing with stealing and aggression.
Demonstrate boundaries, alliances, triangles, and emotional currents that may exacerbate the problem.	Explore family boundaries using sculpturing, a useful technique for understanding triangulation, alliances, and emotional current, (see Behavioral Techniques, Chapter 14).
Family communicates how they handle aggression at home.	Explore sibling rivalry, the ways aggression is handled at home, and acting out behaviors. Explore how family relates to kleptomanic behaviors. Determine if others are stealing. If positive, treat or refer for treatment.
Understand process that gets you into trouble by reacting to acting out.	Teach the family about aggressive behavior: (1) Oversensitive to hostile cues; (2) attribute hostile intentions to others; therefore (3) solve problems with aggressive actions; and (4) become rejected by others; contributing to (5) low self-esteem.

FAMILY'S GOALS	THERAPIST'S INTERVENTIONS
Learn new ways to deal with your aggressive behaviors.	Explore how parents manage their own anger and encourage prosocial behaviors to develop family cohesiveness.
Develop plan of action in case of violence (i.e. get to safe harbor, call 911 etc.).	Explore for physical violence and, if positive, outline plan of action and patterns of escape.
Assume responsibility for changing your behavior.	Target problematic behaviors in the family and patterns of escalation and set realistic goals so family can take responsibility for changing their behaviors.
Develop alternative ways to react to violence.	Explore productive, healthy ways to react rather than act.
Realize that major change is the result of small steps taken one at a time.	Help family identify and prioritize achievable goals.
Shift focus from problem to possible solutions.	Have family imagine a future without the problem and suggest actions that can be taken now to make that future possible.
Reduce negative communication.	Develop a system of positive reinforcement with family to interact better with each other and reduce scapegoating.
Think about what treatment outcome would look like. Explain what you would like to see change in other family members when treatment is completed.	Ask family members to think about what they might want to say about each other when treatment is completed.

FAMILY'S GOALS	THERAPIST'S INTERVENTIONS
Learn to problem solve rather than act out.	Teach client the principles of problem solving: (1) stay calm, take a deep breath; (2) think about what is bothering you; (3) create S.M.A.R.T. action plan—Small, Measurable, Achievable, Realistic, Timelined goals; (4) select three different solutions, pick the best one, do the best you can, if it doesn't work, stay calm and try again. Remember, perseverance works; don't give up (see "Change," Behavioral Techniques, Chapter 14).
Family realizes they have the power to make important changes even if they seem small.	Help family realize they have an opportunity to do some things differently.
Family members are empowered. They recognize that they can create positive change.	Ask family members to relate what they have accomplished in the past week.
Lean new approach to discipline and develop skills to confront and diffuse anger.	Assign family to listen to *6 Essentials of Discipline* to reduce behavioral difficulties at home.
Make use of available community resources.	Refer family to available resources in the community (see Self-Help Groups and 800 Numbers, Chapter 18, and Online Resources, Chapter 19).
Family works together to develop a treatment termination plan.	Discuss treatment termination issues and develop plan to terminate treatment.

KLEPTOMANIA—(312.32)

The essential feature of this disorder is the failure to resist the impulse to steal even when the item is not needed for personal use or its monetary value. The adolescent experiences a sense of tension before the act and a feeling of gratification when the act is completed. The adolescent may hoard the stolen items or return them surreptitiously. The thefts are not preplanned and will generally be avoided if arrest is probable. The individual is usually aware that these acts are wrong and often feels guilty or depressed after the theft. Mood disorders, eating disorders, or personality disorders may be associated.

Kleptomania can cause legal, family, and personal difficulties for the adolescent. It is possible that the adolescent may steal as a rite of passage or rebellion, in which case the diagnosis of Kleptomania would not apply. Kleptomania occurs in less than 5% of identified shoplifters and appears to occur predominantly in females.

Behavioral Symptoms
(severity index: 1–mild; 2–moderate; 3–intense)

		Severity
1.	Unable to resist impulse to steal objects that are not needed	_____
2.	Experiences building tension prior to the act	_____
3.	Feels relief and gratification after the act	_____
4.	Theft is followed by guilt and remorse	_____
5.	Realizes the act is wrong and senseless	_____
6.	Poor self-esteem	_____

KLEPTOMANIA
TREATMENT PLAN

Patient: _____ Date: _____

I. OBJECTIVES OF TREATMENT *(select one or more)*

1. Educate parents about the disorder
2. Explore family history of disorder
3. Help parents develop better parenting styles
4. Reduce stressors that cause adolescent to act out
5. Develop ability to resist aggressive impulses and impulse to steal
6. Understand underlying stressors that lead to assault, or destructive acts
7. Develop strategies to interpose thought between urge and action
8. Help adolescent build self-esteem and reduce tensions
9. Help parents establish and maintain firm boundaries and consistent limits when adolescent acts out
10. Promote socialization
11. Restore family and adolescent to optimum levels of functioning
12. Develop discharge plan for everyday life

II. SHORT-TERM BEHAVIORAL GOALS AND INTERVENTIONS
(Select goals and interventions appropriate for your patient)

NOTE: Separate goals and interventions are provided for Parents, Adolescent, and Family

PARENTS' GOALS	THERAPIST'S INTERVENTIONS
Collaborate with therapist in development of a treatment plan	Attempt to establish a therapeutic alliance with parents in a non-judgmental manner to enhance outcome of treatment.
Help therapist understand your adolescent's development and disorder.	Assess problem with parents and record a comprehensive history of the adolescent's development and the disorder.

PARENTS' GOALS	THERAPIST'S INTERVENTIONS
Become aware of the diagnosis and what to generally expect from your adolescent.	Educate parents about the diagnosis.
Cooperate in building genogram to better understand family patterns.	Construct a genogram to better understand family history and define family behavioral patterns. Explore repetition of dysfunctional behaviors over generations (see Behavioral Techniques, Chapter 14).
Undergo treatment for individual problems, which, in turn, enhances the outcome of your adolescent's therapy.	Explore for parental psychopathology (e.g. antisocial behaviors, marital discord, Kleptomania, or poor impulse control etc.) and refer for treatment or treat.
Learn effective ways to acknowledge feelings, establish boundaries, and de-escalate acting out behavior.	Assign audiotape *6 Essentials of Discipline* to teach effective skills for dealing with adolescent behavior.
Undergo evaluation for psychiatric medication.	If appropriate, refer parents for psychiatric evaluation.
Become aware of maladaptive messages you are sending to the adolescent.	Identify if and how parents model antisocial behaviors that the adolescent translates as permission to defy authority and steal.
Recognize your ineffective or inconsistent disciplinary practices.	Assess ineffective or inconsistent practices of discipline.
Develop awareness of how your personal theory influences cognition of the problem.	Explore parental theory of the problem.
Explain your sense of right and wrong and system of values.	Clarify parental morals and values.

PARENTS' GOALS	THERAPIST'S INTERVENTIONS
Recognize fears and negative self-blame related to the problem.	Evaluate parents' fears and negative self-blame for the adolescent's problem.
Share thoughts, feelings, and fears about your adolescent's behavior.	Encourage parents to vent feelings, thoughts, and fears about the adolescent's behavior.
Learn to reach beyond automatic cognitive reactions in viewing the problem.	Expand parental perspective beyond limited cognitive reactions.
Confront thoughts of exaggerated and unrealistic consequences—"what ifs?"	Guide parents in confronting distorted reactions to trigger situations.
Identify cognitive distortions	Weigh the reactions against evidence-based reality.
Restructure distortions with evidence-based consequences	With parents, reframe distortions with reality-based reactions to stressors.
Learn diaphragmatic breathing as relaxation technique and teach your adolescent to help in relaxation.	Teach parents diaphragmatic breathing to assist the adolescent in relaxation (see Behavioral Techniques, Chapter 14).
Agree to allow therapist to confer with your adolescent's school to help in development of a comprehensive psycho-educational treatment plan.	If appropriate, request and receive parental permission to confer with the adolescent's teachers and school officials.
Attend self-help group to improve parenting skills.	Evaluate parenting skills and, if necessary, refer to parenting skills group. (See Self-Help Groups and 800 Numbers, Chapter 18, and Online Resources, Chapter 19).

PARENTS' GOALS	THERAPIST'S INTERVENTIONS
Read about and improve parenting skills.	Assign reading of books on positive parenting (see *Making Families Work and What to Do When They Don't* or *Parents Do Make a Difference: How to Raise Kids with Solid Character, Strong Minds, and Caring Hearts*, Bibliotherapy, Chapter 17).
Make positive use of community resources.	Educate parents about available community resources (see Self-Help Groups and 800 Numbers, Chapter 18 and Online Resources, Chapter 19).
Discuss a treatment termination plan and resolve termination issues.	Develop a treatment termination plan and discuss issues of separation and dependency.

ADOLESCENT'S GOALS	THERAPIST'S INTERVENTIONS
Enter non-threatening therapeutic interaction geared to appropriate development level.	Attempt to engage the adolescent in an age-appropriate therapeutic relationship that is non-judgmental.
Learn about the diagnosis and develop realistic expectations of self.	Educate the adolescent about the diagnosis and discuss symptomatology so he or she can adjust self-expectations.
Identify triggers that lead to stealing.	With the adolescent, explore the triggers that lead to stealing.
Understand and recognize the warning signs that precede the act.	Investigate the warning signs (i.e. build up of tension) prior to the act.
Identify ways to interrupt escalation of the tension.	Explore different methods he/she can use to interrupt the build up of tension before the act.
Recognize underlying feelings of anger or depression and express appropriately.	Explore for underlying feelings of anger or depression.
Share and ventilate bad feelings related to stealing.	Investigate for feelings of low esteem related to Kleptomania.
Identify irrational beliefs.	Explore for irrational beliefs about stealing.
Reframe beliefs about conduct disorder.	Discuss the beliefs and develop rational alternatives.
Psychodramatically work out ways to deal with triggers and reduce the need to act out.	Role-play methods for dealing with triggers that prompt the adolescent to steal (see Behavioral Techniques, Chapter 14).

ADOLESCENT'S GOALS	THERAPIST'S INTERVENTIONS
Use hypnosis, relaxation techniques, or creative visualization to eliminate stealing and build confidence.	If the adolescent is well motivated, use creative visualization, hypnosis, or relaxation techniques with parental permission to help reduce tension, change imprinted responses, gain control, and improve self-esteem. Provide audiotape for home use (see Behavioral Techniques, Chapter 14).
Understand anxiety and realize that avoidance or acting out does not help.	Teach the adolescent the laws of anxiety: anxiety is not permanent or dangerous; avoidance increases anxiety; confronting the problem can reduce anxiety; exposure can produce growth.
Tell therapist your life's story.	Have the adolescent relate the story of his or her life.
Enter treatment for anxiety, depression, or low self-esteem.	Explore for low self-esteem, anxiety, or depression and treat appropriately (see appropriate treatment plan).
Understand how trauma may have contributed to existing disorder.	Explore the adolescent's background for trauma that may have prompted or exacerbated the disorder.
Discuss personal coping mechanisms developed to handle the disorder.	With the adolescent, investigate possible patterns that trigger acting out.
Learn to identify signals of rising tension and develop possible alternatives.	Help patient identify signals of rising tension and develop alternative solutions (i.e. talk to a safe parent or friend, call therapist, do aerobic exercise).

ADOLESCENT'S GOALS	THERAPIST'S INTERVENTIONS
Recognize and relate how family impacts the problem.	Explore familial impact on the problem.
Learn positive self-talk.	Teach the adolescent positive self-talk to interrupt negative patterns.
Understand the probable consequences of stealing.	Clarify the possible consequences of stealing. (i.e. guilt, remorse, jail etc.).
Learn new technique for dealing with anxiety.	Teach diaphragmatic breathing to control anxiety (see Behavioral Techniques, Chapter 14).
Learn new techniques for dealing with emotional difficulties.	Use the *Positive Thinking Game* to teach how positive self-talk helps control emotional difficulties (see Therapeutic Games, Chapter 15).
Shift focus of attention from problem to accomplishment.	Ask the adolescent to describe his or her accomplishments for the past week.
Feel more confident as self-esteem improves.	Compliment the adolescent to provide positive reinforcement whenever possible.
Release tensions with routine exercise.	Recommend routine exercise to help adolescent release frustrations
Maintain journal to record and intercept automatic thoughts and urges.	Assign the adolescent to maintain an automatic thought log to record urges to steal (see Homework Assignments Chapter 16).

ADOLESCENT'S GOALS	THERAPIST'S INTERVENTIONS
Read assigned book and gain insights into how to conquer self-defeating behaviors.	Assign to read *The Teens' Solutions Workbook* or *Thoughts and Feelings: Taking Control of Your Moods and Your Life* (see Bibliotherapy, Chapter 17).
Learn new strategies for dealing with urges to steal.	Assign handouts from S.E.A.L.S. books or *Life Management Skills* to learn positive ways to relate to others, simple strategies to reduce acting out, and new behaviors.
Recognize regression as a chance to work harder and assume more responsibility.	Reframe regression as an opportunity to take more responsibility.
Learn to self-monitor to prevent relapse.	Help the adolescent develop ability to monitor self and prevent relapse.
Understand that you can deal with these issues and bring therapy to an end successfully.	Develop a treatment termination plan and explain issues of separation anxiety and dependency.

FAMILY'S GOALS	THERAPIST'S INTERVENTIONS
Improve communications among family members.	Conduct family sessions or refer for family therapy to reduce anger and/or alienation, and improve communication skills within the family.
Cooperate in amplifying family genogram.	Amplify family genogram created in first family session to help understand family history.
Discuss genogram openly to fully understand family history as it relates to aggression. aggression.	Discuss genogram to reveal family history and possible family secrets dealing with
Demonstrate boundaries, alliances, triangles, and emotional currents that may exacerbate the problem.	Explore family boundaries using sculpturing, a useful technique for understanding triangulation, alliances, and emotional current, (see Behavioral Techniques, Chapter 14).
Family communicates how they handle aggression at home.	Explore sibling rivalry and the ways aggression is handled at home.
Learn new ways to deal with your aggressive behaviors.	Explore how parents manage their own anger and encourage prosocial behaviors to develop family cohesiveness.
Assume responsibility for changing your behavior.	Target problematic behaviors in the family and set realistic goals so family can take responsibility for changing their behaviors.

FAMILY'S GOALS	THERAPIST'S INTERVENTIONS
Family members learn problem-solving techniques to reduce pathological behaviors.	Teach clients the principles of problem solving: (1) stay calm, take a deep breath; (2) think about what is bothering you; (3) create S.M.A.R.T. action plan—Small, Measurable, Achievable, Realistic, Timelined goals; (4) select three different solutions, pick the best one, do the best you can, if it doesn't work, stay calm and try again. Remember perseverance works; don't give up (see "Change," Behavioral Techniques, Chapter 14).
Realize that major change is the result of small steps taken one at a time.	Help family identify and prioritize achievable goals.
Shift focus from problem to possible solutions.	Have family imagine a future without the problem and suggest actions that can be taken now to make that future possible.
Reduce negative communication.	Develop a system of positive reinforcement with family to interact better with each other and reduce scapegoating.
Think about what treatment outcome would look like. Explain what you would like to see change in other family members when treatment is completed.	Ask family members to think about what they might want to say about each other when treatment is completed.
Family realizes they have the power to make important changes even if they seem small.	Help family realize they have an opportunity to do some things differently.

FAMILY'S GOALS	THERAPIST'S INTERVENTIONS
Members are empowered. They recognize that they can create positive change.	Ask family members to relate what they have accomplished in the past week.
Read assigned book and aid in breaking free of stealing.	Assign homework reading *The Teens' Solutions Workbook* or *The OCD Workbook* (see Bibliotherapy, Chapter 17).
Make use of available community resources.	Refer family to available resources in the community (see Self-Help Groups and 800 Numbers, Chapter 18, and Online Resources, Chapter 19).
Family works together to develop a treatment termination plan.	Discuss treatment termination issues and develop a plan to terminate treatment.

PATHOLOGICAL GAMBLING—(312.31)

Pathological or Compulsive Gambling is exemplified by maladaptive betting that disrupts the adolescent's academic and interpersonal functioning. Youths who suffer from this impulse control disorder are fixated on gambling in much the same way as people who are addicted to drugs or alcohol. Often they claim to be hooked on the gaming "action," and not the financial gain. Although they may initially deny or lie about having a problem, eventually they admit to being unable to control their betting behavior. Distortions in judgment and irrational thinking are commonplace and include superstitions and overconfidence in "good luck." The need for money to gamble with may result in stealing from friends and family or other antisocial acts.

Adolescent gamblers often have parents who are or were gamblers. Difficulties with related disorders are common and include depression, anxiety, anger, and potential suicide.

There has been an alarming rise in younger people gambling because of the Internet. Since Internet gambling is a solitary activity, it can go uninterrupted, and, therefore, untreated, for a long period of time. Treatment of adolescent gambling is complicated. If a familial gambling pattern exists, the family usually acts as an "enabler" and may even cover-up for the adolescent. A different problem is presented when the adolescent runs afoul of the justice system and is mandated into treatment. The youth becomes an unwilling, unmotivated partner in treatment, and formation of a therapeutic alliance is virtually impossible.

Behavioral Symptoms
(severity index: 1–mild; 2–moderate; 3–intense)

		Severity
1.	Preoccupied with gambling or getting money to gamble	_____
2.	Needs to increase the stakes to maintain the excitement	_____
3.	Unsuccessful in repeated attempts to stop or cut down	_____
4.	Habitually lies about gambling to family or therapist	_____
5.	Becomes restless, irritable when trying to stop	_____
6.	Chases losses by doubling up on bets or other methods	_____
7.	Relies on superstition or magical thinking	_____
8.	Resorts to criminal acts to finance gambling	_____
9.	Borrows from family or friends to cover gambling losses	_____
10.	Gambling has created academic and interpersonal problems	_____
11.	Adolescent is depressed or anxious	_____
12.	Adolescent displays poor impulse control in other areas	_____
13.	Gambles secretly online	_____

PATHOLOGICAL GAMBLING TREATMENT PLAN

Patient: _____ Date: _____

I. OBJECTIVES OF TREATMENT *(select one or more)*

1. Educate parents about the disorder
2. Determine family history of gambling
3. Explore denial of pathological gambling
4. Recognize gambling as a maladaptive response behavior
5. Refer to Gamblers Anonymous group to help treatment
6. Help family develop better coping skills
7. Control anger and anxiety over idea of curtailing gambling
8. Reframe denial/superstition/magical thinking with reality
9. Strengthen family support and improve interaction
10. Confront lying and criminal behavior
11. Confront destructive impact on activities of daily living
12. Improve quality of life
13. Understand self-sabotaging behavior
14. Reduce/eliminate shame and guilt
15. Identify persons, places, and things that trigger gambling
16. Reduce pervasive anxiety and worry
17. Explore secretive online gambling
18. Encourage compliance with programs and referrals
19. Restore the adolescent and family to optimum level of functioning
20. Prevent relapse
21. Develop discharge plan for coping with everyday life

II. SHORT-TERM BEHAVIORAL GOALS AND INTERVENTIONS
(select goals and interventions appropriate for your patient)

NOTE: Separate goals and interventions are provided for Parents, Adolescent, and Family

PARENTS' GOALS	THERAPIST'S INTERVENTIONS
Collaborate with therapist in development of a treatment plan.	Establish therapeutic alliance with parents to enhance the outcome of their adolescent's therapy.

PARENTS' GOALS	THERAPIST'S INTERVENTIONS
Help therapist understand your adolescent's history of gambling.	Assess problem with parents and record a comprehensive history of the adolescent's gambling as they know it.
Cooperate in building a genogram.	Construct a genogram to reveal and understand family pattern of gambling.
Become aware of the behavioral symptoms associated with pathological gambling.	Educate parents about the diagnosis and behavioral symptoms.
Enter treatment for your own gambling problems.	Examine possible pathological gambling in parents and treat or refer for treatment (see appropriate treatment plan).
Develop an understanding of the destructive impact of gambling on your adolescent's life.	If the adolescent has been mandated to treatment by the courts, explore parental reaction and confront denial.
Participate in 12-step program to reduce destructive enabling behavior.	Refer parents to Gamblers Anonymous family groups (see Self-Help Groups and 800 Numbers, Chapter 18, and Online Resources, Chapter 19).
Recognize how your feelings about gambling influence your thoughts and behaviors toward your adolescent.	Explore parents' personal theory of gambling and personal gambling behaviors.
Recognize your feelings of self-blame for adolescent's problem.	Evaluate parents' fears and feelings of self-blame for the adolescent's problem.
Go beyond limited cognitive reactions in viewing the problem.	Expand personal perspective beyond limited cognitive or behavioral reactions.

PARENTS' GOALS	THERAPIST'S INTERVENTIONS
Inform your adolescent of gambling triggers to avoid.	Teach parents about gambling triggers (i.e. people, places, and things) that the adolescent should avoid.
Become aware of online gambling in order to monitor whether your adolescent is using the computer to gamble.	Educate parents about online gambling to help them understand the secretive nature of Internet gambling and how easily it can go undetected for years.
Identify enabling behaviors in the family.	Investigate family conflicts and identify enablers who encourage aid gambling behavior.
Help your adolescent replace magical thinking and ritualistic behavior with more rational responses.	Explore ritualistic behaviors and magical thinking the parents can identify in the adolescent and enlist their aid in urging more rational behaviors.
Be prepared to help your adolescent through the five stages of mourning for his or her abandoned addiction.	Explain the mourning process that accompanies giving up an addiction so parents can help the adolescent through the five stages: denial, anger, bargaining, depression, and acceptance.
Lear principles of diaphragmatic breathing and coach your adolescent to help in relaxation.	Instruct parents in diaphragmatic breathing to assist the adolescent in relaxation (see Behavioral Techniques, Chapter 14).
Become aware of how pathological gambling reduces the family's quality of life.	Explore and identify the major impact of gambling on the family.

PARENTS' GOALS	THERAPIST'S INTERVENTIONS
Agree to allow therapist to confer with adolescent's teachers and officials to help in development of a comprehensive psycho-educational treatment plan.	If appropriate, request and receive parental permission to confer with school officials.
Read assigned book/s to increase knowledge and expand coping skills to deal more effectively with your adolescent's gambling.	Assign parents to read *When Someone You Love Gambles* or *Understanding Compulsive Gambling* (see Bibliotherapy, Chapter 17).
Develop new parenting skills.	Assign parents to read *Making Families Work and What to Do When They Don't* (see Bibliotherapy, Chapter 17).
Understand that guilt creates more tension.	Assign parents to read *Releasing Guilt About Gambling* (see Bibliotherapy, Chapter 17).
Discuss a treatment termination plan and resolve related issues.	Develop a treatment termination plan and address issues of separation and dependency.

ADOLESCENT'S GOALS	THERAPIST'S INTERVENTIONS
Adolescent joins in treatment. Outlook improves, feelings of anger and isolation are diminished.	Cultivate therapeutic alliance or collaborative relationship to build trust and enhance outcome of treatment.
Adolescent feels acknowledged rather than blamed.	Acknowledge the adolescent's point of view.
As appropriate, adolescent is hospitalized for safety or enters into pact agreeing to inform therapist of ideations and plans and to provide prior notification before taking action.	Since there is a high incidence of suicidal behavior associated with gambling, assess suicide potential. If actively suicidal, hospitalize immediately. If the adolescent has suicidal ideations, but no active plan, initiate "suicide pact."
Follow through with psychiatric evaluation and comply with prescribed medication.	If appropriate, refer the adolescent for psychiatric evaluation and possible medication.
Create genogram to show genesis and history of gambling.	Investigate chronological history of the adolescent and gambling by creating genogram (see Behavioral Techniques, Chapter 14).
Explore denial and magical thinking related to gambling.	Explore level of magical thinking and denial and assess the adolescent's cognitive and intellectual functioning that contributes to gambling.
Identify gambling method of choice and develop an understanding of how destructive the addiction is.	Explore methods of gambling (i.e. sports, cards, dice, Internet etc.) and help the adolescent recognize how compulsive and destructive it can be.

ADOLESCENT'S GOALS	THERAPIST'S INTERVENTIONS
Join Gambler's Anonymous.	Refer the adolescent to Gambler's Anonymous to reinforce abstinence between therapy sessions.
Understand that relapse may occur, but you can return to abstinence.	Normalize possible relapse and help the adolescent regard it as an opportunity to apply new techniques to restore abstinence.
See new possibilities for change.	Explore a new direction for treatment. What would the adolescent like to see happen in the future?
Describe barriers to continuing therapy.	Identify and explore barriers to moving on.
Face up to other problems in your life created by gambling.	Gently help the adolescent admit to the other problems gambling has caused in his or her life.
Reveal other impairments and undergo treatment for them.	Evaluate the adolescent for other impairments (i.e. depression, anxiety, impulse control) and treat as indicated (see appropriate treatment plan).
Understand role of stress related to gambling.	Investigate gambling patterns as they relate to life stressors.
Recognize the realistic pitfalls of gambling.	Educate the adolescent about the potential dangers of gambling: school problems, financial crisis, stealing to support the habit, the excitement "high" that leads to addiction.

ADOLESCENT'S GOALS	THERAPIST'S INTERVENTIONS
Begin to seriously examine and question gambling.	Provide feedback on consequences of gambling to create negative cognitions toward the habit.
Recognize gambling's role in avoiding other issues that must be addressed.	Suggest that gambling is used to avoid other issues that need to be resolved.
Explore feelings about change.	Help the adolescent understand his or her ambivalence and explore fear of change.
Recognize that gambling is not a panacea for all your problems.	Help the adolescent understand that his or her problems will not suddenly disappear with the next big win.
Realize that relapse may occur, but you can return to abstinence.	Help the adolescent understand that relapse is possible, but should be regarded as an opportunity to try harder rather than a failure.
Apply principles of mourning to the loss of gambling.	Explain mourning process as it applies to abstention from gambling.
Recognize and confront need for ritualistic behaviors.	Investigate ritualistic nature of gambling behavior.
Identify triggers of need to gamble.	Identify people, places, and things associated with the urge to gamble.
Make commitment to someone else to refrain from gambling.	Urge the adolescent to sign a contract to abstain from gambling.

ADOLESCENT'S GOALS	THERAPIST'S INTERVENTIONS
Realize negative aspects of gambling on other areas of your life.	Explore destructive impact of gambling on interpersonal and other important areas of life.
Take your new skills into the real world. Learn to self-reward success. Correct failures, and try again. Persistence works.	Instruct the adolescent to externalize his or her new skills in the real world.
Explore shame and guilt as they diffuse attempts to stop gambling.	Review issues of shame and guilt that may sabotage client's attempts to stop gambling.
Recognize that most gamblers feel shame and/or guilt but these feelings can be destructive to abstinence.	Help the adolescent to understand that shame and guilt create stressors that cause more gambling.
Identify factors that may cause relapse and how to avoid or control them.	Identify high-risk factors that could lead to relapse. Teach the adolescent avoidance, control, and alternate positive behavior.
Actively develop new behaviors.	Encourage, support, and reinforce any positive new behaviors.
Start daily thought and feelings log.	Assign the adolescent to maintain daily thought and feelings journal to record urges to gamble and his or her reactions (see Homework Assignments, Chapter 16).
Learn new anger management techniques.	Teach the adolescent anger management techniques (see Homework Assignments, Chapter 16).

ADOLESCENT'S GOALS	THERAPIST'S INTERVENTIONS
Learn about anxiety and realize that you can manage your anxiety before it manages you.	Teach the adolescent dynamics of anxiety: anxiety is not permanent or dangerous; avoidance increases anxiety; confronting the problem can reduce anxiety; exposure can produce growth.
Practice control of anger while building confidence to overcome gambling.	With parents' permission, use relaxation techniques, creative visualization or self-hypnosis to help the adolescent reduce stressors and build confidence that he or she can overcome gambling. Provide audiotape for home use (see Behavioral Techniques, Chapter 14).
Learn even more about gambling.	Assign the adolescent to read *Understanding Compulsive Gambling* or *Releasing Guilt About Gambling* (see Bibliotherapy, Chapter 17).
Anger toward self and others is diminished.	Guide the adolescent in reducing anger toward self and others.
Develop a treatment termination plan and resolve associated issues.	Develop a treatment termination plan and resolve separation and dependency issues.

FAMILY'S GOALS	THERAPIST'S INTERVENTIONS
Improve communications among family members.	Conduct family sessions or refer for family therapy to improve communication skills and foster intimacy and cooperation.
Cooperate in understanding the dynamics of the family. Participate in amplifying the parental and adolescent genograms.	Expand previous genograms to aid in understanding family history of gambling and better understand physical and emotional boundaries, nodal events, and toxic issues (see Behavioral Techniques, Chapter 14).
Alienation is reduced as family discusses gambling.	Investigate for possible parental gambling and associated shame and guilt.
Each family member describes his or her point of view about gambling.	Acknowledge and validate each family member's point of view about gambling.
Understand how gambling affects the entire household.	Discuss links between gambling and consequences.
Empathize with the adolescent and support change.	Help family understand the ambivalence toward and fear of change.
Family becomes aware that shame and guilt are not constructive.	Educate family about the destructive effects of shame and guilt.
Empower the adolescent to give up gambling.	Explore solutions and obstacles to create realistic achievable steps toward successful recovery for the adolescent.
Family recognizes enabling as destructive.	Teach family about behaviors that are enabling and therefore destructive.

FAMILY'S GOALS	THERAPIST'S INTERVENTIONS
Read assigned books to further understand nature of gambling.	Assign family members to read *When Someone You Love Gambles* or *Understanding Compulsive Behaviors* (see Bibliotherapy, Chapter 17).
Demonstrate boundaries, triangulation, alliances, and emotional currents within family.	Explore family boundaries using sculpturing, a useful technique for understanding triangulation, alliances, and emotional currents (see "Family Sculpturing," Behavioral Techniques, Chapter 14).
Reframe denial, magical thinking, and superstition using evidence-based reality.	Explore familial magical thinking, denial, and ritualistic behaviors.
Realize that faith in the "next win" only creates problems and does not help resolve underlying issues	Help family to understand that betting cannot and will not cure or melt away problems.
Shift focus from the problem to possible solutions.	Have each family member imagine a future without the problem and suggest actions that can be taken now to make that future possible.
Engage in role-playing to help understand the dynamics of the relationship and improve dysfunctional communication.	Conduct role-playing sessions to help family members "walk in the others' shoes" and develop ways to help each other abandon gambling (see Behavioral Techniques, Chapter 14).
Each family member identifies how he or she has been affected by gambling.	Determine destructive impact of gambling on the family.

FAMILY'S GOALS	THERAPIST'S INTERVENTIONS
Identify familial triggers that enable gambling.	Explore family behaviors that trigger gambling.
Realize you have the power to make important changes even if they seem small.	Help family members realize they have the opportunity to do some things differently.
Family members are empowered and realize they can create positive change.	Ask family members to relate what they have accomplished in the past week.
Learn anger management.	Teach family anger management skills to cope with gambling abstention (see Behavioral Techniques, Chapter 14).
Realize that major change is the result of small steps taken one at a time.	Help family identify and prioritize achievable goals.
Understand the mourning process: denial, anger, bargaining, depression, and acceptance.	Explain mourning process to family so they understand the stages the gambler is going through.
Help in preventing relapse.	Explore relapse triggers with the family so they can provide understanding and support.
In event of relapse, family mobilizes to find new solution.	Instruct family that relapse is normal and should be regarded as an opportunity to try a new solution.
Think about what treatment outcome would look like. Explain what you would like to see change in other family members at the end of treatment.	Ask family members what they might want to say about each other when treatment is ended.

FAMILY'S GOALS	THERAPIST'S INTERVENTIONS
Make use of available community resources.	Refer family to available community resources (see Self-Help Groups and 800 Numbers, Chapter 18, and Online Resources, Chapter 19).
Family works on S.M.A.R.T. plan and understands that persistence works.	Develop a S.M.A.R.T. action plan: plan—Small, Measurable, Achievable, Realistic, Timelined goals (see Behavioral Techniques, Chapter 14).
Work together to develop a treatment termination plan.	Discuss treatment termination issues and develop a plan to terminate.

TRICHOTILLOMANIA—(312.39)

Trichotillomania (TTM) refers to the habitual and irrepressible pulling out of one's own body hair, frequently resulting in noticeable hair loss and other physical and emotional damage. The most commonly affected body sites are the head, pubic region, legs, and face, including the scalp, eyelashes, and eyebrows. Less common sites are the underarms, ears, nose, and torso. Behaviors associated with this disorder include visual examination of the pulled hair, chewing the hair or dragging the hair between one's teeth, or ingestion of the hair.

This disorder seems to begin around the age of 12 or later, but has been known to start earlier in childhood. More frequent in children or adolescents than in adults, it is also more common in girls than in boys. For some, the frequency of the behavior and severity of the disorder seem to correlate with stress levels in their lives. Some clinicians associate the initial hair pulling with hormonal changes at puberty.

The affected person typically experiences an increasing tension just before pulling out the hair, followed by a sense of relief during or just after the act. While it was thought that affected individuals experienced gratification, pleasure, or tension relief when pulling out their hair, this has now been shown to be untrue for a large percentage of the sufferers. For adolescents, TTM is a source of significant emotional distress and impairment in their familial and social functioning. Diagnostically, TTM is not attributable to other mental disorders and is not due to a medical or dermatological condition. It is now suspected that this disorder has both behavioral and biochemical underpinnings.

Behavioral Symptoms
(severity index: 1–mild; 2–moderate; 3–intense)

		Severity
1.	Recurrent pulling of hair from the body	_____
2.	Inspects the hair before and after pulling	_____
3.	Chews on the pulled hair	_____
4.	Plays with or twirls hair prior to pulling	_____
5.	Noticeable bald patches on head	_____
6.	Skin irritation or infection	_____
7.	Gastrointestinal difficulties due to ingested hair	_____
8.	Picks the skin	_____

TRICHOTILLOMANIA TREATMENT PLAN

Patient: _____ Date: _____

I. OBJECTIVES OF TREATMENT *(select one or more)*

1. Lessen, and eventually ameliorate, hair-pulling behavior
2. Determine what initiated the disorder and what maintains it
3. Educate family members about TTM
4. Explore family history of the disorder to determine possible antecedents
5. Diminish anxiety and anger associated with TTM
6. Improve self-image and increase levels of self-esteem
7. Reduce irrational beliefs about TTM
8. Promote socialization in school and at home
9. Assure compliance with any needed medical regimen and referrals

II. SHORT-TERM BEHAVIORAL GOALS AND INTERVENTIONS
(select goals and interventions appropriate for your patient)

NOTE: Separate goals and interventions are provided for Parents, Adolescent, and Family

PARENTS' GOALS	THERAPIST'S INTERVENTIONS
Collaborate with therapist in development of a treatment plan.	Establish therapeutic alliance with parents to promote a positive outcome.
Help the therapist understand your adolescent's development to pinpoint possible origins of the disorder.	Discuss problem with parents and record a complete psychohistory of the adolescent's development to accurately assess problems.
Become aware of the diagnosis and what to reasonably expect from the adolescent.	Inform the parents about the implications of the TTM diagnosis and the prognosis.

PARENTS' GOALS	THERAPIST'S INTERVENTIONS
Cooperate in building a genogram to identify familial history and its relationship to TTM.	Construct a genogram to better understand the family history with regard to the disorder, and its impact on the family (see Behavioral Techniques, Chapter 14).
Become aware of how partial facts and misunderstandings influence your thoughts and actions.	Explore the validity of what the parents think to be true about the disorder and, if appropriate, replace irrational thinking.
Challenge fears and feelings of blame related to the problem.	Evaluate parents' fears and negative perceptions of themselves, and each other for the adolescent's problem.
Develop a more tempered response repertoire to the disorder.	Help parents to act appropriately to the situation, rather than react out of frustration.
If present, receive treatment for underlying physical and/or emotional problems, which may intensify the adolescent's condition.	Determine if the parents are suffering from some physical and/or emotional disorder that may be affecting the adolescent and treat or refer for therapy.
Have the adolescent evaluated for medical problems that may exacerbate the disorder.	If appropriate, have the adolescent evaluated for physical problems related to TTM.
Agree to allow therapist to confer with the adolescent's school to help in development of a comprehensive psychoeducational treatment plan.	After interviewing the adolescent, and with his or her permission, request and receive parental permission to discuss the situation with the adolescent's teachers and school administrators.

PARENTS' GOALS	THERAPIST'S INTERVENTIONS
Have the adolescent evaluated by dermatologist, neurologist. and/or psychiatrist to best determine most comprehensive treatment.	After interviewing the adolescent, provide referral for him or her to be evaluated by dermatologist, neurologist, and/or psychiatrist for evaluation and possible medication.
Comply with referrals to medical and psychiatric evaluations.	Work through any parental objections to referrals for medical and psychiatric evaluations.
Use games to improve communications with your adolescent.	Suggest activities or games to improve communication between parents and the adolescent (i.e. *Life Stories*, see Therapeutic Games, Chapter 15).
Become a positive change agent for your adolescent through environmental shaping.	Teach parents how to provide a positive environment for the adolescent that will reinforce his or her healthy and constructive behaviors.
To increase knowledge and lessen impact of false impressions and conclusions, meet with parents of other afflicted adolescents.	Have parents discuss their pain and confusion over the situation. Refer to appropriate self-help group (see Self-Help Groups and 800 Numbers, Chapter 18, and Online Resources, Chapter 19).
Enhance parenting skills.	Assign books on improving parenting skills (see *Good Kids, Difficult Behavior* or *Parenting Toward Solutions*, in Bibliotherapy, Chapter 17).

PARENTS' GOALS	THERAPIST'S INTERVENTIONS
Reduce the sense of isolation by becoming involved in community organizations that deal with this disorder.	Explain the availability of community resources to provide both concrete and emotional support (see Self-Help Groups, and 800 Numbers, Chapter 18, and Online Resources, Chapter 19).
Parents are educated in ways to reinforce healthier expressions of feelings in their adolescent.	Teach parents basic behavioral techniques for reinforcing alternative behaviors to hair pulling.
Discuss and approve a treatment termination plan and resolve termination issues.	Once the hair pulling has abated, develop a treatment termination plan and discuss issues of separation anxiety and dependency.

ADOLESCENT'S GOALS	THERAPIST'S INTERVENTIONS
Begin to feel safe with and to trust the therapist.	Develop a therapeutic relationship with the adolescent to instill trust and enhance treatment outcome.
Learn about the problem and begin to get ideas about how to deal with it.	Educate the adolescent about the diagnosis, discuss symptomatology so he or she can better understand what is happening, and begin to develop problem-solving strategies.
See new ways of behaving that may lessen the urge to pull hair.	Modify the adolescent's behavior through role-playing and other self-expressive techniques (see Behavioral Techniques, Chapter 14).
Learn what your body feels like before hair pulling begins.	Have the adolescent recognize somatic indicators that he or she associates with hair pulling.
Continually learn that you can control your behaviors and are not a victim of them.	Teach the adolescent relaxation techniques to lessen the stress associated with resisting the hair-pulling impulse (see Behavioral Techniques, Chapter 14).
Understand you do not have to act on feelings.	Teach the adolescent to place thought before action to interrupt hair-pulling behaviors.
Develop internalized guide to help perform self-regulatory tasks.	Instruct the adolescent how to develop an internal, self-monitoring guide or ally to help stop the hair pulling. Initially, the therapist may represent the internalized figure.

ADOLESCENT'S GOALS	THERAPIST'S INTERVENTIONS
Reframe beliefs about TTM.	Change irrational beliefs by having the adolescent discuss his or her beliefs and develop rational alternatives.
Learn from role modeling and shape new behaviors.	Provide cognitive restructuring and role model appropriate behavior (see Behavioral Techniques, Chapter 14).
Using hypnosis, guided imagery, or relaxation techniques, learn to gain control over feelings. Use audiotape to learn to interrupt urges.	With parents' permission, use hypnosis, creative visualization or relaxation techniques to help master troublesome feelings. Provide audiotape for home use (see Behavioral Techniques, Chapter 14).
Develop and discover alternate ways to counteract urges to pull hair.	Help the adolescent develop actions to replace hair pulling (i.e., When urge appears, place pointer finger and thumb together rather than pull hair.
Learn to self-monitor and exercise the power of your mind to override hair-pulling behavior.	Teach the adolescent that his or her hair-pulling behaviors are subject to volition.
Learn that it is healthier to verbally convey feelings than to express them through hair pulling.	Reinforce behaviors that the adolescent uses to express feelings other than hair pulling.
Expand vocabulary to express thoughts and feelings that may have gone unexpressed.	When necessary, provide the adolescent with words or phrases that may aid in his or her self-expression.
Underlying feelings of anger or depression are treated to reduce acting out behaviors.	Explore for underlying feelings of anger or depression and treat (see appropriate treatment plan).

ADOLESCENT'S GOALS	THERAPIST'S INTERVENTIONS
Put words to your feelings to reduce negative impact on behavior.	Explore for feelings of despair and of low self-esteem related to TTM. Have the adolescent tell how he or she feels and discuss what to do about the situation.
Learn the meaning the hair pulling has taken on. Begin to see possible alternatives.	With the adolescent, discuss the meaning of the hair-pulling behaviors.
Identify irrational and negative beliefs about self-worth and how TTM may be a way of punishing yourself.	Without using punitive or derogatory language, enable the adolescent to see the self-destructive nature of his or her behavior. Explore for underlying self-hatred.
Using guided imagery and other relaxation techniques, learn to gain control over feelings.	With parents' permission, use hypnosis, relaxation techniques or guided imagery to help master troublesome or dangerous feelings (see Behavioral Techniques, Chapter 14).
Understand anxiety and realize that avoidance does not help.	Teach client the dynamics of anxiety: anxiety is not permanent or dangerous; avoidance increases anxiety; confronting the problem can reduce anxiety; exposure can produce growth.
Communicate personal experience of the disorder to the therapist	Help the adolescent to communicate his or her personal experience through the use of *The Storytelling Game* (see Therapeutic Games, Chapter 15).

ADOLESCENT'S GOALS	THERAPIST'S INTERVENTIONS
Learn that it is safe to discuss your problems with someone in a non-threatening environment	Have the adolescent play *The Talking, Feeling, Doing Game* to understand underlying processes in a non-threatening way (see Therapeutic Games, Chapter 15).
Understand how trauma may have contributed to the existing disorder.	Explore the adolescent's background for trauma that may have exacerbated the disorder.
Discuss how the behaviors associated with TTM may have begun.	Investigate ways the behaviors associated with TTM may have begun as a misguided solution to another issue.
Significantly reduce hair-pulling and related behaviors.	Aid the adolescent in recognizing that previously uncontrollable behaviors can be controlled through increased awareness.
Make use of a journal or behavioral log to document when and for how long hair pulling was successfully avoided.	Assign the adolescent to maintain a journal to record success in resisting the urge to pull hair.
Recognize triggers of impulsive behavior and learn to consciously respond rather than react automatically.	Help the adolescent to recognize and confront internal and environmental triggers of impulsive behavior.
Attend self-help group to increase understanding and control and get feedback from others who share the same problem.	Refer the adolescent to self-help group (see Self-Help Groups and 800 Numbers, Chapter 18, and Online Resources, Chapter 19).
Recognize the causal relationship between hair pulling and emotional pain.	Help the adolescent to see the connection between hair pulling and the physical and emotional pain he or she feels.

ADOLESCENT'S GOALS	THERAPIST'S INTERVENTIONS
Continue to intensify sense of mastery over the condition.	Help the adolescent tolerate the impulse to pull hair for increasingly longer periods of time.
Learn methods to control anxiety and offer practical suggestions to reduce tension and stress.	Assign the adolescent to read *How to Control Your Anxiety Before It Controls You* or *You Must Relax* (see Bibliotherapy, Chapter 17).
Determine the factors that enable the adolescent to successfully resist the hair-pulling urge.	Explore with the adolescent the ways that he or she has been able to resist the urge to pull.
Understand that you can effectively deal with TTM and bring treatment to a successful conclusion.	Develop a treatment termination plan and resolve issues of separation anxiety and dependency.

FAMILY'S GOALS	THERAPIST'S INTERVENTIONS
Improve communications among all family members.	Conduct family sessions or refer for family therapy to improve communication skills and foster intimacy and cooperation.
Cooperate in understanding the dynamics of the family. Participate in the construction of a family genogram.	Discuss family history to help understand relational dynamics with a focus on how they affect the adolescent. Create family genogram to better understand physical and emotional boundaries, nodal events, and toxic issues surrounding the adolescent (see Behavioral Techniques, Chapter 14).
Discuss genogram openly to fully understand family history as it relates to TTM.	Discuss genogram to uncover family history and possible prior involvements with TTM.
Understand the roles that the family members may individually and collectively play in the problem.	Recognize and discuss how the family members may influence the problem.
Identify if other family members have TTM.	Explore if other family members have TTM and if positive, treat or refer for treatment.
Demonstrate boundaries, alliances, triangles, and emotional currents through family choreography to help understand how the family impacts the problem.	Explore boundaries using family sculpturing to understand triangulation, alliances, and emotional currents (see Behavioral Techniques, Chapter 14).
Emphasize your past success in positive interaction to deal with serious issues in the past. Shift the focus from problems to possible solutions.	Discuss with family members and reinforce the ways that they have successfully dealt with serious issues in the past.

FAMILY'S GOALS	THERAPIST'S INTERVENTIONS
Reduce negative communication.	Develop a system of positive reinforcement with family to interact better with each other and reduce scapegoating.
Realize you can help each other make important and necessary changes for the benefit of everyone.	Help family realize that they can do many things differently if they work together.
Family learns to problem solve.	Teach the adolescent the principles of problem solving: (1) stay calm, take a deep breath; (2) think about what is bothering you; (3) create a S.M.A.R.T. action plan: plan—Small, Measurable, Achievable, Realistic, Timelined goals; (4) select three different solutions, pick the best one, do the best you can, if it doesn't work, stay calm and try again. Remember, perseverance works; don't give up (see "Change," Behavioral Techniques, Chapter 14).
Recognize you can be effective change agents.	Explore accomplishments the family has achieved.
Enhance sense of mastery or competence in the accomplishment of stated goals.	Help family identify and prioritize achievable goals.
Promote understanding of how to control ritualistic behaviors.	Assign reading of *Mastery of Obsessive-Compulsive Disorder: A Cognitive-Behavioral Approach* (see Bibliotherapy, Chapter 17).

FAMILY'S GOALS	THERAPIST'S INTERVENTIONS
Make use of available community resources.	Refer family to available resources in the community (see Self-Help Groups and 800 Numbers, Chapter 18, and Online Resources, Chapter 19).
Family works together to develop a treatment termination plan.	Discuss treatment termination issues and develop a plan to successfully complete treatment.

11
RELATIONAL PROBLEMS

PARENT–ADOLESCENT RELATIONAL PROBLEM—(V61.20)

Since V-codes are not usually reimbursable by most insurance companies, it is important to identify a behavioral impairment under treatment on Axis I of the DSM *(DSM-IV)* Multiaxial Assessment System. Some of the behavioral symptoms that should be coded on Axis I or II include anxiety disorders, conduct disorder, mood disorders, or personality disorders. V-codes are coded on Axis IV. However, the focus of treatment should be on the recurrent patterns of dysfunctional interactions among family members (i.e. inadequate parenting, the "too good" or "not good enough" mother or father syndrome, overprotection, underprotection, or dysfunctional communication).

If indicated by the symptomatology, one or both members of the dyad should be considered candidates for individual or family treatment. If both parents are emotionally impaired, they should be considered for individual or conjoint treatment. Some of the behavioral symptoms that occur are products of unresolved parental conflicts. Since parents are role models for their children, it is not surprising to find these problems reappearing in the next generation.

The problems of separation and divorce are so endemic in our society today that they are covered in a separate plan.

Behavioral Symptoms
(severity index: 1–mild; 2–moderate; 3–intense)

NOTE: Behavioral impairment should be coded on Axis I or II and the associated V-code on Axis IV

                                                                  Severity

1. Parent or adolescent persistently acts out   _____
2. Parent and adolescent engage in heated quarreling   _____
3. Parent or adolescent displays significant anxiety
    and/or stress-related problems   _____
4. Parent or adolescent is constantly irritable   _____
5. Parent or adolescent suffers from mood disorder   _____
6. Neurological disorder of parent or adolescent
    is exacerbated   _____
7. Adolescent has serious academic problems   _____
8. Parent or adolescent has eating disorder   _____
9. Parent or adolescent has sleep disturbance   _____
10. Parent or adolescent has personality disorder   _____
11. Parent exhibits inadequate parenting skills   _____
12. Parent or adolescent show marked inability
    to empathize with each other   _____
13. Patterns of discipline are irrational, confused,
    or lacking   _____

SIBLING RELATIONAL PROBLEM—V61.8

Sibling rivalry is a normal part of growing up. However, it is considered pathological when it becomes uncontrollable, tension arises among family members, and recurring arguments get out of hand. Such rivalry may occur when parents have unresolved childhood problems of their own with their siblings. It can also occur because of marital problems (children acting out their parents' problems), role confusion, communication difficulties, or other conflicts with extended family. Other contributing factors may be parental failure to set appropriate boundaries and provide consistent, respectful discipline, or parental over-involvement in their own lives.

No two children in a family are exactly alike. Some of the major differences include birth order, genetics and gender. As a result, parents do not act the same with each of them. Siblings often learn to test strong love and hate relations with each other rather than express their feelings to their parents.

Behavioral Symptoms
(severity index: 1–mild; 2–moderate; 3–intense)

Severity

1. Significant impairment in academic and interpersonal functioning _____
2. Depressed most of the time _____
3. Persistent anxiety _____
4. Difficulty falling and staying sleep _____
5. Displays social phobia _____
6. Adjustment disorder _____
7. Personality disorder _____
8. Developmental delays _____
9. School or learning problems _____
10. Somatization _____
11. Oppositional defiant behavior _____
12. Acts out _____
13. Distorted parenting _____
14. Poor disciplining _____
15. Physical or sexual abuse _____
16. Scapegoating _____
17. Marked inability to empathize with sibling _____

PARENT–ADOLESCENT RELATIONAL PROBLEM
SIBLING RELATIONAL PROBLEM
TREATMENT PLAN

Patient: _____   Date: _____

I. OBJECTIVES OF TREATMENT *(select one or more)*

1. Develop better parenting skills
2. Investigate family history of problem/problems
3. Reduce overall intensity of quarreling
4. Ameliorate behavioral symptoms
5. Improve communication skills
6. Reduce dysfunctional interactions
7. Restore rational discipline
8. Increase ability to empathize with each other
9. Reduce familial alienation
10. Restore adolescent and family to optimum level of functioning

II. SHORT-TERM BEHAVIORAL GOALS AND INTERVENTIONS
(select goals and interventions appropriate for your patients)

FAMILY'S GOALS	THERAPIST'S INTERVENTIONS
Improve communications within the family system to reduce anger and alienation.	Conduct family sessions with focus on reducing anger and/or alienation.
Cooperate with therapist to improve treatment outlook.	Develop therapeutic alliance or collaborative relationship with parents and children to instill trust and enhance treatment outcomes.
Discuss treatment plan and agree on target problems.	Formulate treatment plan and discuss with the family. Agree on target problems.
Cooperate in construction of a family genogram. Begin to understand historical communication patterns and contributions of ancestors to dysfunctional patterns.	Prepare complete genogram to uncover and display family interactions, patterns, roles, and secrets (see Behavioral Techniques, Chapter 14).

FAMILY'S GOALS	THERAPIST'S INTERVENTIONS
Discuss genogram openly to understand pathological patterns of interaction.	Discuss genogram to reveal family history and toxic issues that may have contributed to current pathology.
Identify the things you think have created or contributed to the family problems.	Explore and acknowledge each family member's personal view of the problems that have brought him or her into therapy.
Identify behavioral symptoms and enter individual therapy as required.	Explore individual behavioral symptoms and evaluate potential effectiveness of current modality or the need for individual therapy. If required, provide or refer for treatment.
Identify impact of extended family.	Explore impact of extended family.
Identify crisis that may have created unusual family stress.	Investigate for environmental stressors that may have exacerbated the problem (i.e. death, relocation, loss of employment, financial issues etc.).
Demonstrate boundaries, alliances, triangulation, and emotional currents that may undermine family functioning.	Explore family boundaries using Family Sculpturing, a useful technique for revealing triangulation, alliances, and emotional currents (see Behavioral Techniques, Chapter 14).
Children and adolescents clearly understand what is expected of them and the consequences for out-of-bounds behavior.	Help parents establish appropriate boundaries, clear rules, and methods of positive reinforcement.

FAMILY'S GOALS	THERAPIST'S INTERVENTIONS
Increase emotional awareness by walking in another family member's shoes and expand your repertoire of behavior.	Conduct role-playing sessions with each member playing the part of another and switching parts as necessary (see Behavioral Techniques, Chapter 14).
Familial homeostasis is established.	Identify and rectify disruptive relational patterns.
Explore impact of rivalry on each child and determine strategy for dealing with it.	Explore sibling rivalry, how it is handled, and the impact on each child and/or adolescent. Brainstorm methods of dealing with it.
Help develop family solution and become part of the solution instead of the problem.	Preclude a "search for the guilty" by requiring the family to stay solution-focused.
Realize that anxiety and awkwardness are normal accompaniments to family change.	Instruct the family on barriers and resistance to change.
Learn to listen to one another and ask for clarification when necessary.	Teach active family listening and clarification skills.
Reduce scapegoating of "identified patient."	Determine if there is an "identified patient" within the family system.
All family members assume responsibility for improvement.	Assist family in understanding that current difficulties may be the result of systemic dysfunctions and not the fault of any one individual.
Follow-up with referrals for evaluation.	If appropriate, refer family member(s) for medical and psychiatric evaluations.

FAMILY'S GOALS	THERAPIST'S INTERVENTIONS
Maintain a medication log to monitor medication schedule and reactions. Discuss in session with therapist.	If medication is prescribed, assure compliance with regimen. Identify need for dosage adjustment.
Keep journal and discuss during session.	Instruct each family member to maintain a thought and feelings log to record events and reactions between visits.
If necessary, family member(s) enter treatment for substance abuse.	Explore possibility of substance abuse and, if positive, treat or refer to 12-step rational recovery program.
Improve parenting skills.	Refer mother and/or father to parenting group to improve parenting skills (See Self-Help Groups and 800 Numbers, Chapter 18, and Online Resources, Chapter 19).
Identify and evaluate existing irrational beliefs.	Help family members examine their irrational beliefs
Reframe your irrational beliefs.	Reframe family members' irrational beliefs with evidence-based reality.
Work toward changing the way you speak to each other.	Educate family about "indoor" (chronic tone) behavior and "outdoor" (social tone) behavior. Encourage family to reduce indoor behavior.
Reduce negative behaviors and interaction.	Explore negative self-talk and familial negative talk and encourage more positive ways to communicate.
Learn new rational perspective.	Further clarify rational distortions in family members' perceptions.

Read assigned book to enhance parenting skills.	Assign parents to read *Making Families Work and What to Do When They Don't* or *Try and Make Me: A Revolutionary Program for Raising Your Defiant Child Without Losing Your Cool* (see Bibliotherapy, Chapter 17).
Read books together that address behavioral problems and how to deal with them.	Assign family to read together *When Living Hurts: For Teenagers and Young Adults* or *An Ounce of Prevention* (see Bibliotherapy, Chapter 17).
Describe your view of what the future should be.	Have each family member describe what he or she would like the future to be like.
Acknowledge your personal barriers and available resources.	Identify barriers and available internal and external resources to overcome them and create change.
Family works together to create S.M.A.R.T. action plan.	Develop a S.M.A.R.T. action plan—Small, Measurable, Achievable, Realistic, Timelined goals (see "Change," Behavioral Techniques, Chapter 14).
Learn to abandon old patterns and develop new ways of thinking.	Discuss what actions are going to be taken and encourage the family to persist until the goals are reached.
Receive positive reinforcement for success.	Provide positive reinforcement for success.
Imagine what life might be like after treatment and how the lives of all family members will be changed.	Ask family members to verbalize three things they would like to be able to say about each of the others when therapy is completed.

FAMILY'S GOALS	THERAPIST'S INTERVENTIONS
Play and share *Life Stories*.	Have entire family play *Life Stories* to share family tales and bring them closer together (see Therapeutic Games, Chapter 15).
Use family outing to practice new knowledge and insights and enhance relationships.	Assign family outings to include all family members.
Discuss treatment termination issues and end treatment.	Develop a treatment termination plan and discuss related issues of dependency and separation anxiety.

DIVORCE OR SEPARATION-RELATED PROBLEMS

This is a difficult time for traditional institutions, especially the family. It is estimated (Kurdck, 1986; Knell 2000) that almost 40% of all children in America will experience parental disruption by their fifteenth birthday. In divorce or separation, some disturbance is common in the interaction between the child and one or both parents, as well as a period of adjustment that may require therapeutic intervention.

Although there is no category in *DSM-IV* for Children of Divorce or Separation, I believe this growing problem deserves special attention. It is assumed that the diagnosis would be coded as V61.20 on Axis IV of the *DSM-IV* Multiaxis Assessment System with the associated behavioral impairments coded on Axis I.

Divorce or separation often create major life changes for all members of the family (i.e. financial problems, new homes or schools, increased mother-child conflict, and others). Adjustment to post-divorce lifestyle changes is challenging for both parent and child.

Behavioral Symptoms
(severity index: 1–mild; 2–moderate; 3–intense)

		Severity
1.	Elimination disorders–children 2½–5 years old	_____
2.	Depression	_____
3.	Aggressive behaviors	_____
4.	Withdrawal	_____
5.	Decreased frustration tolerance	_____
6.	Separation anxiety	_____
7.	Fear of interaction with others	_____
8.	Difficulty concentrating	_____
9.	Self-esteem issues	_____
10.	Self-blame, guilt, shame	_____

There may be many more symptoms resulting from divorce as a traumatic event.

DIVORCE OR SEPARATION-RELATED PROBLEMS TREATMENT PLAN

Patient: _____ Date: _____

I. OBJECTIVES OF TREATMENT *(select one or more)*

1. Educate parents about the possible reactions their child/children may have to divorce (i.e. self-blame, magical thinking about reconciliation, fear of abandonment, avoidance behavior, peer ridicule)
2. Teach parents importance of showing mutual respect in front of their children
3. Determine family history of divorce and separation
4. Eliminate blame
5. Help family develop better coping skills
6. Help parents develop a reasonable visitation schedule
7. Reduce pervasive anxiety and worry
8. Treat elimination disorders associated with stress of the divorce
9. Reduce depression
10. Diminish acting out
11. Eliminate fears of abandonment
12. Reduce and eliminate fear of ridicule in social interactions
13. Increase frustration tolerance
14. Encourage compliance with educational programs and referrals
15. Reframe irrational beliefs
16. Eliminate anxieties
17. Help children and adolescent(s) develop a realistic view of the divorce or separation
18. Reduce "too good" syndrome
19. Reduce alienation, promote socialization
20. Treat other disorders related to trauma
21. Restore the adolescent and his or her family to optimum level of functioning
22. Develop discharge plan for coping with everyday life

II. SHORT-TERM BEHAVIORAL GOALS AND INTERVENTIONS
(select goals and interventions appropriate for your patient)

NOTE: Separate goals and interventions are provided for Parents, Adolescent, and Family

PARENTS' GOALS	THERAPIST'S INTERVENTIONS
Separately collaborate with therapist in development of a treatment plan.	Establish therapeutic alliance separately with each custodial and noncustodial parent.
If there is any hope of reconciliation, enter couples therapy or marriage counseling.	Identify any hope of reconciliation and if positive refer for couples therapy or marriage counseling.
Help therapist understand your adolescent's developmental issues and concerns before and after the divorce or separation.	Assess problem separately with both parents and record a comprehensive history of the adolescent's development before and after the divorce or separation.
Recognize what to reasonably expect from the adolescent.	Educate parents about the possible pitfalls for their adolescent related to the divorce or separation.
Cooperate in building a genogram.	Construct a genogram to better understand the physical and emotional boundaries, toxic issues, and familial support network (see Behavioral Techniques, Chapter 14).
Enter treatment for individual psychopathology, in appropriate, to support your adolescent's treatment and enhance outcome.	Evaluate parents for individual psychopathology and refer for treatment, if appropriate, to reduce negative effects on the adolescent.

PARENTS' GOALS	THERAPIST'S INTERVENTIONS
Develop awareness of how your personal theory influences cognition of how your adolescent deals with divorce or separation.	Explore parental cognitions of the divorce or separation and identify how they have discussed it with the adolescent. What did they explain and what did they withhold?
Recognize your fears and feelings of responsibility for the divorce or separation.	Evaluate parents' fears and feelings of personal responsibility for the divorce or separation.
Learn to reach beyond automatic cognitive reactions in viewing the problem.	Expand parental perspective beyond limited cognitive reactions.
Identify and explain how well you think your adolescent is coping with the divorce or separation.	Explore parents' understanding of how the adolescent is coping with the divorce or separation. Is the adolescent angry with one or the other parent, both parents, or himself?
Identify conflicts and realize the impact they can have on your adolescent's recovery.	Explore the dynamics of marital conflict and how its intensity impacts the adolescent.
Confront reactions that can lead to catastrophic outcomes.	Confront parents' distorted reactions that trigger destructive behaviors.
Control your stress to protect your adolescent from the conflict.	Teach parents to reduce the stress during the marital breakup and ultimate family separation in order to protect the adolescent from their hostilities and conflict.

PARENTS' GOALS	THERAPIST'S INTERVENTIONS
Feel acknowledged instead of blamed.	Acknowledge each parent's point of view (see "Change," Behavioral Techniques, Chapter 14).
Identify cognitive distortions and correct them.	Have parents weigh their reactions against evidence-based reality.
Collaborate in development of a direction-based plan	Develop a direction-based plan for a controlled, non-hostile separation and divorce.
Parents become aware of the possibility of change.	Explore possibilities of change (i.e. internal barriers, old patterns) and identify resources for making modifications.
Identify financial concerns and actions to limit the impact on your adolescent.	Explore financial situation and identify actions to reduce negative impact.
Cooperate with therapist's efforts to enlist the school's assistance in developing a psychoeducational treatment plan for your adolescent.	When indicated, request and receive parental permission to confer with the adolescent's teachers and school officials.
Comply with referral for evaluations.	If necessary, after interviewing the adolescent, provide referral for medical and psychiatric evaluations.
Read assigned book(s) to help understand and deal with feelings triggered by the divorce or separation.	Assign books for parents to read (see Bibliotherapy, Chapter 17).
Learn new skills and strategies for managing the adolescent's anxieties related to the divorce or separation.	Assign parents to read *Helping Your Kids Cope With Divorce* (see Bibliotherapy, Chapter 17).

PARENTS' GOALS	THERAPIST'S INTERVENTIONS
Understand common behavioral pitfalls to help the adolescent cope if it becomes necessary.	Educate parents about problematic reaction by the adolescent (i.e. peer avoidance or ridicule, interfamilial blame, personal blame, abandonment issues, unfounded hopes of reconciliation).
Meet with other parents who are going through the same difficulties and share solutions for dealing with the problems.	Refer parents to appropriate self-help group (see Self-Help Groups and 800 Numbers, Chapter 18, and Online Resources, Chapter 19).
Expand your repertoire of strategies to help your adolescent cope with divorce or separation.	Assign parents to read: *Helping Your Kids Cope With Divorce*, or *Caught in the Middle* (see Bibliotherapy, Chapter 17).
Discuss a treatment termination plan and resolve related issues.	Develop a treatment termination plan and discuss issues of separation and dependency.

ADOLESCENT'S GOALS	THERAPIST'S INTERVENTIONS
Engage in a therapeutic alliance with therapist to improve outcome of treatment.	Engage the adolescent in a non-threatening therapeutic relationship
Discuss symptoms openly with therapist.	Identify the adolescent's symptoms and determine the most appropriate course of treatment.
Recognize and explain your reactions to the divorce or separation.	Explain the common reactions to divorce or separation (i.e. self-blame, parental blame, abandonment issues, separation anxiety, social ostracism, and unfounded hopes of reconciliation).
Understand underlying dynamics that lead to maladaptive behavior and stress.	Explore ways in which anxieties manfest themselves.
Undergo treatment for sleep disorder.	Investigate for sleep disorder and treat if necessary (see appropriate treatment plan).
Ease the blame and increase self-acceptance.	Teach the adolescent that human beings are less than perfect.
Psychodramatically practice new ways to handle visitations.	Role-play awkward and difficult situations (see Behavioral Techniques, Chapter 14).
Identify feelings about stepparent and siblings.	If parent(s) are remarried after divorce, discuss with the adolescent his or her feelings about the new stepparent and stepsiblings.

ADOLESCENT'S GOALS	THERAPIST'S INTERVENTIONS
Realize you are not alone. Others also feel bad.	Investigate for low self-esteem relates to the divorce or separation.
Begin to see possible solutions to your negative feelings and anxiety.	Discuss how negative feelings are dealt with and develop a plan of action.
Identify beliefs related to marital dissolution.	Explore relevant attitudes, fears, and anxieties regarding marital dissolution.
Increase repertoire of adaptive responses.	Develop effective alternatives to reduce negative emotions and behaviors triggered by stressors.
Realize that you didn't cause your parents' problems.	Discuss how the adolescent might feel the divorce or separation was his or her fault because he or she was "bad."
Use relaxation techniques and guided imagery to handle anxieties.	With permission of custodial parent, teach the adolescent relaxation techniques and guided imagery to master anxieties (see Behavioral Techniques, Chapter 14).
Understand anxiety and realize that avoidance does not help.	Teach child dynamics of anxiety: anxiety is not permanent or dangerous; avoidance increases anxiety; confronting the problem can reduce anxiety; exposure can produce growth.
Lessen impact of socioeconomic change.	Discuss how changes in the family's financial status have affected the child.

ADOLESCENT'S GOALS	THERAPIST'S INTERVENTIONS
Relate life story to therapist or play *Life Stories*.	Ask the adolescent to relate his or her life story, or play *Life Stories* (see Therapeutic Games, Chapter 15).
Develop better coping skills to lessen the impact of painful emotions.	Play *Bounce-Back* or *My Two Homes* to help adjust to parents' divorce or separation.
Discuss personal coping mechanisms used to handle the divorce or separation.	Wth the adolescent, investigate possible patterns of withdrawal used to avoid shame of divorce or separation.
Identify magical thinking and replace it with rational expectations.	Explore for magical thinking (e.g. "Mommy and Daddy will reconcile, if I am exceptionally good, and we will all be together again"). Replace with rational expectations.
Discuss how extended family impacts the problem.	Explore impact of extended family (grandparents, aunts, uncles etc.) on the divorce or separation.
Recognize that violence is wrong, that violence happens in other families too, and that it is okay to talk about it.	Investigate for physical or emotional abuse before or after separation.
Learn positive self-talk.	Teach the adolescent positive self-talk to interrupt negative patterns.
Admit fear of abandonment and clarify rational responses.	Facilitate the adolescent's admission of fears of abandonment and clarify reality.

ADOLESCENT'S GOALS	THERAPIST'S INTERVENTIONS
Learn new technique for dealing with anxiety.	Teach child diaphragmatic breathing to control anxiety (see Behavioral Techniques, Chapter 14).
Learn new ways to nurture yourself and deal with emotional difficulties.	Use the *Positive Thinking Game*, or *The Ungame* to practice positive self-talk and control negative emotions (see Therapeutic Games, Chapter 15).
Shift focus of attention from the problem to accomplishment.	Ask the adolescent to describe his or her accomplishments of the past week.
Feel more confident as self-esteem improves.	Compliment the adolescent to provide positive reinforcement whenever possible.
Use routine aerobic exercise to relieve frustrations and anger.	Suggest the adolescent start a regular aerobic exercise program to relieve frustration.
Report results to therapist.	Provide positive reinforcement when the adolescent reports back that he or she has challenged anxiety-provoking situations. Praise attempt and reward success.
Learn to problem solve.	Teach the adolescent the principles of problem solving: (1) stay calm, take a deep breath; (2) think about what is bothering you; (3) create S.M.A.R.T. action plan—Small, Measurable, Achievable, Realistic, Timelined goals; (4) select three different solutions, pick the best one, do the best you can, if it doesn't work, stay calm and try again.

ADOLESCENT'S GOALS	THERAPIST'S INTERVENTIONS
	Remember perseverance works; don't give up (see "Change," Behavioral Techniques, Chapter 14).
Learn methods that you can be use to advocate for yourself.	Instruct the adolescent in the techniques of self-advocacy.
Understand that you can deal with these issues and bring treatment to a successful conclusion.	Develop a treatment termination plan and explain issues of separation anxiety and dependency.

FAMILY'S GOALS	THERAPIST'S INTERVENTIONS
Improve communications among family members to reduce levels of anger and alienation.	Conduct family sessions with either one or both parents present, or refer for family therapy to reduce anger and/or alienation, and improve communication skills within the family.
Cooperate in amplifying family genogram.	Expand genograms created in earlier sessions to help understand family history (see Behavioral Techniques, Chapter 14).
Discuss genogram openly to develop consensus.	Compare and discuss genogram to reveal possible family secrets dealing with divorce or separation.
Family works out conflicts psychodramatically and attempts to share and understand.	Role-play family dynamics, having family members switch roles to clarify dynamics and improve communications (see Behavioral Techniques, Chapter 14).
Demonstrate boundaries, alliances, triangles, and emotional currents that may exacerbate divorce or separation difficulties.	Explore boundaries using family sculpturing (see Behavioral Techniques, Chapter 14).
Family members share how divorce has affected their lives.	Discuss symptoms of divorce or separation (i.e. self-blame, ridicule, avoidance behavior, fear of abandonment, magical thinking of reconciliation).

FAMILY'S GOALS	THERAPIST'S INTERVENTIONS
Each family member feels acknowledged and blame is reduced.	Acknowledge and validate each family member's point of view about the problem(s).
Identify internal and external barriers (i.e., fears, irrational beliefs, old habits, finances, lack of information) that lead to maladaptive behaviors.	Investigate internal and external barriers to developing a better future.
Identify resources that will help each other and reduce the stress of divorce or separation.	Investigate possible available resources to help make change possible (i.e. support systems, other extended family members who might be helpful, tasks older children and adolescents might assume).
Shift focus from problem to possible solutions.	Have family imagine a future without these problems and suggest actions that can be taken now to best approximate that possibility.
Family realizes they have the power to make important changes even if they seem small.	Help family realize they have an opportunity to do some things differently.
Family members are empowered. They recognize that they can create positive change.	Ask family members to relate what they have accomplished in the past week.
Enhance understanding of parenting and divorce, and see how other families have handled similar problems.	Assign homework reading and discuss: *Making Families Work and What to Do When They Don't* or *Does Wednesday Mean Mom's House or Dad's?* (see Bibliotherapy, Chapter 17.)

FAMILY'S GOALS	THERAPIST'S INTERVENTIONS
Make use of available community resources.	Refer family to available resources in the community (see Self-Help Groups and 800 Numbers, Chapter 18, and Online Resources, Chapter 19).
Reduce negative communication.	Develop a system of positive reinforcement with family to interact better with each other and reduce scapegoating.
Family works together to develop a treatment termination plan.	Discuss termination issues and develop a plan to terminate treatment.

ADOLESCENT ABUSE OR NEGLECT—(995.5X)

Although not a disorder, adolescent abuse or neglect is coded on Axis I of the *DSM-IV* Multiaxial Assessment System as the focus of clinical attention along with the impairment being treated (i.e. anxiety, depression, post-traumatic stress disorder etc.). Included in this category are: physical abuse—(995.54), sexual abuse—(995.53), or neglect—(995.52) of an adolescent.

Adolescent sexual abuse cuts across all socioeconomic, racial, and ethnic lines. It is estimated that almost 3 out of every 10 adult females and about 2 out of every 10 adult males were abused before age 18.

Behavioral Symptoms
(severity index: 1–mild; 2–moderate; 3–intense)

		Severity
1.	Physical signs of abuse	_____
2.	Acts out sexually or aggressively	_____
3.	Impaired ability to trust	_____
4.	Problems with control and self-mastery	_____
5.	Post-traumatic stress disorder	_____
6.	Depression or anxiety	_____
7.	Psychiatric symptoms	_____
8.	"Damaged goods" syndrome ("I'm not worth love, kindness, respect etc.")	_____
9.	Low self-esteem	_____
10.	Suicidal ideations or attempt	_____
11.	Guilt	_____
12.	Repressed anger	_____
13.	Role confusion and blurred role boundaries	_____
14.	Pseudomaturity	_____
15.	Failure to accomplish developmental tasks	_____
16.	Regressive behavior (baby talk, enuresis, thumb sucking)	_____
17.	Poor social skills	_____
18.	Social withdrawal	_____
19.	Nightmares	_____
20.	Runs away from home to escape further abuse	_____

ADOLESCENT ABUSE OR NEGLECT—VICTIM TREATMENT PLAN

Patient: _____   Date: _____

I. OBJECTIVES OF TREATMENT *(select one or more)*

1. Preclude further abuse or neglect
2. Prevent recurrence of symptoms
3. If parents are perpetrators, relocate child to safe environment
4. Educate parents about the problem
5. Investigate family history of the problem
6. Encourage family to establish rules regarding privacy and boundaries
7. Help family develop better coping skills
8. Reduce pervasive anxiety and worry
9. Eliminate denial
10. Diminish symptoms of depression and reduce guilt
11. Eliminate sexual or aggressive acting out
12. Build self-esteem
13. End nightmares or night terrors
14. Reduce role confusion and blurred boundaries
15. Treat post-traumatic stress disorder
16. Encourage compliance with educational programs and referrals
17. Eliminate regressive behaviors
18. Reduce irrational beliefs
19. Eliminate "damaged goods" syndrome
20. Promote socialization, reduce alienation
21. Reduce pseudomaturity
22. Treat sexual problems if age appropriate
23. Restore child and family to optimum level of functioning

II. SHORT-TERM BEHAVIORAL GOALS AND INTERVENTIONS
(select goals and interventions appropriate for your patient)

NOTE: Separate goals and interventions are provided for Parents, Adolescent, and Family

PARENTS' GOALS	THERAPIST'S INTERVENTIONS
Collaborate with therapist in development of a treatment plan.	Establish therapeutic alliance with parents to enhance outcome of treatment.
Identify if authorities have been notified and if the adolescent has been treated medically or psychiatrically.	Determine if abuse has been reported and if the adolescent has been treated medically or psychiatrically.
Help therapist understand your adolescent's level of development before and after the abuse.	Assess problem with parents and record a comprehensive history of the abuse identifying the adolescent's level of functioning prior to the abuse, his or her current symptomatology, feelings toward the abuse, and parents' reaction.
Become aware of the diagnosis and symptomatology associated with abuse or neglect what to appropriately expect from your adolescent	Educate parents about the diagnosis and symptomatology associated with abuse.
Become aware of reporting requirements for abusive behavior.	Discuss therapist's obligation to report deviant behavior if and when mandated.
Cooperate in building a genogram to identify familial history and its relationship to abusive or neglectful behaviors.	Construct a genogram to understand the family history and identify physical and emotional boundaries to get a better idea of the "Ghosts of the Past" in order to break pathological cycles (see Behavioral Techniques, Chapter 14).

PARENTS' GOALS	THERAPIST'S INTERVENTIONS
Enter treatment for abusive or neglectful behavior to enhance your adolescent's therapy.	If parents are the abusers, the adolescent must be removed from the home to a safer environment while they are referred out for treatment.
Identify level of support the adolescent can get from non-offending parent.	Determine role of non-offending parents and level of support they can provide for the adolescent.
Understand that it is "normal" to feel crazy after an abusive event.	Explore symptoms with parents. Are they or their adolescent experiencing shock, confusion, anxiety, or fear?
Develop awareness of how your personal theory of the problem influences cognition of the problem in your adolescent.	Explore parental theory of the problem and the level of belief that abuse occurred and the level of its seriousness.
Recognize fears and feelings of self-blame related to the problem.	Evaluate parental fears and feelings of self-blame related to the problem.
Realize that failure to deal with your own abuse may inhibit your ability to support recovery of your adolescent.	Determine whether parent/parents were abused. (Failure to deal with their own abuse may inhibit ability to support their adolescent's recovery.)
Learn to reach beyond automatic cognitive reactions in viewing the problem.	Expand parental perspective beyond limited cognitive reactions.
Understand the need for appropriate boundaries and privacy	Explore rules regarding boundaries and privacy within the family.
Parents are treated for marital discord to reduce tension in the family.	Evaluate for marital discord and, if appropriate, treat or refer for treatment.

PARENTS' GOALS	THERAPIST'S INTERVENTIONS
Learn how to deal with child's sleep problems.	Investigate for sleep problems in child and teach parents how to deal with the problem.
Identify other symptoms the adolescent may be exhibiting.	Explore for other symptoms in the adolescent that the parents have noticed (i.e. depression, anxiety).
Confront thoughts of exaggerated and unrealistic consequences regarding the abuse.	Guide parents in confronting distorted reactions to the adolescent's problems.
Undergo evaluation for substance or sexual addictions and, if positive, enter treatment.	Investigate for substance or sexual addictions in parents and treat or refer for treatment.
Parents feel validated and enter treatment for their own problems related to their adolescent's abuse.	Acknowledge and validate parental problems with the abuse. Determine need for treatment of anxiety, depression, or other reactions (see appropriate treatment plan).
Feel empowered to help your adolescent.	Help develop a plan of action for parents to empower them and reduce helplessness.
Recognize abusive nature of certain behaviors.	If abuse is emotional and parents are the perpetrators, address and identify abusive behaviors.
Help develop action plan to avoid abusive behaviors.	Develop an action plan to interrupt pathological behaviors before they get out of control.

PARENTS' GOALS	THERAPIST'S INTERVENTIONS
Learn better parenting skills.	If abuse is between siblings, help parents develop techniques for interrupting abusive behaviors and restoring appropriate boundaries.
Recognize that change is possible and you can make a difference.	Help parents understand that change is possible.
Understand how hypnosis can eventually broaden responses to a traumatic event and modulate responses to anxiety and give permission to use this technique.	If adolescent is experiencing flashbacks due to abuse, request parental permission to treat adolescent with hypnosis (see Behavioral Techniques, Chapter 14).
Follow through with referral for psychological testing of your adolescent.	Provide referral for psychological testing of the adolescent to assess current level of functioning.
Agree to allow therapist to confer with your adolescent's school to help in development of a comprehensive psycho-educational treatment plan.	After interviewing the adolescent, if appropriate, request and receive parental permission to confer with teachers and school officials.
Learn to encourage positive behaviors through better parenting. Physical and mental abuse is reduced.	Explore methods of parenting and, if aversive (i.e. insults, physical punishment, abuse) help parents understand these methods only suppress negative behavior and teach children aggression. Refer to parenting class (see Self-Help Groups and 800 Numbers, Chapter 18, and Online Resources, Chapter 19).

PARENTS' GOALS	THERAPIST'S INTERVENTIONS
Parents develop new parenting skills and learn healing rituals to help their adolescent over	Assign parents to read *Making Families Work and What to Do When They Don't* (see Bibliotherapy, Chapter 17).
Monitor your adolescent's medication schedule and report all reactions or failures to take meds.	If the adolescent is on meds, instruct parents on need for a regular schedule and feedback that may indicate need for revised dosage.
Read about ways in which you and your adolescent can deal with sexual abuse.	If appropriate, assign books on molestation, such as *When Your Child Has Been Molested* (see Bibliotherapy, Chapter 17).
Discuss a treatment termination plan and resolve related issues.	Develop a treatment termination plan and discuss issues of separation anxiety and dependency.

ADOLESCENT'S GOALS	THERAPIST'S INTERVENTIONS
Enter non-threatening therapeutic interaction.	Encourage the adolescent to join in a therapeutic relationship to enhance treatment outcome.
Realize why you are in treatment.	Determine whether the adolescent understands why he or she is in treatment and discuss if he or she is uncomfortable talking about the abuse at this time.
Take time, if needed, to rebuild trust and control before discussing the abuse.	If advisable, postpone talking about the abuse until the adolescent is more comfortable in treatment, and trust has started to rebuild.
Develop understanding of underlying feelings associated with abuse. Understand it is "normal" to feel crazy after abuse.	Educate the adolescent about the diagnosis and discuss symptomatology so he or she can better understand what they are feeling (i.e. denial, anger, depression, guilt, or "damaged goods" syndrome).
Adolescent understands need to report the abuse and the need for a safe environment.	If it has not yet been reported, report the abuse to authorities. Help the adolescent understand your concerns for his or her future well-being and that of siblings.
Verbalize the facts about the abuse to break through the denial and receive therapist support while reducing alienation.	If ready, encourage the adolescent to overcome the denial and explain the facts associated with the abuse.

ADOLESCENT'S GOALS	THERAPIST'S INTERVENTIONS
Cooperate in construction of genogram and compare it with parental genogram.	Construct a genogram to identify and understand physical and emotional boundaries over generations. (If parents are the abusers, explain to the adolescent that parents learn parenting skills from parents; abused children grow up to abuse. Compare the adolescent's view with his or her parent's genogram (see Behavioral Techniques, Chapter 14).)
Validate the adolescent's viewpoint.	Acknowledge the adolescent's point of view concerning abuse.
Understand the emotional reactions usually associated with abuse.	Explore for symptoms related to the abuse. Reactions usually fall into one of four categories: (1) Reexperiencing the event as in flashbacks or Post-traumatic Stress Disorder; (2) Numbing or denial; (3) Hyperarousal; and (4) Avoidance of people, places, or activities that are cues to the trauma or abuse. Treat as necessary (see appropriate treatment plan).
Identify symptoms indirectly if necessary.	Ask indirect questions to identify symptoms, since some adolescents may appear asymptomatic in direct questioning.
Recognize that it is "normal" to feel crazy after such an event. Common reactions include shock, confusion, helplessness, anger, depression, guilt, anxiety, Post-traumatic Stress Disorder, nightmares or night terrors, enuresis, and others.	Explain that these post-abuse symptoms are normal.

ADOLESCENT'S GOALS	THERAPIST'S INTERVENTIONS
Become aware that alcohol, drugs, or overeating to deal with abuse only creates further problems. Treat substance abuse or eating disorder as necessary.	Investigate for substance abuse since many adolescents turn to self-medicating to deal with abuse. (If positive, see appropriate treatment plan.)
Reduce anxieties related to pending medical examination.	Help reduce the adolescent's anxiety related to the imminent physical examination.
Identify irrational beliefs about sexuality and dating.	Developmentally, adolescents are consolidating their attitudes about sexuality and dating. Help the adolescent identify ways in which abuse has influenced his or her thoughts and behaviors. Dispute irrational cognitions.
Identify negative cues and avoidance behavior used to handle fear.	Explore for negative cues associated with abuse (i.e. fear of darkness, certain kinds of clothes etc.) and avoidance behaviors used to deal with the fear.
Learn that avoidance is not the answer to fears and anxieties.	Indicate how avoidance may result in long-term maladaptive behaviors if used as a coping response.
Learn to "feel the fear and do it anyway."	Teach dynamics of anxiety: anxiety is not permanent or dangerous; avoidance increases anxiety; confronting the problem can reduce anxiety; exposure can produce growth.
Recognize that action in the face of fear can promote growth.	Assign the adolescent to read *Feel the Fear and Do It Anyway* (see Bibliotherapy, Chapter 17).

ADOLESCENT'S GOALS	THERAPIST'S INTERVENTIONS
Learn to rebuild your life, reduce irrational ways of dealing with the pain, and reject avoidance behaviors that don't work.	If the adolescent has been sexually abused, explore and dispute irrational thoughts and beliefs regarding sex (i.e. sex is dirty, I will never do it etc.) Provide adequate healthy educational material about sexuality.
Recognize if and how non-offending parents reinforce difficulties or respond appropriately.	Discuss with the adolescent how non-offending parent/s teach behavioral skills that effectively respond to abuse-related difficulties or disclosures.
Through role-playing, identify skills to deal with abuse and dysfunctional responses.	Use role-playing to help the adolescent identify internal resources to deal with the trauma (see "Role-playing," Behavioral Techniques, Chapter 14).
Learn to overcome barriers and recover from trauma.	With parental permission, use hypnosis or creative visualization to help the adolescent break through barriers, improve self-esteem, and recover from trauma.
Recognize flashbacks as a cry for help.	If the adolescent is suffering from flashbacks, help him or her recognize them as a dissociated cry for help.
Agree to use hypnosis to reconceptualize and broaden the memory of the abuse, reducing fear and/or hyperarousal.	Propose the use of hypnosis, actually self-hypnosis, to eventually broaden responses to the traumatic event and modulate reactions while increasing cognitive flexibility to deal with anxiety and flashbacks.

ADOLESCENT'S GOALS	THERAPIST'S INTERVENTIONS
Tell therapist your life story and realize that you are much more than a case of abuse.	Have the adolescent relate his or her life story, or play *Life Stories* to reinforce other parts of the adolescent's life (see Therapeutic Games, Chapter 15).
Understand process that may trigger abusive behavior.	Teach adolescent about aggressive behavior: (1) Oversensitive to hostile cues; (2) Attribute hostile intentions to others; therefore (3) solve problems with aggressive actions; and (4) become rejected by others; and that (5) contributes to low self-esteem.
Learn positive self-talk to interrupt negative patterns or flashback.	Teach the adolescent positive self-talk to interrupt negative patterns or post-traumatic stress disorder.
Learn new technique for dealing with anxiety.	Teach diaphragmatic breathing to control anxiety (see Behavioral Techniques, Chapter 14).
Shift focus of attention from problem to accomplishment.	Ask the adolescent to describe accomplishments for the past week.
Feel more confident as self-esteem improves.	Compliment the adolescent to provide positive reinforcement whenever possible.
Develop routine aerobic exercise program to release anxiety and frustration.	Recommend routine exercise to help release frustrations.
Learn methods that can be used to advocate for yourself.	Instruct the adolescent in the techniques of self-advocacy.

ADOLESCENT'S GOALS	THERAPIST'S INTERVENTIONS
Understand that you can deal with these issues and bring treatment to an end successfully.	Develop a treatment termination plan and resolve issues of separation anxiety and dependency.

FAMILY'S GOALS	THERAPIST'S INTERVENTIONS
Abuse is identified and acknowledged among family members.	Conduct family sessions or refer for family therapy in order to address the abuse.
Identify and review the five key cognitions of the problem.	Explore family cognitions of the problem: (1) selective perceptions of what occurred; (2) attributions of blame; (3) expectations of a recurrence; (4) assumptions of the characteristics of family members; and (5) standards each members expects of the others.
Discuss your view of central family problems.	Investigate communication problems, role conflicts, and influence of extended family.
Express your thoughts and emotions regarding aberrant behaviors.	Explore individual thoughts and emotions regarding aberrant behaviors.
Acknowledge actions taken.	Review actions taken to deal with abusive behaviors.
Identify triggers of the abusive event.	Investigate the triggers that led to the abusive event.
Family is educated about available resources and creates a safety plan.	With family, develop a plan to assure safety of all members if abuse continues or is possible. Suggest they call an 800 number or the police, etc., (see Self-Help Groups and 800 Numbers, Chapter 18, and Online Resources, Chapter 19).
Identify substance use in family and urge treatment for guilty member(s).	Investigate possible substance use within family that may contribute to abuse and, if appropriate, treat or refer for treatment.

FAMILY'S GOALS	THERAPIST'S INTERVENTIONS
Learn better communication skills and conflict resolution.	Explore for communication deficits and discrepancies that may result. Teach new methods of conflict resolution.
Cooperate in amplifying family genogram.	Augment genogram created in parental and adolescent sessions to help understand family history of abusive behaviors (see Behavioral Techniques, Chapter 14).
Discuss genogram openly to fully understand family history as it relates to abuse.	Discuss genogram to reveal family history and possible family secrets regarding abusive behavior.
Demonstrate boundaries, alliances, triangles, and emotional currents that may exacerbate the abusive behavior.	Explore family boundaries using sculpturing, a useful technique for understanding triangulation, alliances, and emotional currents (see "Family Sculpturing," Behavioral Techniques, Chapter 14).
Work together to reduce denial, anger, and shame.	Develop therapeutic alliance with family to increase understanding of abusive behaviors, break through the denial, and reduce anger and shame.
Become aware of the diagnosis of the adolescent.	Educate family members about the diagnosis.
Understand the emotional reactions usually associated with abuse.	Explore with family members for symptoms related to the abuse. Reactions usually fall into one of four categories: (1) Reexperiencing the event as in flashbacks or Post-traumatic Stress Disorder; (2) Numbing or denial; (3) Hyperarousal; or

FAMILY'S GOALS	THERAPIST'S INTERVENTIONS
	(4) Avoidance of people, places, or activities that are cues to the trauma or abuse.) Treat as necessary (see appropriate treatment plan).
Recognize that it is "normal" to feel crazy after such an event. Common reactions include shock, confusion, helplessness, anger, depression, guilt, anxiety, Post-traumatic Stress Disorder, nightmares or night terrors, enuresis, and others.	Explain that these post-abuse symptoms are normal.
Understand symptoms as a normal reaction to abuse.	Educate family members about the symptomatology so they can better understand what they are feeling.
Learn problem solving.	Teach family the principles of problem-solving: (1) stay calm, take a deep breath; (2) think about what is bothering you; (3) create S.M.A.R.T. action plan—Small, Measurable, Achievable, Realistic, Timelined goals; (4) select three different solutions, pick the best one, do the best you can, if it doesn't work, stay calm and try again. Remember perseverance works; don't give up (see "Change," Behavioral Techniques, Chapter 14).
Shift focus from problem to possible solutions.	Have family imagine a future without the problem and suggest actions that can be taken now to best approximate that possibility.

FAMILY'S GOALS	THERAPIST'S INTERVENTIONS
Think about what treatment outcome would look like. Explain what you would like to see change in other family members when treatment is completed.	Ask family members to think about what they might want to say about each other when treatment is completed.
Become aware of cues that stimulate aberrant behavior.	If parent or family member is the perpetrator, investigate cues that stimulate aberrant behavior.
Family members realize they have the power to make important changes even if they seem small.	Help family realize they have an opportunity to do some things differently.
Family members are empowered. They recognize that they can create positive change.	Ask family members to relate what they have accomplished in the past week.
Realize that major change is the result of small steps taken one at a time.	Help family identify and prioritize achievable goals.
Enhance understanding of abuse and its behavioral and emotional symptoms.	Assign homework reading *Making Families Work and What to Do When They Don't*, or *Trust After Trauma* (see Bibliotherapy, Chapter 17).
Make use of available community resources.	Refer family to available resources in the community (see Self-Help Groups and 800 Numbers, Chapter 18, and Online Resources, Chapter 19).
Reduce negative communication.	Develop a system of positive reinforcement with family to interact better with each other to reduce scapegoating and abuse.

FAMILY'S GOALS	THERAPIST'S INTERVENTIONS
Family works together to develop a treatment termination plan.	Discuss termination issues and develop a plan to terminate treatment.

12
SLEEP DISORDERS

There are two principal types of sleep disorders: Dyssomnias and Parasomnias.

DYSSOMNIAS

Dyssomnias include disturbances in the amount of sleep, falling asleep, and staying asleep. In Primary Insomnia—(307.42), the problem is maintaining sleep, compared with Primary Hypersomnia—(307.44), which is marked by excessive sleepiness. In the recurrent form of Primary Hypersmonia, known as Kleine-Levin syndrome, individuals may spend 18–20 hours in bed or asleep. Primary Hypersomnia and Kleine-Levin syndrome may begin in early adolescence, while Primary Insomnia usually does not appear until early adulthood.

Narcolepsy—(347) includes the presence of cataplexy or daily, uncomfortable attacks of sleep. Breathing-Related Sleep Disorders—(780.59) feature excessive sleep or insomnia, or sleep apnea. Circadian Rhythm Sleep Disorder—(307.45) is caused by an environmentally imposed sleep-wake schedule.

PARASOMNIAS

Parasomnias include Nightmare Disorder—(307.47), Sleep Terror Disorder—(307.46), and Sleepwalking Disorder—(307.46) in which abnormal events occur during sleep. These may be characterized by repeated or sudden awakenings, frightening dreams, or sleepwalking which usually occurs during the first third of major sleep episodes. Parasomnias cause inappropriate activation of cognitive processes in the nervous and motor systems.

All Dyssomnias and Parasomnias can cause significant distress or impairment in school and other major areas of functioning. In addition, sleep disorders can be related to other Axis I and Axis II mental disorders. Characteristically, children have trouble falling asleep and experience problems with bad dreams. Systematic assessment of sleep disorders includes evaluation of other comorbid mental disorders, general medical conditions, and substance abuse, including prescribed medications.

Although there are no formal studies, there appears to be a familial disposition associated with sleep problems.

Behavioral Symptoms
(severity index: 1–mild; 2–moderate; 3–intense)

	Severity
Dyssomnias	
1. Difficulty falling asleep	_____
2. Difficulty staying asleep	_____
3. Irresistible attacks of refreshing sleep (Narcolepsy)	_____
4. Daytime fatigue	_____
5. Excessive sleepiness	_____
6. Uncontrollable attacks of sleep	_____
7. Sudden loss of muscle tone (Cataplexy)	_____
8. Intrusions in REM sleep	_____
9. Breathing-related sleep problems (Apnea)	_____
10. Restless leg syndrome	_____
Parasomnias	
11. Nightmares	_____
12. Recurrent, abrupt awakenings due to night terrors	_____
13. Signs of autonomic arousal	_____
14. Terror related to unrecalled dream	_____
15. Sleepwalking	_____
16. Sleepwalking with blank starring face, difficult to awaken	_____
17. Amnesia of sleepwalking event	_____

SLEEP DISORDERS TREATMENT PLAN

Patient: _____ Date: _____

I. OBJECTIVES OF TREATMENT *(select one or more)*

1. Educate parents about the disorder
2. Determine family history of the disorder
3. Help family develop better coping skills
4. Reduce pervasive anxiety and worry
5. Reduce symptoms of separation anxiety
6. Identify any medical disorders and treat or refer for treatment
7. Identify any psychological problems and treat or refer for treatment
8. Reduce nightmares or sleep terrors
9. Eliminate sleepwalking episodes
10. Establish healthy sleep patterns, regular sleep schedule
11. Reduce irrational beliefs about sleep
12. Rule out other mental disorders, general medical conditions, and substance abuse, including prescribed medications
13. Restore adolescent and family to optimum level of functioning.
14. Develop a discharge plan for coping with everyday life.

II. SHORT-TERM BEHAVIORAL GOALS AND INTERVENTIONS
(select goals and interventions appropriate for your patient)

NOTE: Separate goals and interventions are provided for Parents, Adolescent, and Family

PARENTS' GOALS	THERAPIST'S INTERVENTIONS
Collaborate with therapist in development of a treatment plan.	Establish a therapeutic alliance with parents to enhance outcome of the adolescent's treatment.
Help therapist understand the development of your adolescent's sleep problems.	Assess problem with parents and record a comprehensive history of the adolescent's development of sleep-related problems.

PARENTS' GOALS	THERAPIST'S INTERVENTIONS
Identify specific nature of the problem.	Does the adolescent have problems falling asleep or staying asleep (i.e. Dyssomnias or Parasomnias)?
Help identify origin of problem and predominant sleep patterns of your adolescent.	Determine origin of sleep problem and the sleep stage in which it occurs.
Describe your adolescent's sleep terrors or sleepwalking.	Determine if the adolescent has sleep terrors or is sleepwalking.
Disclose possible problems with separation anxiety.	Explore for separation anxiety and treat (see appropriate treatment plan).
Assist in building a family genogram.	Construct a genogram to better understand the family history of sleep problems and how the family deals with them (see Behavioral Techniques, Chapter 14).
Undergo evaluation for sleep disorder and enter treatment as indicated.	Examine parents for sleep disorders and treat or refer for treatment.
Develop awareness of how your personal theory of the problem influences cognition of the problem in your adolescent.	Explore parental theory of the problem.
Recognize fears and feelings of self-blame for your adolescent's sleep disorder.	Evaluate parents' fears and negative feelings of self-blame for the adolescent's problems.
Realize that sleep is a habit, and develop a more appropriate sleep schedule.	Teach parents that sleep is a habit, and help them establish an appropriate sleep schedule.

PARENTS' GOALS	THERAPIST'S INTERVENTIONS
Teach the adolescent that napping to make up for lost sleep is ineffective.	Teach parents that napping to compensate for lost sleep does not work.
Understand the need to restrict use of certain stimulants that may impair sleep.	Advise parents about the effects of certain stimulants (i.e. sugar, chocolate, caffeine, cola) on sleep patterns.
Confront thoughts of exaggerated reactions and unrealistic consequences—"what ifs?"	Guide parents in confronting distorted reactions that can trigger sleep problems.
Identify cognitive distortions and weigh against reality.	Evaluate cognitive distortions against evidence-based reality.
Restructure distortions with evidence-based consequences.	With parents, reframe distortions with reality-based reactions to stressors.
Understand the importance of REM sleep.	Educate parents about the importance of REM sleep in healing the body physically and psychologically.
Restrict use of bed to sleep only.	Educate parents about the importance of limiting the adolescent's use of his or her bed for sleep only (i.e. no TV, reading, or doing homework in or on the bed).
Help develop awareness of other problems that may cause or contribute to sleep problems.	Identify other problems that may exacerbate sleep disorder (i.e. trauma, troubled relationships, sexual abuse, Post-traumatic Stress Disorder).
Learn diaphragmatic breathing as a relaxation technique and teach your adolescent to use it.	Teach parents diaphragmatic breathing to assist the adolescent in relaxation and sleep (see Behavioral Techniques, Chapter 14).

PARENTS' GOALS	THERAPIST'S INTERVENTIONS
Sexual abuse uncovered. Child removed to safe environment. Undergo treatment as appropriate.	Investigate for sexual abuse and, if necessary, revise diagnosis (see appropriate treatment plan). Refer parents (if they are the perpetrators) for treatment and advise of the need to notify proper authorities.
Cooperate in protecting your adolescent from accidental injury during sleepwalking episodes.	Explore sleepwalking episodes and assess potential physical danger to the adolescent.
Develop new parenting skills.	Assign parents to read *How to Make Families Work and What to Do When They Don't* or *The Relaxation and Stress Reduction Workbook* (see Bibliotherapy, Chapter 17).
Read assigned book.	Assign parents to read *Your Anxious Child* to better understand how to deal with problem (see Bibliotherapy, Chapter 17).
Monitor your adolescent's medical schedule and report all reactions or failures to comply.	If the adolescent is on mediation, instruct parents on importance of a regular schedule and feedback that may indicate need for dosage adjustment.
Learn suggestions for sleeping better.	Assign parents to read *All I Want is a Good Night's Sleep* to learn better sleep habits and help the adolescent (see Bibliotherapy, Chapter 17).

PARENTS' GOALS	THERAPIST'S INTERVENTIONS
Meet with other parents who experience similar problems and share coping strategies.	Refer parents to self-help group or group on parenting skills (see Self-Help Groups and 800 Numbers, Chapter 18, and Online Resources, Chapter 19).
Discuss a treatment termination plan and resolve related issues.	Develop a treatment termination plan and discuss issues of separation anxiety and dependence.

ADOLESCENT'S GOALS	THERAPIST'S INTERVENTIONS
Develop therapeutic relationship to improve treatment outcome.	Engage the adolescent in an age-appropriate therapeutic relationship to enhance treatment outcome.
Improve treatment outcome and diminish feelings of isolation.	Cultivate a therapeutic alliance or collaborative working relationship to build trust and enhance treatment outcome.
Understand underlying dynamics that may lead to sleep disorders.	Explore ways in which sleep disorder manifests itself (i.e., Dyssomnia or Parasomnia) and clarify underlying dynamics.
Understand need for a regular, calming sleep routine.	Teach the adolescent the importance of a regular, calming sleep routine.
Observe limitations on use of bed exclusively for sleeping.	Instruct the adolescent that his or her bed is to be used only for sleeping—no TV, reading, homework, or play.
Begin to see new solutions for dealing with sleep problems.	Discuss normal sleep patterns and appropriate sleep durations.
Reject napping as a way to make up for lost sleep.	Dissuade the adolescent from napping to make up for lost sleep.
Recognize underlying feelings of anger or depression and express appropriately.	Explore for underlying feelings of anger or depression and treat (see appropriate treatment plan).
Enter treatment for substance abuse.	Explore for substance abuse and, if positive, treat or refer for treatment (see appropriate treatment plan).

ADOLESCENT'S GOALS	THERAPIST'S INTERVENTIONS
Become aware of the triggers that lead to night terrors or nightmares.	Investigate and interpret nightmares and the triggers that contribute to night terrors.
Feel empowered to create new dreams.	Help the adolescent understand that we create our dreams in our heads and we can make up new dreams using creative visualization or hypnosis (see "Bad Dreams," Behavioral Techniques, Chapter 14).
Realize that sleep problems can result in feelings of low self-esteem.	Investigate for feelings of low self-esteem related to sleep disorder.
Comply with referrals.	If appropriate, refer the adolescent for medical and psychiatric evaluations.
Discuss evaluations with therapist. Follow through with recommended medical treatment or revised diagnosis.	Discuss evaluations with the adolescent. If necessary, refer him or her for stabilization of medical condition and revise diagnosis.
Discuss new treatment plan, if necessary, and agree on target problems to be addressed.	Revise treatment plan and target problems, if necessary (see appropriate treatment plan).
Reconfirm original treatment plan.	Absent a general medical problem, another mental disorder, or substance abuse, reconfirm the original treatment plan.
Identify pattern of sleep problems in your family.	Construct genogram to explore family history of sleep disorders (see Behavioral Techniques, Chapter 14).

ADOLESCENT'S GOALS	THERAPIST'S INTERVENTIONS
Understand and confront contributing stressors.	Identify stressors that interfere with sleep.
Practice diaphragmatic breathing to help relax and aid sleep.	Teach the adolescent diaphragmatic breathing for relaxation prior to sleep (see Behavioral Techniques, Chapter 14).
Develop more rational thoughts about sleep.	Explore cognitive distortions the adolescent may have about sleep.
Understand the importance of REM sleep.	Teach the adolescent the importance of REM sleep in healing the body physically and psychologically.
Become aware of the effects of caffeine on sleep patterns.	Advise client on the negative effects of caffeine stimulants (coffee, tea, cola) on sleep.
Use relaxation techniques to prepare for sleep.	Teach the adolescent relaxation or hypnosis techniques. Provide audiotape for home use (see Behavioral Techniques, Chapter 14).
Understand how hypnosis can help.	Help parents understand how hypnosis is actually self-hypnosis that can help the adolescent develop strategies to facilitate deep muscle relaxation, control cognitive overactivity, and explore unconscious fears or conflicts that can interrupt sleep (see Behavioral Techniques, Chapter 14).

ADOLESCENT'S GOALS	THERAPIST'S INTERVENTIONS
If appropriate, undergo treatment for sexual abuse.	Investigate for possible sexual abuse and treat, if necessary (see appropriate treatment plan).
Enlist parental assistance in reducing potentially dangerous situations associated with sleepwalking.	Explore sleepwalking episodes and assess accompanying activities for level of danger.
Identify irrational beliefs.	Explore irrational beliefs about sleep.
Reframe beliefs about fears and anxieties.	Change irrational beliefs by developing rational alternatives based on evidence-based reality.
Understand the dynamics of anxiety and understand that avoidance does not help.	Teach client the dynamics of anxiety: anxiety is not permanent or dangerous; avoidance increases anxiety; confronting the problem can reduce anxiety; exposure can produce growth.
Communicate your life story to therapist.	Have the adolescent relate the story of his or her life, or play *Life Stories* (see Therapeutic Games, Chapter 15).
Learn sophisticated techniques to help you relax.	Play *Stress Attack* to teach the adolescent stress management (see Therapeutic Games, Chapter 15).
Identify life stressors that may contribute to sleep disorder.	Explore for any stressful situations in the adolescent's life that may contribute to sleep disorder (i.e. school, family, personal life).

ADOLESCENT'S GOALS	THERAPIST'S INTERVENTIONS
Understand how trauma may have contributed to existing disorder.	Explore the adolescent's background for trauma that may have exacerbated the disorder.
Discuss personal coping mechanisms developed to handle the disorder.	Investigate patterns of behavior used to avoid sleep anxieties.
Recognize and relate how family impacts the problem.	Explore familial impact on the disorder.
Learn to cope with your family when your basic needs are not met.	If family is dysfunctional, assign the adolescent to read books on coping skills (see Bibliotherapy, Chapter 17).
Learn positive self-talk.	Teach the adolescent positive self-talk to interrupt negative patterns especially prior to sleep.
Learn new technique for dealing with anxiety.	Teach the adolescent diaphragmatic breathing to control anxiety (see Behavioral Techniques, Chapter 14).
Learn to nurture yourself and overcome emotional difficulties.	Play the *Positive Thinking Game* or *Bounce-Back* to teach how positive self-talk helps control emotional difficulties (see Therapeutic Games, Chapter 15).
Shift focus of attention from problem to accomplishment.	Ask the adolescent to describe his or her accomplishments of the past week.
Feel more confident as self-esteem improves.	Compliment the adolescent to provide positive reinforcement whenever possible.

ADOLESCENT'S GOALS	THERAPIST'S INTERVENTIONS
Use aerobic exercise to release frustrations and produce endorphins that stimulate seratonin level that is thought to be involved in neural mechanisms important to sleep.	Recommend routine exercise to help the adolescent release frustrations.
Report results to therapist.	Provide positive reinforcement whenever possible. Praise attempts and reward success.
Learn other techniques for reducing stress and increasing your ability to cope and sleep better.	Assign the adolescent to read *All I Want is a Good Night's Sleep* and *Ready...Set... R.E.L.A.X.* (see Bibliotherapy, Chapter 17).
Learn strategies for dealing with your inner critics and expand your personal strengths.	Assign the adolescent to read *The Self-Esteem Companion* (see Bibliotherapy, Chapter 17).
Develop a S.M.A.R.T. action plan for dealing with sleep disorder.	Develop a S.M.A.R.T. action plan—Small, Measurable, Achievable, Realistic, Timelined goals (see "Change," Behavioral Techniques, Chapter 14).
Learn to advocate for yourself.	Instruct the adolescent in the techniques of self-advocacy.
Understand you can deal with these issues and bring treatment to an end successfully.	Develop a treatment termination plan and address issues of separation anxiety and dependency.

FAMILY'S GOALS	THERAPIST'S INTERVENTIONS
Improve communication among family members to reduce familial anxiety and sleep problems.	Conduct family sessions or refer for family therapy to reduce sleep problems and improve communication skills within the family.
Cooperate in building a family genogram.	Amplify the family genogram construct in earlier sessions to help understand family history of the disorder (see Behavioral Techniques, Chapter 14).
Learn details of the disorder.	Educate family about the disorder. Most sleep disorders are not medical, but the result of cognitive overactivity or habit patterns that are incompatible with sleep (i.e. (1) worry, compulsive thinking about the day's events or future concerns; (2) anxiety and tension in central nervous system; or (3) unconscious or underlying conflicts that disturb or interrupt sleep patterns.
Help compare parental and family genograms.	Compare with parental genogram to reveal family history and secrets dealing with sleep.
Recognize that sleep is a habit and develop a more appropriate sleep schedule.	Teach family that sleep is a habit and help them establish a reasonable sleep schedule.
Become aware of family tensions that may exacerbate the adolescent's sleep disorder.	Assess family tensions that may contribute to the sleep problem.
Learn to reach beyond automatic cognitive reactions in viewing the problem.	Expand parental perspective of the problem beyond limited cognitive reactions.

FAMILY'S GOALS	THERAPIST'S INTERVENTIONS
Demonstrate boundaries, alliances, triangles, and emotional currents that may exacerbate sleep problem.	Explore family boundaries using family sculpturing to understand triangulation, alliances, and emotional currents (see Behavioral Techniques, Chapter 14).
Become aware of family tensions that may exacerbate sleep disorder in the adolescent.	Assess family tensions that may contribute to the problem.
Learn how to establish healthy sleep routines.	Teach family that sleep is a habit and help them develop a regular bedtime routine.
Shift focus from problem to possible solutions.	Have family imagine a future without the sleep problem and suggest actions that can be taken now to make that future possible.
Think about what treatment outcome would look like. Explain what you would like to see change in other family members when treatment is completed.	Ask family members to think about what they might want to say about each other when treatment is completed.
Family members realize they have the power to help the adolescent deal with his or her nightmares.	Discuss "Bad Dreams" (see Behavioral Techniques, Chapter 14) to help deal with the adolescent's nightmares. Do not use this exercise with suspected sex abuse victims.
Recognize that major change is the result of small steps taken one at a time.	Help family identify and prioritize achievable goals.
Enhance understanding of the disorder and see how other families have handled similar problems	Assign family homework reading *Making Families Work and What to Do When They Don't* and *Can't You Sleep, Little Bear?* (see Bibliotherapy, Chapter 17).

FAMILY'S GOALS	THERAPIST'S INTERVENTIONS
Make use of available community resources.	Refer family to available resources in the community (see Self-Help Groups and 800 Numbers, Chapter 18, and Online Resources, Chapter 19).
Reduce negative communication.	Develop a system of positive reinforcement with family to interact better with each other and reduce scapegoating.
Family works together to develop a treatment termination plan.	Discuss termination issues and develop plan to end treatment.

13
SUBSTANCE DISORDERS

Substance Disorders include those conditions related to the use of a drug of abuse, the side effects of a prescribed or over-the-counter medication, and toxin exposure. They are divided into two general groups: Substance Use Disorders (Dependence and Abuse) and Substance-Induced Disorders (Intoxication and Withdrawal).

This guide deals only with Substance Use Disorders (Dependence and Abuse) since Substance Intoxication and Withdrawal are typically treated by immediate hospitalization to ensure the safety of the client. Many hospitals conduct treatment programs ranging from in-patient detoxification to outpatient treatment and support groups focused on abstinence. There are four levels of treatment for Substance Use Disorders: (1) outpatient; (2) intensive outpatient with partial hospitalization and structured programs; (3) around-the-clock inpatient care; and (4) acute in-patient care with 24-hour monitoring.

SUBSTANCE DEPENDENCE

Substance dependence disorders are coded by substance:

alcohol—(303.90)
amphetamines—(304.40)
cannabis—(304.30)
cocaine—(304.20)
hallucinogens—(304.50)
inhalants—(304.60)
nicotine—(305.10)
opioids—(304.00)
phencyclidine—(304.60)

sedatives, hypnotics, or anxiolytics—(304.10)
polysubstances—(304.80)

The symptoms of dependence are generally similar across the categories, although in some instances the symptoms are less pronounced, and all symptoms may not apply, (i.e. withdrawal). Substance Dependence is characterized by a cluster of physical, mental, and behavioral symptoms indicating that the individual continues use of the substance despite significant substance-related problems with three or more of the symptoms occurring at any time in a 12-month period. Global impairment of functioning is clinically significant.

Behavioral Symptoms
(severity index: 1–mild; 2–moderate; 3–intense)

Specify: With or without physiological dependence
           In early full or partial remission
           In sustained full remission
           In agonist therapy
           In controlled environment

To qualify for this diagnosis, three or more of the following symptoms must be present at any time in a 12-month period.

		Severity
1.	Need for increased amount of the substance to achieve the desired effect	_____
2.	Diminished effect with continued use of the same amount of substance	_____
3.	Characteristic Withdrawal Syndrome	_____
4.	Same or related substance taken to avoid withdrawal symptoms	_____
5.	Substance taken in larger amounts or there is a shorter period of time between doses	_____
6.	Persistent desire with unsuccessful effort to reduce or control use of substance	_____
7.	Inordinate amount of time spent to obtain, use, or recover from substance	_____
8.	Important social, occupational, or recreational activities are abandoned or reduced	_____
9.	Substance use continues despite awareness of persistent related physical or psychological problem	_____
10.	Uses the defense mechanism of denial *(not yet in DSM)*	_____

SUBSTANCE ABUSE

Substance Abuse Disorders are also coded by substance:

    alcohol—(305.00)
    amphetamines—(305.20)
    cannabis—(305.20)
    cocaine—(305.60)
    hallucinogens—(305.30)
    inhalants—(305.90)
    opioids—(305.50)
    phencyclidines—(305.90)
    sedatives, hypnotics or Anxiolytics—(305.40)

In contrast to Substance Dependence, a diagnosis of Substance Abuse covers a maladaptive pattern of substance use resulting in clinically significant impairment manifested by only one symptom over a 12-month period. A significant negative life event (e.g. personal failure, loss of job, death of parent) may trigger abuse. Substance Abuse does not apply to caffeine or nicotine. In most cases of substance abuse in younger adolescents, the youth is removed from the home.

Behavioral Symptoms
(severity index: 1–mild; 2–moderate; 3–intense)

To qualify for this diagnosis, the patient must exhibit one or more of the following over a 12-month period.

		Severity
1.	Repeated substance use leading to failure to fulfill major home or school obligations	_____
2.	Repeated substance use in physically dangerous situations	_____
3.	Recurrent substance-related legal problems	_____
4.	Continued substance use despite resulting social or interpersonal problems	_____

SUBSTANCE DEPENDENCE/ABUSE—(_____)
Indicate Substance

TREATMENT PLAN

Patient: _____ Date: _____

I. OBJECTIVES OF TREATMENT *(select one or more)*

1. Educate parents about disorder
2. Determine possible family history of the disorder
3. Explore denial of substance abuse
4. Recognize dependence or abuse as a maladaptive response
5. Refer to AA, NA, Alateen, or Rational Recovery Group to aid treatment
6. Help family develop better coping skills
7. Sustain sobriety
8. Improve quality of life
9. Understand self-sabotaging behavior
10. Reduce or eliminate shame and guilt
11. Identify people, places, or things that trigger abuse
12. Prevent relapse
13. Help heroin-dependent person reduce potential for self-harm (e.g. AIDS, sexually transmitted diseases).
14. Reduce pervasive anxiety and worry
15. Encourage compliance with programs and referrals
16. Restore adolescent and family to optimum level of functioning
17. Develop discharge plan for coping with everyday life

II. SHORT-TERM TREATMENT GOALS & INTERVENTIONS
(select goals & interventions appropriate for your patient)

NOTE: Separate goals and interventions are provided for Parents, Adolescent, and Family

PARENTS' GOALS	THERAPIST'S INTERVENTIONS
Collaborate with therapist in development of an initial treatment plan.	Establish therapeutic alliance with parents to enhance the outcome of their adolescent's treatment.

PARENTS' GOALS	THERAPIST'S INTERVENTIONS
Help parents and therapist understand your adolescent's history of substance abuse.	Assess problem with parents and record a comprehensive history of the adolescent's history of substance abuse as they see it.
Understand and accept possible need for initial hospitalization and subsequent referral to long-term substance abuse programs.	Evaluate with parents, possible hospitalization to treat withdrawal symptoms and provide medical detoxification with supervision.
Cooperate in building a genogram to identify family history and problems with substance abuse.	Construct a genogram to better understand the family history of alcohol or drug abuse (see Behavioral Techniques, Chapter 14).
Become aware of what to appropriately expect from the adolescent once he or she is in treatment.	Educate the parents about the diagnosis. Include the known course of the disorder and possible treatment outcomes.
Enter treatment for your own substance abuse problems that may exacerbate your adolescent's disorder.	Determine possible parental involvement with alcohol or drugs and treat, or refer for treatment, as deemed appropriate.
Adolescent's substance abuse is confirmed or denied. The specifics of the abuse are identified.	Advise parents to have the adolescent tested using Substance Abuse Subtle Screening Inventory (SASSI) to more accurately identify chemical dependency.
Agree to follow through with psychiatric evaluation and accept hospitalization and detoxification if deemed necessary.	Advise parents of the possibility of psychiatric evaluation and/or hospitalization if required.

PARENTS' GOALS	THERAPIST'S INTERVENTIONS
When necessary, the adolescent will be hospitalized.	Assess possible homicidal or suicidal effects of substance dependence.
Enable parents to develop an awareness of how their current understanding of the problem influences their thoughts and behaviors with regard to their adolescent.	Explore parents' personal theory of the problem. Include their own resultant substance abuse practices and behaviors.
Recognize fears, feelings of self-blame, and other negative self-assessments as related to the problem.	Evaluate parents' fears and feelings of negative self-blame for the adolescent's problem.
Grow beyond limited automatic cognitive and emotional reactions in viewing the problem.	Expand parental perspective beyond limited cognitive or behavioral reactions.
Instruct your adolescent about which people, places, and things to avoid.	Teach parents about triggers (i.e., people, places, and things associated with substance use) the adolescent should avoid.
Parents identify enabling behaviors within their family.	Investigate family conflicts and identify who enables or promotes the adolescent's substance abuse.
Help your adolescent replace ritualistic behaviors with more rational responses.	Explore with parents any ritualistic behaviors they can identify in the adolescent and teach them rational substitutes.
Learn diaphragmatic breathing, as relaxation technique, and teach your adolescent to help in relaxation.	Teach parents diaphragmatic breathing to assist the adolescent in relaxation (see Behavioral Techniques, Chapter 14).

PARENTS' GOALS	THERAPIST'S INTERVENTIONS
Become aware of how substance abuse reduces the family's quality of life.	Explore and identify the major impact of substance abuse on the family.
Agree to allow therapist to confer with your adolescent's school to help in development of a comprehensive psychoeducational treatment plan.	After interviewing the adolescent, and with his/her permission, if appropriate, request and receive parental permission to confer with the adolescent's teachers and school officials.
Read assigned books to increase knowledge and coping skills to more appropriately deal with the adolescent when he or she is acting out.	Assign books for parents to read to enhance their knowledge of drug abuse and increase their coping skills, such as *Choices and Consequences: What to Do When a Teenager Uses Alcohol/Drugs*, or other selections (see Bibliotherapy, Chapter 17).
Develop new parenting skills.	Assign parents books on how to deal with their anxiety and increase parenting skills, such as *Making Families Work and What to Do When They Don't* and other selections (see Bibliotherapy, Chapter 17).
Parents are aware of the dangers of mixing drugs and alcohol.	If the adolescent is on medication, instruct parents on the dangers of mixing drugs and/or alcohol.
Meet other parents and receive support from others with similar problems.	Refer parents to self-help group (see Self-Help Groups and 800 Numbers, Chapter 18, and Online Resources, Chapter 19).
Discuss a treatment termination plan and related issues.	Develop a treatment termination plan and discuss issues of separation anxiety and dependence.

ADOLESCENT'S GOALS	THERAPIST'S INTERVENTIONS
Adolescent joins in treatment. Outlook is improved and feelings of anger and isolation are diminished.	Cultivate therapeutic alliance or collaborative relationship with the adolescent to build trust and enhance outcome of treatment.
Resolve fears. Understand and accept possible need for hospitalization.	Explain possible need for hospitalization to treat withdrawal symptoms and provide medical detoxification with supervision.
Undergo testing to confirm or deny substance abuse and to isolate drugs of choice.	Refer for or administer the Substance Abuse Subtle Screening Inventory (SASSI) to accurately identify chemical dependency.
As appropriate, the adolescent is hospitalized or enters into "suicide pact" agreeing to inform therapist of ideations and plans, and to provide prior notification before taking action.	Assess possible homicidal or suicidal effects of substance dependence. If homicidal, notify parents and authorities. If actively suicidal, hospitalize immediately and notify parents. If the adolescent has suicidal ideations, but no active plan, enter into a "suicide pact."
With parental assistance, follow through with psychiatric evaluation, and accept hospitalization and detoxification if necessary.	Refer the adolescent for psychiatric evaluation and/or hospitalization if required.
Follow-up on medical referral. Understand existing or potential physical problems related to substance.	Refer for medical evaluation to identify physical problems caused or exacerbated by substance use.
Identify potential genesis of substance abuse in family of origin.	Investigate chronological history of family and adolescent substance abuse.

ADOLESCENT'S GOALS	THERAPIST'S INTERVENTIONS
Explore denial and understand factors contributing to substance abuse.	Explore level of "distressed thinking" or denial, and assess the adolescent's cognitive and intellectual functioning that contributes to substance abuse.
Understand that relapse may occur, but you can return to abstinence.	Normalize possible relapse and help the adolescent regard it as a learning opportunity for therapist and the adolescent to develop new techniques to restore abstinence.
Face the problems caused by your substance abuse. Take responsibility for the consequences.	Help the adolescent look at the facts of substance abuse and the problems it has caused. Predict probability of relapse.
If medication has been prescribed, maintain a strict medication schedule.	If medication has been prescribed, discuss importance of a strict medication regimen and warn against mixing prescribed drugs with alcohol or street drugs.
Work on underlying issues that contribute to substance abuse.	Evaluate the adolescent for dual diagnosis and treat other symptoms such as anxiety, depression, social phobia, etc. (see appropriate treatment plan).
Comply with referral.	If appropriate, refer for acupuncture and/or other supplementary treatments.
Understand patterns of stress that lead to substance use.	Explore past patterns of substance use in relation to life stressors.
Become aware that substance abuse can rapidly become dependency or addiction.	Educate the adolescent about the potential dangers of dependency.

ADOLESCENT'S GOALS	THERAPIST'S INTERVENTIONS
Begin to seriously examine and question your substance abuse.	Provide feedback on consequences of drug or alcohol abuse to create negative cognitions about use.
Explore feelings toward change.	Help the adolescent understand ambivalence and explore fear and other feelings about change.
Cooperate with therapist in developing a plan of action.	Explore obstacles while organizing a plan so the adolescent can see it develop in small, achievable steps.
Actively develop new behaviors.	Encourage, support, and reinforce any positive new behaviors
Understand process you must go through to become "clean."	Explain mourning process and help the adolescent "mourn" the loss of the substance of choice.
Recognize and avoid potential triggers for relapse.	Identify persons, places, and things that may cause backsliding or relapse.
Maintain daily journal to monitor feelings rather than act them out.	Assign the adolescent the responsibility of keeping a daily journal of his or her feelings and reactions.
Recognize family triggers to substance abuse and avoid enablers within the family.	Investigate family conflicts and identify enablers that promote the adolescent's substance use.
Attend NA or AA and obtain a sponsor, or attend rational recovery group	Refer the adolescent to 12-step program (NA, AA, Alateen or Rational Recovery Group (see Self-Help Groups and 800 Numbers, Chapter 18, and Online Resources, Chapter 19).

ADOLESCENT'S GOALS	THERAPIST'S INTERVENTIONS
Replace ritualistic behavior with more rational response.	Investigate ritualistic behaviors related to substance use and teach client more rational behaviors.
Realize destructive effects of substance abuse on the quality of your relationships.	Explore and identify the effects of substance use on the adolescent's social, family, school, and occupational relations.
Become more knowledgeable about the disorder,	Assign reading of books on substance disorders such as *101 Ready-to-Use Drug Prevention Activities*, or other selections (see Bibliotherapy, Chapter 17).
Learn new techniques for dealing with destructive urges.	Teach the adolescent relaxation techniques, hypnosis, or visualization to cope with feelings. Provide audiotape for home use (see Behavioral Techniques, Chapter 14).
Understand that this disorder is not your fault and that you must constantly work at maintaining your recovery.	Review issues of shame and guilt that may cause or contribute to substance abuse.
Make a commitment to someone else that you will remain sober.	Obtain a contract or commitment for sobriety with the understanding that relapse is common, but that abstinence can be achieved.
Develop a S.M.A.R.T. plan to deal with recovery.	Develop a S.M.A.R.T. action plan: Small, Measurable, Achievable, Realistic, Timeline goals (see "Change," Behavioral Techniques, Chapter 14).

ADOLESCENT'S GOALS	THERAPIST'S INTERVENTIONS
Develop alternate behaviors to substance abuse.	Suggest and discuss alternate behaviors to substance abuse (i.e. exercise, sports, hobbies etc.).
Anger toward self and others is diminished.	Guide the adolescent in reducing anger toward self and others.
Discuss and resolve treatment termination issues and help develop a treatment termination plan.	Develop a treatment termination plan and resolve separation anxiety and dependence issues.

FAMILY'S GOALS	THERAPIST'S INTERVENTIONS
Improve communications among family members to reduce familial misunderstandings and the resultant anger and anxiety.	Conduct family sessions or refer for family therapy to reduce anger and/or alienation, and improve communication skills within the family.
Cooperate in amplifying family genogram and getting a more complete view of family history.	Amplify family genogram created in early parental session to aid in understanding family history. See how other members view family issues.
Discuss genogram to fully understand family history of substance abuse.	Discuss genogram to reveal family history and possible secrets related to substance abuse.
Understand how substance abuse affects the entire household.	Discuss links between drug use and consequences and the benefits of change within the family.
Family empathizes with the adolescent and helps support change.	Help family understand the ambivalence and fear of change.
Family explores solutions and challenges obstacles to change in order to empower the adolescent to give up substance abuse.	Explore solutions and obstacles to create realistic, achievable steps to successful recovery.
Family works together to help the adolescent become abstinent.	Assign family members to read *The Addiction Workbook* to learn new ways of dealing with the problem (see Bibliotherapy, Chapter 17).

FAMILY'S GOALS	THERAPIST'S INTERVENTIONS
Demonstrate boundaries, triangles, alliances, triangles, and emotional currents that exacerbate anxieties.	Explore family boundaries using sculpturing, a useful technique for understanding triangulation and family emotional currents (see Behavioral Techniques, Chapter 14).
Identify enablers and enabling behaviors to diminish their effects.	Discuss enabling behaviors within the family to reduce unnecessary influences.
Shift focus from problem to possible solutions.	Have family imagine a future without the problem and suggest actions that can be taken now to make that future possible.
Think about what treatment outlook would look like. Explain what you would like to see change in other family members when treatment concludes.	Ask family members to think about what they might want to say about each other when treatment is concluded.
Family members realize they have the power to make important changes, even if they are small.	Help family members realize they have an opportunity to do some things differently.
Family members are empowered. They realize they can create positive change.	Ask family members to relate what they have accomplished in the past week.
Realize that major change is the result of small steps taken one at a time.	Help family identify and prioritize achievable goals.
Accept help from family in preventing relapse.	Explore relapse triggers with the family. Provide support and understanding.

FAMILY'S GOALS	THERAPIST'S INTERVENTIONS
In the event of relapse, family mobilizes to find new solutions.	Instruct the family that relapse is normal and should be regarded as a learning tool to uncover new solutions as opposed to a disgraceful action that must be harshly disciplined.
Each member individually develops a S.M.A.R.T. plan.	Develop a S.M.A.R.T. action plan—Small, Measurable, Achievable, Realistic, Timelined goals (see "Change," Behavioral Techniques, Chapter 14).
Make use of available community resources	Refer family to available resources in the community (see Self-Help Groups and 800 Numbers, Chapter 18, and Online Resources, Chapter 19).
Reduce negative communication.	Develop a system of positive reinforcement with family to interact better with one another and reduce scapegoating.
Family works together to develop a treatment termination plan.	Discuss termination issues and develop a plan to terminate treatment.

PART III
TREATMENT AIDS

14
BEHAVIORAL TECHNIQUES

BAD DREAMS

"Bad Dreams" by L. G. Agre

(From *101 Favorite Play Therapy Techniques* edited by H. Kaduson and C. Schaefer. Copyright © 1997 by Jason Aronson and reprinted with permission.)

Introduction

Bad dreams sometimes come up in the play situation. This technique was derived from reading about dream work in *The Centering Book* by Gay Hendricks and Russell Wills (1975) and about neuro-linguistic programming (NLP) in books by Grinder and Bandler (1982, 1985).

Rationale

Using this technique allows a child to understand that each of us creates our dreams and that we can choose to change our dreams if we so desire. A child is empowered by this technique, and this technique is open-ended.

Depending on the child's intellectual capacity, a child can go on to use NLP principles to develop goals and visualize himself performing tasks the way he would like to perform tasks. When a child brings up nightmares, I talk about how we make up our dreams in our own heads and about how we can change our dreams. We can pretend to have our own remote control to squeeze to change our dreams.

Description

First, the child is asked to describe his dream. Then, we talk about how he would like his dream to end, how he could change his dream. Then, I have the child draw a picture of how he wants his dream to end. Next, I have the child close his eyes and tell me about the dream. When the child gets to the scary part of the dream, I have him squeeze his hand as if it held a remote control, and then the child finishes the dream the way he wants it to end.

When the child tells me he can see the new ending, I touch him lightly on the wrist or arm to anchor the new ending. The child is then told to open his eyes. We repeat this process at least three times I have the child take home his picture of the new ending to put under his pillow. I check with the child the next two or three days to see if we were successful. If not, we repeat the process.

Applications

I use this technique with a child whose nightmare appears to be the result of scary movies or fall tales told by older siblings. The dreamer and dream cue me into whether or not the dream is of benign origin. This technique seems to work with almost all children. However, it did not work with a severely emotionally disturbed child (as defined by special education guidelines) or with one other child. I rarely use this technique with children I know or suspect of having been sexually abused.

References

Bandler, R. (1985). *Using Your Brain—for a Change.* Moab, UT: Real People Press.
Bandler, R., and Grinder, J. (1982). *Reframing—Neuro-Linguistic Programming and the Transformation of Meaning* Moab, UT: Real People Press.
Hendricks, G., and Wills, R. (1975). *The Centering Book.* Englewood Cliffs, NJ: Prentice-Hall.

CHANGE

"How to Change 101," by Bill O'Hanlon, MS.

(From *Possibilities E-mail,* April 2001, by W. H. O'Hanlon, and reprinted with permission.)

Step 1: Acknowledge

- Acknowledge people and validate their points of view.
- Don't blame or make them wrong.
- Get specific: Use action talk (videotalk*) to avoid labeling or generalizing.
- Acknowledge concerns (yours and others).
- Acknowledge problems.
- Acknowledge what has worked: no need to throw the baby out with the bathwater.

Step 2: Find and agree on a direction/mission/vision

- If you don't know where you're going, you'll probably end up somewhere else.
- If possible, paint a vivid picture of the future, again in action talk (videotalk*).
- Get consensus or at least mutual understanding of that future.
- Use possibility talk (expect change, open up possibilities for change etc.).

Step 3: Acknowledge barriers and identify resources to achieving that future

- What has stopped you or tripped you up in moving toward that future?
- What are internal barriers (fears, old habits, outdated or unhelpful beliefs) to moving on?
- What are real world barriers (money, lack of consensus, lack of information, actions that haven't been taken) to moving on?
- What or who are resources available to overcome or resolve the barriers?
- What has worked well in the past?

---

* *Videotalk* means to describe something only in terms of what one could see or hear if watching and listening to a videotape.

- Identify patterns of thinking, focus, and action that do not help the situation change.

Step 4: Make an action plan

- Start small.
- SMART (Small, Measurable, Achievable, Realistic, Timeline) goals and directions are more likely to succeed.

Step 5: Act (Just Do It!)

- Take action, notice results, adjust action if needed.
- Break patterns of thinking, focus, and action.
- Decide who is going to take what action by when.
- Get a promise and arrange to follow-up.
- Persist until goal is achieved.

Step 6: Acknowledge and celebrate progress and success

- Give lots of credit.
- Rituals/awards/celebrations to acknowledge milestones achieved and goals met.

FAMILY SCULPTURING

(From *Behavioral Management Guide: Essential Treatment Strategies for Adult Psychotherapy* by M. P. Warren. Copyright © 2001 by Jason Aronson and reprinted with permission.)

Family sculpturing is a technique that emerged from attempts to translate systems theory into physical form through special arrangements. It uses space as a metaphor for understanding human relationships.

Sometimes called Family Choreography, sculpturing depicts emotional relationships that are always in motion. In a sense it choreographs important transactional patterns such as alliances, triangles and shifting emotional currents. The technique can be used with any theoretical modality and modified to implement a variety of goals. Virginia Satir used family sculpturing to demonstrate what she called the four most common stances of family members: the accuser, the placatory, the rational one and the irrelevant one. The technique is also used to realign family relationships, create new patterns and change the family system.

In practice, after defining or describing the family problem, each family member is asked to arrange family members as the individual experiences them or show a visual picture of the way he or she experiences the problem, to arrange the family members according to their emotional relationship with each member, and to identify their characteristic way of coping with this relationship. The technique can also be used to show how major stressors (death, illness) have altered the relationships over time. To help move the process along, the therapist might ask questions aimed at shedding light on the traditional patterns. Each member is asked to arrange the other family members, as they would like to interact with them.

In this way, family sculpting or family choreography can be used to reveal human relationships within a social, psychological, and physical system and to realign those relationships when necessary. It is a silent motion picture of the family that removes the linguistic traps and cuts through the barrage of attack and counterattack that often characterizes family sessions.

GENOGRAMS

(From *Behavioral Management Guide: Essential Treatment Strategies for Adult Psychotherapy* by M. P. Warren. Copyright © 2001 by Jason Aronson and reprinted with permission.)

A genogram is a diagram that depicts the relationships between family members over three generations. The genogram uses symbols to illustrate the relationships with the units and major stressors in chronological order. The diagram is used to help understand the family dynamics over time. The symbols include:

Genogram Symbols:

□	Male	|	Offspring
○	Female	– – –	Marriage
△	Child	D/	Divorce
Ø	Abortion/Stillbirth	X	Death

Construction of a genogram begins with the collection of facts about each member, their position in the family and their relationships to other family members. Physical location is important for tracking distance and boundaries. Analysis of the genogram provides information about how conflicts are resolved as well as family secrets such as abortion. It is also helpful in identifying whether the family is cohesive or explosive. The genogram is used to spell out physical and emotional boundaries, characteristics of the membership, modal events, toxic issues, emotional cut-offs, a general openness/closedness index, and the available relationship options within the family.

The resulting diagram allows one to see at a glance the basic structural framework of the family including triangulation and repetitive family issues. Such information might otherwise require a lengthy document to record. General questions that should be explored include cultural, ethnic and religious affiliations, socioeconomic level, and the way the family relates to the community socially and economically, and whether the family is cohesive or isolated.

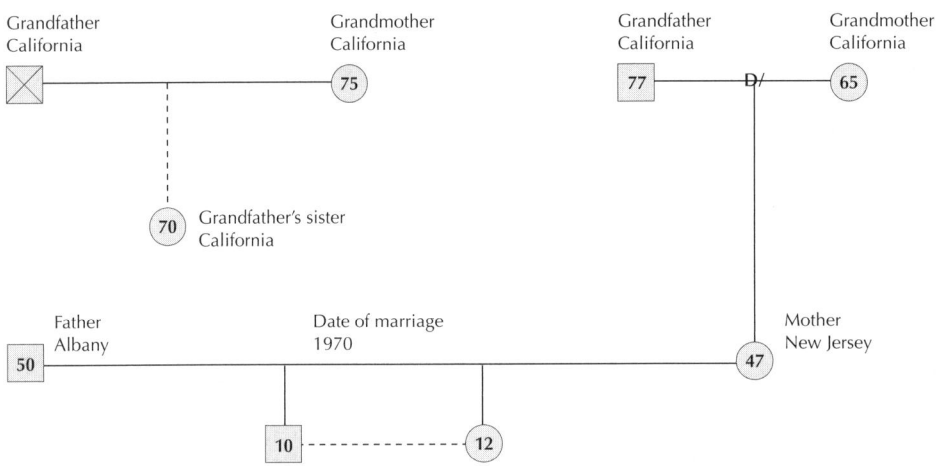

Example of a Genogram

Once the basic information is collected, including names, ages, births, deaths, divorces, the structure is expanded to include other significant data that points up critical nodal points. As patterns of interaction emerge, other universal issues are exposed such as money, sex, power, control, parenting, children, and others. Does the family discuss problems or is there a conspiracy of silence? What events in the life cycle will shape the future? The genogram has proven to be an important tool for family therapists.

HYPNOSIS

(From *Behavioral Management Guide: Essential Treatment Strategies for Adult Psychotherapy* by M. P. Warren Copyright © 2001 by Jason Aronson and reprinted with permission.)

Hypnosis is an induced altered state of consciousness or trance state in which the individual is more susceptible to suggestion. People are imprinted with mindsets that originate in their families of origin and are incorporated into the unconscious. People organize their personalities and act around these imprints. We do not operate directly on the world, but through a map or model of the world, a created representation of what we believe. In hypnosis, the therapist aims at changing or otherwise influencing the maps we hold in our minds. All hypnosis is essentially self-hypnosis, which can broaden responses and increase cognitive flexibility.

Hypnosis can be a highly effective therapeutic tool. When the client has slipped into trance after induced relaxation, the client may be instructed to imagine himself or herself the way they would like to be. For example, in hypnosis, an adolescent with low self-esteem may be asked to imagine himself/herself as capable, valuable, and confident, and through visualization begin to change their belief systems.

Hypnosis appears to work well with the cognitive-behavioral modality. However, insurance company reaction to the technique is mixed. Although many find it an acceptable psychotherapeutic technique, some prefer to call it relaxation technique rather than hypnosis. It is best to find out where the insurance company stands on the issue.

LEARNING

Identifying Modality Strengths

Understanding one's preferred modalities helps children discover their strengths. Using the chart overleaf, review the styles with the child and help him/her identify their modality strengths and improve their learning styles.

RELAXATION

Relaxation Exercise—Diaphragmatic Breathing

(Adapted from *Specific Phobias: Clinical Applications of Evidence-Based Psychotherapy* by T. J. Bruce and W. C. Sanderson. Copyright © 1998 by Jason Aronson and used with permission.)

Commonly known as stomach or body breathing, diaphragmatic breathing can be used as an effective coping skill for anxiety. This exercise should be practiced at least once a day because the first step in developing a coping skill is getting your body acquainted with and used to it.

Observable Characteristics
Indicative of Modality Strength

(From "Observable Characteristics Indicative of Modality Strength," in *Teaching Through Modality Strengths: Concepts and Practices* by R.H. Swassing, and W. B. Barbe (eds). Copyright © 1979 by Zaner Bloser and reprinted with permission.)

	Visual	Auditory	Kinesthetic
Learning Style	Learns by seeing; watching demonstrations	Learns through verbal instructions from others or self	Learns by doing; direct involvement
Reading	Likes description; sometimes stops reading to stare into space and imagine scene; intense concentration	Enjoys dialogue, plays; avoids lengthy description, unaware of illustrations; moves lips or subvocalizes	Prefers stories where action occurs early, fidgets when reading, handles books, not an avid reader
Spelling	Recognizes words by sight; relies on configuration of words	Uses a phonics approach; has auditory word attack skills	Often is a poor speller, writes words to determine if they "feel" right
Handwriting	Tends to be good, particularly when young; spacing and size are good; appearance is important	Has more difficulty learning in initial stages; tends to write lightly; says strokes when writing	Good initially, deteriorates when space becomes smaller; pushes harder on writing instrument
Memory	Remembers faces, forgets names; writes things down, takes notes	Remembers names, forgets faces; remembers by auditory repetition	Remembers best what was done, not what was seen or talked about
Imagery	Vivid imagination; thinks in pictures, visualizes in detail	Subvocalizes, thinks in sounds; details less important	Imagery not important; images that do occur are accompanied by movement
Distractibility	Generally unaware of sounds; distracted by visual disorder or movement	Easily distracted by sounds	Not attentive to visual, auditory presentation so seems distractible
Problem Solving	Deliberate; plans in advance; organizes thoughts by writing them; lists problems	Talks problems out, tries solutions verbally, subvocally; talks self through problem	Attacks problems physically, impulsive; often selects solution involving greatest activity

After you feel comfortable with this exercise, your therapist can show you how a briefer version can be used to cope during public encounters.

Let's take a moment to think about breathing. Our lungs sit in our chest in a space that is surrounded on the top and sides by our rib cage and on the bottom, by our diaphragm. The diaphragm is a sheet of muscle that bows upward like a dome beneath our lungs and separates the lung space from the abdominal cavity. As we breathe in, we must increase this lung space. Yet when we are anxious, the muscles of our shoulders and chest tighten and can make us feel that our breathing is labored, which in turn, increases our feelings of anxiety. While there are several ways of increasing our lung space, diaphragmatic or stomach breathing requires the least effort and, therefore, can serve as the most effective coping skill for managing anxious situations.

While some people achieve diaphragmatic breathing naturally and with ease, others may need to practice for a while before they feel comfortable with the exercise. But don't worry, practicing can be very relaxing and enjoyable! To see what it feels like to breath diaphragmatically, lie with your stomach down on a bed or on the floor and cross your arms beneath your head. You might even imagine that you are lying on the beach sunning your back as you look at the waves swell and crash at the shore. Now relax your stomach muscles and breath normally, inhaling through your nose. In this position, you are most likely to breath diaphragmatically. If you feel pressure from the floor or bed on your stomach as you inhale, you are breathing diaphragmatically. Try this for a few moments until you feel comfortable doing it without having to think about what you are doing so intensely. Now practice it as follows: sit in a comfortable chair with both feet on the floor. If you like, you can place one hand lightly on your chest and the other on your stomach just above your navel. Now breath slowly through your nose, relaxing your stomach and using only your diaphragm. You might even feel as if you are inhaling with your stomach. Inhale as deeply as is comfortable and then exhale through pursed lips as if you were blowing through a straw. When you are breathing correctly, your stomach will rise as you breath in, and slowly fall when you exhale. Now try to exhale for as long as it took you to inhale. This is called paced breathing.

When you feel comfortable with the paced diaphragmatic breathing, you can add one more component to this exercise. After you have taken a few breaths, mildly contract the muscles of your face and neck and then relax them again during the most convenient exhale. When you feel comfortable with this coordination component, try it with your neck and then back. This can be a great way to stretch and relax all of your major muscle groups! You may have to do some of the more tense muscle groups a few times before they fully unwind.

You should do this exercise at least once and preferably twice a day. Begin with 5 minutes of paced diaphragmatic breathing and then spend approximately 10–20 minutes combining it with the muscle stretching and relaxing followed by five more minutes of breathing. During those last five minutes allow your breathing to slow considerably and your muscles to feel heavy. Now indulge yourself in this quiet and calm place, you are finally fully relaxed!

A shorter version of this exercise can be used as a practical coping skill to manage anxiety before or during exposure. If you find yourself in such a situation, don't panic! You have all of the tools necessary to cope with your anxiety. Just take a deep diaphragmatic breath through your nose. Hold it for a second or so, then exhale slowly through pursed lips. Then pace your diaphragmatic breathing with the goal of slowing your rate of breathing. This may not seem so easy at first but just begin by extending your exhale and taking a deep breath when you can. You can even try holding your breath for a moment.

Eventually, you will be able to slow your breathing. As you are slowing your breathing rate, begin stretching and relaxing your major muscle groups, this will help you overcome the natural inclination to "freeze" when anxious. This will help you to regroup and feel as if you can cope at your own pace. Remember that the goal is not to stop your feeling of anxiety, but rather to cope with the feelings that anxiety induces. Back at the beach, it would be like riding out an ocean wave, allowing it to pick you up, and then set you back down. Your goal is not to stop it, but rather to flow with it and cope with it. You may also find it helpful to focus on your thoughts while you cope with your anxiety. Talk to your therapist about creating coping self-statements and other coping strategies that can be used with this exercise.

Reference

Bruce, T.J. and Sanderson, W.C. (1998). *Specific Phobias: Clinical Applications of Evidence-Based Psychotherapy.* Northvale, NJ: Aronson.

ROLE-PLAYING

"Role-Playing" by Richard L. Levinson, Jr., and Jack Herman

(From *Play Therapy Techniques* by C. E. Schaefer and D. M. Conglosai (eds). Copyright © 1997 by Jason Aronson and reprinted with permission.)

The goal of child psychotherapy is to help alleviate a child's difficulty in affective, cognitive, or behavioral areas that impede developmental adaptations. According to Dodds (1985), child psychotherapy "is designed to change the child in some way either to ease internal pain, change undesirable behavior or improve relationships between the child and other people who are important in the child's life" (p. 15). Interventions typically have ranged from the direct type, for example, analytic, behavioral, client-centered, and family therapies, to the indirect type, which include consultation and "parent counseling" (Dodds, 1985), as well as other methods.

As in adult psychotherapy, the relationship between therapist and child is crucial in order to set the stage for the intervention to have a successful outcome. There must be a working alliance and the establishment of a supportive, nonjudgmental atmosphere with emphatic understanding, in which the child can feel respected, non-threatened, and free to think, act (within limits), and say what he or she feels, There must be regularly scheduled sessions ranging from one to three sessions per week. Yet, psychotherapy with children differs from adult psychotherapy in that children do not possess the cognitive abilities to assimilate that which is heavily language oriented. Harter (1977) noted that, within Piaget's (1952) concept, the child is in the midst of a developmental shift from prelogical to logical thought. As Harter (1977) stated: "for it is this particular transition, and the gradual development and solidification of logical operations during the concrete operational period, that seem intimately related to the child's comprehension and construction of a logical system of *emotional* concepts that define the affective spheres of his/her life" (pp. 418–19).

For this reason, play therapy techniques, as well as numerous other primarily nonlanguage-oriented methods were developed (e.g. A. Freud 1965, Klein 1975). The therapeutic playing out of inner experience, ideas, affects, and fantasies associated with life events seems to aid the child in becoming more aware of the feelings and thoughts, conflicts, and ego dysfunctions that may underlie problematic or disturbed behaviors and affects and that provides an opportunity for the child to revise and resolve psychological and psychosocial problems.

Reisman (1973) provided a brief, but excellent theoretical history of play therapy. Allen (1942) believed play therapy served to help the child become aware of his or her identity as an individual in relation to the therapist and the nature of their relationship. Moustakas (1953) reported that play therapy was "a progression [of] the child's expression of feelings" (p. 111). Anna Freud (1965) saw a similarity between play therapy and psychoanalysis and theorized that "there is movement from surface to depth, from the interpretation of unconscious impulses, wishes, and fears or id content" (in Reisman 1973, p. III). Anna Freud believed that play therapy reduced anxiety and emotional (neurotic) disturbance by helping the child become more aware of unconscious conflicts and hidden material.

Waelder (1933) wrote an interesting and early paper on psychoanalytic play therapy with a special emphasis on the repetition theme. Of course, Sigmund Freud (1920) was the first to posit that some forms of play are repetitious acts, possibly to gain mastery over some particular event that was anxiety producing or frustrating, by reversal of roles from passive to active. Erikson (1950) described play as a form of hallucinatory mastery over life experiences that induced feelings of anxiety and helplessness. When children use repetition or repeat an act or game, they are, in a sense, working through, possibly undoing or redoing via displacement and symbolization, and thereby articulating, assimilating, and integrating that which is unconscious and connected to a special set of circumstances. These circumstances might range from separation anxiety to protection against unconscious wishes or feelings of dread or hostility, for example, in relation to a parent.

Some children have imaginary playmates or friends; others may act out roles or take the part of a significant person in their environment. Repetition or role reversal, however, does not seem to be a pathological set of behaviors or solutions to anxiety or conflictual issues, but rather is curative in that it serves to repair hurts and losses. It helps the child separate and individuate by inculcating a sense of mastery and competence, by giving an "illusion of accomplishment" (J. L. Herman, personal communication, February 23, 1987) and by contributing to the healthy adaptation and resolution of the normally stressful or anxiety-producing events that must occur during childhood.

It seems logical, then, that some forms of child psychotherapy incorporate techniques involving repetition. An indirect example of is Gardner's Mutual Storytelling Techniques (1971). Gardner's method involves encouraging the child to tell a story into a tape recorder. According to Schaefer and Milliman (1977), "the child is asked to be guest of honor on a make-believe television program in which stories to be told" (p. 38). The therapist then tells a parallel story; but after a psychoanalytic fashion, "healthier adaptations and resolutions of conflicts are introduced" (p. 38). Gardner's method is essentially a projective technique in which, with a minimum of structure, the child is asked to make up a story that is apprehended psychodynamically by the therapist and then relayed back to the child with more adaptive solutions. We know that in the process the child is going to construct a story based on her construction of herself in relation to the world and her characteristic adaptive or maladaptive ways of emotional problem solving. The issue of Gardner's technique is that, while it may be a useful diagnostic device, it may be questionable (from a psychoanalytic standpoint) as a therapeutic technique. The psychoanalytic concept of therapy relies on creating a therapeutic climate that promotes natural, evolving moment-to-moment spontaneous self-expression through play and verbalization with a *minimum* of structuring and interference by the therapist. The therapist aims to enable the patient to express himself *in his own way*, in a stream of consciousness fashion, whether via verbalization, play, or both. The therapist's job is to help the patient expand on whatever the patient initiated, not to introduce anything new. Introducing an artificial task for the child patient, extraneous to what might be on the child's mind at the moment, is to distract the child from whatever he or she might be immediately experiencing and expressing. It is important to stay within the immediate experience and not disrupt an ongoing experiential process that might bear fruit if followed.

The therapist attempts to follow and expand on whatever the child has introduced rather than distract the child by suggesting a game make-believe television show, even when a child may be resisting. In the latter case, the therapist attempts to follow the resistance and verbalize what it might mean, rather than to introduce a device to try to bypass it. The therapist acknowledges, clarifies, and interprets his or her understanding of the defensive reasons for the resistance, rather than trying to distract the child by introducing a new activity. The child's attention must be in the realm of everyday experience or occurrences so that there will be some connection between therapeutic interpretations and the child's incorporation of a corrective emotional experience.

The technique of role-playing has had a long history in various psychotherapeutic approaches. Traditionally, role-playing has been used by gestalt psychotherapists and in behavioral methodologies for reasons ranging from increasing emotional awareness to expanding repertoires of behaviors. Social psychological theorists such as McGuire (1961) and his "inoculation theory" have sought methods of cognitive-behavioral rehearsal to increase the individual's ability to deal with new and unfamiliar situations. Moreno (1969) utilized psychodrama, a psychotherapeutic technique of structuring, or partially structuring a real or hypothetical life situation, which the patient, along with assistants, is encouraged to dramatize in an improvisational manner while the therapist directs and comments upon the action. Perhaps the most important effort to utilize role-playing in psychotherapy was put forth by George Kelly within his Psychology of Personal Constructs. Kelly (1955) defined fixed-role therapy as "a sheer creative process in which therapist and client conjoin their talents" (p, 380). Rychlak (1973) reported that prior to fixed-role therapy the client is asked to write a self-descriptive sketch of his own character, which the therapist then rewrites in a role "based upon what the client has said of himself," but in contrasting themes, a role that the client knows he or she can act within as "experimental fantasy" (p. 496). Fixed-role therapy is then carried out for as many as eight sessions during which the client gains insight into the way he or she normally construes events and others, and thereafter he or she may decide to incorporate new behaviors and/or affective changes.

Within a social learning paradigm, Gottman, Gonso, and Shuler (1976) used modeling, role-playing, and behavioral rehearsal to improve social interactions among "isolated children." LaGreca (1983) discussed the efficacy of "role-play assessments" that serve to give the clinician insight into a child's repertoire of behaviors in contrived versus "structured observation formats." The contrived format is of particular interest here in that the patient is "asked to respond to a 'pretend' situation as if the situation were really occurring" (p. 121). Kendall and Braswell (1985), in their work with impulsive children, stated that "one reason for even including role-play tasks is to heighten the child's level of emotional involvement and arousal" (p. 135). Kendall and Braswell (1985), like LaGreca (1983), also reported that, "hypothetical problem situations" which are role-played should be practiced prior to real problem situations (p. 136).

Gresham (1986) routinely uses role-playing when remediating social skills deficits in children. He reported that "behavioral role play tests or performances in analogue situations have essentially become mark of assessment in social skills research" (p. 161). Among the advantages of using role-playing is that the technique depicts "actual behavioral enactment of a skill rather than a rating or perception of that skill" (p. 161). Irwin (1983) reported that role-playing and pretending may be used as a diagnostic technique in order to discern "the child's, ability to present and solve a problem, tolerance for frustration, capacity for language ... the ability to talk about and reflect on the experience including a discussion of feelings about the product which has just been created" (p.164).

Irwin also highlighted that role-playing gives insight into the quality of the child's ability to relate with his or her therapist.

More recently, research has focused on using role-play as a direct therapeutic intervention. Goldstein and Glick (1987) reported successful interventions occurred from the use of role-play within their program for "anger control" for adolescents who are "chronically delinquent" (p. 13). Goldstein and Glick's intervention is based, in part on the premise that these youngsters often demonstrate "impulsiveness and overreliance on aggressive means for goal attainment ... and characteristically reason at more egocentric, concrete, and in a sense, more primitive levels of moral reasoning" (p. 13). The program for anger control includes the role-playing of situations that have led previously to inappropriate expressions of anger. Role-plays focus upon achieving insight into underlying cognitive and affective issues that are triggered either internally or externally. Trainers use modeling, clear descriptions of conflict situations, and behavioral rehearsal with repetitive demonstrations of appropriate behaviors that lead to nonaggressive, positive outcomes.

In child psychotherapy, we are not so much interested in using role-play for the traditional uses of learning and rehearsal *per se*, but rather for its experiential value in promoting an internal corrective emotional experience, in which repressed affects can be integrated with cognitions of the self. We contend that what has been called *catharsis* is really a form of integration and mastery since, in apparently discharging pent-up affects, the child patient is undoing via reversal of roles or identities situations that created feelings of helplessness, but now serve to create a sense of completeness and control. It is suggested that children may not be especially insightful, but are willing to directly examine problematic areas in their emotional life. As noted, the necessary cognitive, language-based structures may not be sufficiently mature to allow for direct verbal intervention. Children, especially troubled children, lack the capacity for psychosynthesis, that is, the integration of intellectual and affective data. For these reasons, the technique of role-playing in child psychotherapy is seen as a valuable aid in reducing psychopathology and increasing awareness, understanding, and mastery in children and adolescents.

Preliminary reasons for the positive potential of this method are straightforward. First, it is simple to employ and involves the child in direct, everyday experiences in which they have interacted. Second, although it is a verbal technique and requires some sophistication in language use and comprehension, it taps the stream of consciousness and underlying conflictual material by allowing the child to use repetition as a tool toward mastery over an event that stimulated unresolved issues or conflicts. Unlike Gardner's (1971) Storytelling Technique, role-playing with children allows for direct participation and discussion in an area of conflict, and, through controlled therapeutic guidance, an implicit insightful experience might be achieved.

15
THERAPEUTIC GAMES

ANGER

Exploring My Anger, Western Psychological Services.
Breaking the Chains of Anger, Western Psychological Services.
I Can Control My Anger, Childswork/Childsplay.

BEHAVIOR

The Conscience Game, GoRu, Dallas, TX.
The Good Behavior Game, Childswork/Childsplay.
The Helping, Sharing, And Caring Game, Western Psychological Services.
The Odyssey Islands Game, Childswork/Childsplay.
The Storytelling Game, Childswork/Childsplay.

COGNITIVE SKILLS

Bop It, Parker Bros., Beverly, MA.
Captain's Log, BrainTrain, Richmond, VA.
Personal Trainer, BrainTrain, Richmond, VA.
Smart Driver, BrainTrain, Richmond, VA.
Simon, Milton Bradley, Springfield, MA.

COMMUNICATION

Communicate, Western Psychological Services.
Life Stories, Western Psychological Services.
The Ungame, Western Psychological Services.

The Parent Report Card for Teens, Western Psychological Services.
Chicken Soup for the Teen's Soul, Childswork/Childsplay.
Personality Probe, Childswork/Childsplay.

FAMILY ISSUES

Duplo Home, Western Psychological Services.
My Two Homes, Childswork/Childsplay.

LOSS

The Goodbye Game, Childswork/Childsplay.
The Grief Game, Childswork/Childsplay.

FEELINGS

The Talking, Feeling, Doing Game, Western Psychological Services.

MOTIVATION

Never Say Never, Childswork/Childsplay.

RESILIENCY

Bounce-Back, Childswork/Childsplay.

SELF-CONTROL

Teaching Self-Control, Childswork/Childsplay.

SELF-CONFIDENCE

The Bridge of Self-Confidence Game, Western Psychological Services.

SELF-ESTEEM

Self-Esteem Game, Childswork/Childsplay.

Turn Low Self-Esteem Into Positive Self-Image, Childswork/Childsplay.
Personal Power! Pow!, Childswork/Childsplay.

SEXUAL ABUSE

"Real People"™ Dolls, Los Angeles, CA: Western Psychological Services, Creative Therapy Store.

STRESS

Less Stress Ball, Childswork/Childsplay.
Positive Attitude Ball, Childswork/Childsplay.
Stress Attack, Childswork/Childsplay.

THINKING AND FEELNG

Positive Thinking Game, Childswork/Childsplay.
Futurestories, Childswork/Childsplay.
Stop Being So Mean, Childswork/Childsplay.
Clear Thinking, Childswork/Childsplay.

There are many therapeutic games designed by professionals for use in child psychotherapy. A few are listed here. For a catalog or more information, contact the distributor listed below.

Childswork/Childsplay
135 Dupont Street, PO Box 760, Plainview, NY 11803-0760
800-962-1141; Fax 1-800-262-1886

Creative Therapy Store
Western Psychological Services
12031 Wilshire Blvd., Los Angeles, CA 90025-1251
800-648-8857; Fax 1-310/478-7838

Teach-A-Body Dolls
7 Doris Drive, Mission, TX 78572
888-228-1314; Fax 1-956/585-3089

BrainTrain
727 Twin Ridge Lane, Richmond, VA 23235
800-822-0538; Fax: 804-320-0242

16
HOMEWORK ASSIGNMENTS

Homework assignments grew out of managed care's strategy that patients take a more active role in their treatment to provide a quicker outcome. Homework is a technique that facilitates change outside of sessions and encourages adolescent patients to explore changes on their own. The provider recertification form distributed by merit behavioral care specifies that "patients are expected to take an active part in their own therapy, often completing assignments between sessions."

In order to help providers deal more effectively with that request, this chapter offers some suggestions for homework as well as a list of available books that contain homework assignments.

Table 1
AUTOMATIC THOUGHT LOG

Fill out when you have a negative feeling or if a negative feeling becomes worse.

1. **FEELING**
   How do you feel now? Check ✔ and rate how much on a scale of 0 (usual) to 100 (worst I can imagine.)

   anxious   – (   )
   sad   – (   )
   guilty   – (   )
   angry   – (   )
   other   – (   )   specify which one _____

2. SITUATION
   What were you doing when you felt this way?

3. AUTOMATIC THOUGHT
   What went through your mind that could have made you feel this way? List all thoughts here and rate each thought on how much you believe it—0 (not at all) to 100 (completely).

4. BEHAVIOR
   What did you do? How did you cope with the situation?

(From *Treatment of Obsessive-Compulsive Disorder* by L. K. McGinn and S. C. Sanderson, Copyright © 1999 by Jason Aronson and used with permission.)

Table 2
THE STEPS TO CONSTRUCTING A RATIONAL RESPONSE

AUTOMATIC THOUGHTS

_____

_____

Rate belief in automatic thoughts (0–100):

What evidence do you have to support your automatic thoughts?

What evidence do you have against your automatic thoughts?

What are some alternative explanations?

Have you made any cognitive distortions?

Can you design a test of your automatic thoughts?

Have you identified a realistic problem? If so, go through the steps of the problem-solving exercise, and write the results here. What solution have you chosen? What steps can you take to carry out this solution?

Has one of your schemas been triggered? Which one? What do you need to do to battle the schema in this case?

Summarized rational response: _____

_____

_____

Rerate belief in automatic thoughts (0–100) _____

(From *Cognitive–Behavioral Treatment of Depression* by J. S. Klosko and W. C. Sanderson. Copyright © 1999 by Jason Aronson and used with permission.)

CHALLENGING COGNITIONS

This exercise involves identifying existing patterns of cognitive distortion and replacing them with rational thinking. Clients are given the challenging distortions worksheet (Table 3) and a list of common cognitive distortions (Table 4). They are asked to identify their distortions and then to use the worksheet to get immediate feedback and discover their own ways to change their thinking based on evidence-based reality. They are then asked to bring the completed worksheet to the next session and discuss it with the therapist.

Table 3
CHALLENGING COGNITIONS WORKSHEET

Initial thought (belief rating 1–100):

Associated behavior (or behavioral urge):

Cognitive distortion:

Weigh the evidence:

Challenge: (what are other possible ways of looking at this?)

(From *Marital Distress* by J. H. Rathus and W. C. Sanderson, Copyright © 1999 by Jason Aronson and used with permission.)

Table 4
COMMON COGNITIVE DISTORTIONS

Can you identify those cognitive distortions that apply to you?

- *All or nothing thinking*: either your behavior is perfect or it is awful. Things are either black or white.
- *Emotional reasoning*: you imagine that negative emotions are real. (i.e. John just doesn't like me).
- *Ignoring the positive*: you disqualify positive experiences as if they don't count, yet hold on to negative beliefs (i.e. I am just unlucky. The fact that my boss gave me a raise is a quirk).
- *Magical thinking*: thinking that if you do something or don't do something, it will cause some problem in someone else's life (i.e. if I step on this crack in the sidewalk, so and so will get sick).
- *Maximization or catastrophizing*: making a mountain out of a molehill.
- *Minimization*: making a molehill out of a mountain.
- *Negative interpretation*: you assume that someone is acting negatively toward you without checking it out.
- *Negative labeling*: attaching names to errors rather than describing the event. I am stupid because I forgot to lock the door.
- *Overgeneralization*: taking one event and viewing it as a pattern that never ends.
- *Personalization*: giving yourself credit for being the cause of a negative or positive event for which you are not really responsible (i.e. I didn't remind her, so she left the car unlocked).
- *Personification*: a form of projection in which the desirable or undesirable properties of reality are attributed to some other person even if they are unrelated to what happened (i.e. you send a letter to someone that is not delivered and accuse someone else of intercepting the letter).
- *Shoulds:* using the word "should" to motivate yourself and others. Using "should" directed at yourself creates guilt. When directed at others, it results in anger and frustration.

(From *Marital Distress* by J. H. Rathus and W. C. Sanderson, Copyright © 1999 by Jason Aronson, and used with permission).

17
BIBLIOTHERAPY

SELF-HELP BOOKS FOR ADOLESCENTS

Addiction

Fanning, Patrick, and O'Neill, John. (1996). *The Addiction Workbook.* Oakland, CA: New Harbinger.

101 Ready-to-Use Drug Prevention Activities: http://www.lcps.k12.nm.us/Departments/FedPrograms/Inventory%20list.htm

Abuse

Copeland, Mary Ellen, and Harris, Maxine. (2000). *Healing The Trauma of Abuse.* Oakland, CA: New Harbinger.

Alzheimers

Lokvig, Jytte, and Becker, John D. (2004). *Alzheimers A to Z.* Oakland, CA: New Harbinger.

Anger

Kassinove, Howard, and Tafrate, Raymond Chip. (2002). *Anger Management.* Atascadero, CA: Impact Publishers.

McKay, Matthew, and Rogers, Peter. (1995). *The Anger Control Workbook.* Oakland, CA: New Harbinger.

Mason, Paul T., and Kreger, Randi. (1998). *Stop Walking on Eggshells*. Oakland, CA: New Harbinger.
Potter-Efron, Ronald. (2005). *Angry All The Time*. Oakland, CA: New Harbinger.
Potter-Efron, Ronald, and Potter-Efron, Pat. (1995). *Letting Go of Anger*. Oakland, CA: New Harbinger.
Santoro, Joseph, and Cohen, Ronald. (1997). *The Angry Heart*. Oakland, CA: New Harbinger.

Anxiety

Barlowe, D., and Crooke, M. G. (2000). *Mastery of Your Anxiety and Panic*. San Antonio, TX: The Psychological Group.
Bassete, L. (1995). *From Panic to Power*. New York: HarperCollins.
Bodger, C. (1999). *Smart Guide to Relieving Stress*. New York: Wiley.
Bourne, E. J. (1998). *Healing Fear*. Oakland, CA: New Harbinger.
Bourne, E. J. (2001). *The Anxiety and Phobia Workbook*. Oakland, CA: New Harbinger.
Bourne, E. J. (2001). *Beyond Anxiety and Phobia*. Oakland, CA: New Harbinger.
Bourne, Edmund, and Garano, Lorna. (2001). *Coping With Anxiety*. Oakland, CA: New Harbinger.
Clarke, Lynn. (2001). *SOS Help for Emotions: Managing Anxiety, Anger and Depression*. Berkeley, CA: Parents Press.
Copeland, M. E. (1998). *The Worry Control Workshop*. Oakland, CA: New Harbinger.
Ellis, A. (1999). *How to Control Your Anxiety Before It Controls You*. Secaucus, NJ: Carol Publishing.
Gerzon, R. (1997). *Finding Serenity in the Age of Anxiety*. New York: Bantam.
Jacobson, E. (1978). *You Must Relax*. New York: McGraw-Hill.
Jeffers, S. (1988). *Feel the Fear and Do It Anyway*. New York: Fawcett Columbine.
Kopp, S. (1988). *Raise Your Right Hand Against Fear, Extend the Other One In Compassion*. Minneapolis, MN: Compcare.
Wetherill, M. J. (2000). *The Eye of the Storm: Discovering Inner Calm Amidst Inner Pressure*. Holbrook, MA: Adams.
White, John. (1998). *Overcoming Generalized Anxiety Disorder*. Oakland, CA: New Harbinger.
Wilson, R. R. (1996). *Don't Panic: Taking Control of Anxiety Attacks*. New York: HarperCollins.
Ziegler, R. G., and Ziegler, P. (1992). *Homemade Books to Help Kids Cope*. New York: Magination.

Attention Deficit Disorder

Christ, J. J. (1997). *ADHD—A Teenager's Guide*. Plainview, NY: Childswork/Childsplay.
Hartman, T. (1995). *Healing ADD: Simple Exercises That Will Change Your Daily Life*. Grass Valley, CA: Underwood.
Hartman, T. (1995). *Success Stories: A Guide to Fulfillment with Attention Deficit Disorder*. Grass Valley, CA: Underwood.
Honos-Webb, Lara. (2005). *The gift of ADHD*. Oakland, CA: New Harbinger.
Morrison, J. (1996). *Coping With ADD/ADHD*. New York: Rosen.
Roberts, S., and Jansen, G. J. (1997). *Living With ADD*. Oakland, CA: New Harbinger.

Behavior Management

Korb-Khalsa, K. L., and Leutenberg, E. A. (2002). *Life Management Skills*. Plainview, NY: Wellness Reproductions & Publishing.
Korb-Khalsa, K. L., Azok, S. D., and Leutenberg, E. A. (1992). S.E.A.L.S. book series. Plainview, NY: Wellness Reproductions & Publishing.
Warren, Muriel P. (2001). *Behavioral Management Guide: Essential Treatment Strategies for Adult Psychotherapy*. Northvale, NJ: Jason Aronson.
Warren, Muriel P. (2001). *Behavioral Management Guide: Essential Treatment Strategies for the Psychotherapy of Children, Their Parents, and Families*. Northvale, NJ: Jason Aronson.

Bereavement

Caplan, S., and Lang, G. (1995). *Grief's Courageous Journey*. Oakland, CA: New Harbinger.
Grollman, E.A. (1993). *Straight Talk About Death for Teenagers*. Boston, MA: Beacon.
Harris, M. (1995). *The Loss That Is Forever: The Lifelong Impact of the Early Death of a Mother or Father*. New York: Penguin.
Jozefowski, J. T. (1999). *The Phoenix Phenomenon: Rising from the Ashes of Grief*. Northvale, NJ: Aronson.
Romain, T. (1999). *What On Earth Do You Do When Someone Dies?* Minneapolis, MN: Free Spirit.
Tyson, J. N. (1997). *Common Threads of Teenage Grief: A Handbook For Healing*. Helm Seminars.

Bipolar Disorder

Fast, Julie A., and John D. Preton. (2003). *Loving Someone With Bipolar Disorder.* Oakland, CA: New Harbinger.

Coping Skills

Lewis, B.A. (1998). *What Do You Stand For?* Minneapolis, MN: Free Spirit.
McKay, M., Davis, M., and Fanning, P. (1997). *Thoughts and Feelings: Taking Control of Your Moods and Your Life.* Oakland, CA: New Harbinger.
Napier, N. J. (1993). *Getting Through the Day: Strategies for Adults Hurt as Children.* New York: Norton.
Shapiro, L. E. (1996). *The Teens' Solutions Workbook.* Plainview, NY: Childswork/Childsplay.
Taubman, S. (1994). *Ending the Struggle Against Yourself.* New York: Putnam.

Conflict Resolution

Doyle, T. (1991). *Why is Everybody Always Picking on Me?: A Guide to Handling Bullies.* Middlebury, VT: Atrium.

Critical Incident Stress Management

Mitchell, J. T., and Everly, G. S. (1999). *Critical Incident Stress Debriefing: An Operations Manual. 3rd. Ed.* Ellicott City, MD: Chevron Publishing.
Mitchell, J. T., and Everly, G. S. (2001). *Critical Incident Stress Management: A New Era and Standard of Care in Crisis Intervention. 2nd Ed.* Ellicott City, MD: Chevron Publishing.

Cyclothymia

Price, Prentiss. (2005). *The Cyclothymia Workbook.* Oakland, CA: New Harbinger.

Depression

Burns, D. (1999). *Feeling Good.* New York: Avon.

Cobain, B. (1998). *When Nothing Matters Anymore*. Minneapolis, MN: Free Spirit.
Copeland, M. E. (1992). *The Depression Workbook: A Guide for Living with Depression and Manic Depression*. Oakland, CA: New Harbinger.
Copeland, M. E. (1992). *Living Without Depression and Manic Depression*. Oakland, CA: New Harbinger.
Copeland, M. E. (1998). *Adolescent Depression Workbook*. Oakland, CA: New Harbinger.
Emery, Gary. (2000). *Overcoming Depression*. Oakland, CA: New Harbinger.
Martell, Christopher R., and Addis, Michael E. (2004). *Overcoming Depression One Step at a Time*. Oakland, CA: New Harbinger.
Williams, K. (1995). *A Parent's Guide to Suicide and Depressed Teens*. Center City: MN: Hazelden.

Defiant Child

Levy, R., and O'Hanlon, William H. (2001). *Try and Make Me: A Revolutionary Program for Raising Your Defiant Child Without Losing Your Cool*. Emmaus, PA: Rosedale.
Tower, T., and Van Patter, B. (1995). *Self Control Patrol Workbook*. Plainview, NY: Childswork/Childsplay.

Dissociative Disorder

Steinberg, M. (2000). *The Stranger in the Mirror: Dissociation, the Hidden Epidemic*. New York: HarperCollins.

Domestic Violence

Kubany, Edward, McCaig, Mari, and Laconsay, Janet R. (2004). *Healing the Trauma of Domestic Violence*. Oakland, CA: New Harbinger.

Eating Disorders

Apple, R. F., and Agras, W. S. (1977). *Overcoming Eating Disorders: Bulimia Nervosa and Binge-Eating Disorders*. San Antonio, TX: Harcourt Brace.
Danowski, D., and Lazaro, P. (2000). *Why Can't I Stop Eating?* Center City, MN: Hazelden.
Ebbett, J. (1994). *The Eating Illness Workbook*. Center City, MN: Hazelden.

Edell, D. (1999). *Eat, Drink and Be Merry*. New York: HarperCollins.
Heffner, Michelle, and Eifert, Georg H. (2004). *The Anorexia Workbook*. Oakland, CA: New Harbinger.
Lobue, A., and Marcus, M. (1999). *The Don't Diet, Live It! Workbook: Healing Food, Weight & Body Issues*. Carlsbad, CA: Gurze.
McCabe, Randi E., McFarlane, Traci L., and Olmstead, Marion P. (2003). *The Overcoming Bulimia Workbook*. Oakland, CA: New Harbinger.
Nash, J. D. (1999). *Binge No More*. Oakland, CA: New Harbinger.
Sandbek, T. (1993). *The Deadly Diet*. Oakland, CA: New Harbinger.
Schroder, C. R. (1992). *Fat Is Not a Four-Letter Word*. New York: Chronemed.
Sherman, R. T., and Thompson, R. T. (1996). *Bulimia: A Guide for Family and Friends*. San Francisco, CA: Jossey-Bass.
Virtue, D. (1994). *Losing Your Pounds of Pain*. Carson, CA: Hay House.
Zerbe, K. J. (1993). *The Body Betrayed: Eating Disorders and Their Treatment*. Washington, DC: American Psychiatric.

Gambling

Heineman, M. (1988). *When Someone You Love Gambles*. Center City, MN: Hazelden.
Horvath, A. T. (2000). *Sex, Drugs, Gambling, and Chocolate*. Atascadaro, CA: Impact.
Lesieur, H. R. (1986). *Understanding Compulsive Gambling*. Center City, MN: Hazelden.
Lorenz, V. (1988). *Releasing Guilt About Gambling*. Center City, MN: Hazelden.

Guilt/Shame

Black, S., and Drozd, L. (1995). *The Missing Piece: Solving the Puzzle of Self*. New York: Ballantine Publishing Group.
Breitman, P., and Hatch, C. (2000). *How To Say No Without Feeling Guilty*. New York: Broadway.
Elton, R. P., and Elton, F. P. (1989). *Letting Go of Shame*. Center City, MN: Hazeldon.

Hypnosis, Relaxation, Visualization and Feedback

Allen, J. S., and Klein, R. J. (1996). *Ready...Set...R.E.L.A.X*. Watertown, WI: Inner Coaching.

Austin, V. (1998). *Free Yourself from Fear: Self-Hypnosis for Anxiety, Panic Attacks, and Phobias*. London: HarperCollins.

Davis, M., Eshelman, E., and McKay, M. (1988). *The Relaxation and Stress Reduction Workbook*. Oakland, CA: New Harbinger.

Epstein, G. (1987). *Healing Visualizations: Creating Health Through Imagery*. New York: Bantam.

Fisher, S., and Ellison, J. (1991). *Discovering the Power of Self-Hypnosis: A New Approach for Enabling Change and Promoting Healing*. San Antonio, TX: HarperCollins.

Gawain, S. (1982). *Creative Visualization*. New York: Bantam.

Clayton, L. (1999). *Coping With a Learning Disability*. New York: Rosen.

Medical

Caufield, J., Hansen, M.V., Aubry, P., and Mitchell, N. M. (1996). *Chicken Soup for the Surviving Soul*. FL: HCI.

Doka, K. J. (1998). *Living with Life-Threatening Illness: A Guide for Patients, Their Families, and Caregivers*. San Francisco, CA: Jossey-Bass.

Fennell, Patricia. (2001). *The Chronic Illness Workbook*. Oakland, CA: New Harbinger.

Kabat-Zinn, J. (1990). *Full Catastrophe Living: Using the Wisdom of Your Body and Mind to Face Stress, Pain, and Illness*. New York: Dell.

Pitzele, S. K. (2000). *Finding the Joy in Today*. Center City, MN: Hazelden.

Register, C. (2000). *Living with Chronic Illness*. Center City, MN: Hazelden.

Obsessive-Compulsive Disorder

Hyman, Bruce M., and Pedrick, Cherry. (2003). *Helping Your Child With OCD*. Oakland, CA: New Harbinger.

Hyman, Bruce M., and White, K. (1990). *The OCD Workbook*. Oakland, CA: New Harbinger.

McGinn, L. K., and Sanderson, W. C. (1999). *Treatment of Obsessive-Compulsive Disorder*. Northvale, NJ: Jason Aronson.

Rathus. J. M., and Sanderson, W. C. (1999). *Marital Distress*. Northvale, NJ: Jason Aronson.

Steketee, Gail. (1998). *Overcoming Obsessive-Compulsive Disorder*. Oakland, CA: New Harbinger.

Parenting

Borba, M. (1999). *Parents Do Make a Difference: How to Raise Kids With Solid Character, Strong Minds, and Caring Hearts.* San Francisco, CA: Jossey-Bass.
Ford, A. (1994). *Wonderful Ways to Love a Child.* Berkeley, CA: Conari.
Nowicki, S. A., and Duke, M. P. (1992). *Helping The Child Who Doesn't Fit In.* Atlanta, GA: Peachtree.
Renshaw-Joslin, K. (1994). *Positive Parenting From A to Z.* New York: Ballantine Publishing Group.

Phobias

Anthony, M. M., Craske, M. G., and Barlow, D. H. (1995). *Mastering Your Special Phobia.* San Antonio, TX: Harcourt Brace.
Bourne, Edmund. (1998). *Overcoming Specific Phobia.* Oakland, CA: New Harbinger.
Colas, E. (1988). *Scenes from the Life of an Obsessive-Compulsive.* New York: Pocket.
Foa, E. B., and Kozak, M. J. (1997). *Mastery of Obsessive-Compulsive Disorder: A Cognitive-Behavioral Approach.* San Antonio, TX: Harcourt Brace.
Gravitz, H. L. (1998). *New Help for the Family.* Santa Barbara, CA: New Visions.
Robinson, B.E. (2000). *Don't Let Your Mind Stunt Your Growth.* Oakland, CA: New Harbinger.
Schwartz, J. M., and Bigette, B. (1996). *Brain Lock.* New York: HarperCollins.
Zuercher-White, E. (1997). *Taming Panic Disorder and Agoraphobia.* Oakland, CA: New Harbinger.

Post-traumatic Stress Disorder

Alexander, D. W. (1999). *Children Changed by Trauma: A Healing Guide.* Oakland, CA: New Harbinger.
Matsakis, A. (1998). *Trust After Trauma.* Oakland, CA: New Harbinger.
Matsakis, A. (1999). *I Can't Get Over It.* Oakland, CA: New Harbinger.
Matsakis, A. (1999). *Survivor Guilt.* Oakland, CA: New Harbinger.
Matsakis, A. (2003). *The Rape Recovery Handbook.* Oakland, CA: New Harbinger.
O'Hanlon, W. H., and Bertolino, B. (2000). *Even from a Broken Web: Brief, Respectful, Solution-Oriented Therapy For Sexual Abuse and Trauma.* New York: Wiley.

Rothblum, B. O., and Foa, E. B. (2000). *Reclaiming Your Life After Rape*. San Antonio, TX: Harcourt Brace.

Smyth, Larry. (1998). *Overcoming Post-traumatic Stress Disorder*. Oakland, CA: New Harbinger.

Williams, Mary Beth, and Podula, Soili. (2002). *The PTSD Workbook*. Oakland, CA: New Harbinger.

Problem-Solving

Zimmerman, T. (1995). *The Problem Solving Workbook*. Plainview, NY: Childsswork/Childsplay.

Schizophrenia

Muesler, K., and Gingerich, L. (1994). *Coping with Schizophrenia*. Oakland, CA: New Harbinger.

School Issues

Davis, L., and Sirotowitz, S. (1996). *Study Strategies Made Easy: A Practical Plan for School Success*. Plantation, FL: Specialty.

Hernes-Silverman, S. (1998). *13 Steps to Better Grades*. Plainview, NY: Childswork/Childsplay.

McCutcheon, R. (1998). *Get Off My Brain*. Minneapolis, MN: Free Spirit.

Self-Esteem

Benson, P.L., Espeland, P., and Galbraith, J. (1998). *What Teens Need to Succeed: Proven, Practical Ways to Shape Your Own Future*. Minneapolis, MN: Free Spirit Publishing.

Clark, J. I. (1978). *Self-Esteem: A Family Affair*. Center City, MN: Hazelden.

Covey, S. (1998). *The 7 Habits Of Highly Effective Teens* (book and journal). New York: Simon & Schuster.

Gordon, S. (1981). *The Teenage Survival Book*. New York: Three Rivers.

Loomans, D., and Loomans, J. (1994). *Full Esteem Ahead: 100 Ways to Build Self-Esteem in Children and Adults*. Tiburon, CA: H. J. Kramer.

McDermott, D., and Snyder, C. R. (1999). *Making Hope Happen: A Workbook for Turning Possibilities Into Reality*. Oakland, CA: New Harbinger.

McKay, M., and Fanning, P. (1987). *Self-Esteem*. NY: MJF Books.

McKay, M., Fanning, P., Honeychurch, C., and Sutker, C. (1999). *The Self-Esteem Companion*. Oakland, CA: New Harbinger.

Mosatche, H. S., and Unger, K. (2000). *Too Old for This, Too Young for That*. Minneapolis, MN: Free Spirit.

O'Hanlon, W. H. (2000). *Do One Thing Different and Other Uncommonly Sensible Solutions to Life's Problems*. New York: HarperCollins.

Schraldi, Glenn R. (2001). *The Self-Esteem Workbook*. Oakland, CA: New Harbinger.

Zack, L. R. (1995). *Building Self-Esteem Through the Museum of I: 25 Original Projects That Explore and Celebrate the Self*. Minneapolis, MN: Free Spirit.

Sexual Abuse

Bean, B., and Bennett, S. (1997). *The Me Nobody Knows*. San Francisco, CA: Jossey-Bass.

Carter, William L. (2002). *It Happened To Me*. Oakland, CA: New Harbinger.

Copeland, M. E. (2000). *Healing the Trauma of Abuse: A Woman's Workbook*. Oakland, CA: New Harbinger.

Katherine, A. (1991). *Boundaries: Where You End and I Begin*. New York: Simon & Schuster.

Loiselle, M. B., and Wright, L. (1997). *Back On Track: Boys Dealing With Sexual Abuse*. Brandon, VT: Safer Society.

Loiselle, M. B., and Wright, L. (1997). *Shining Through: Pulling It Together After Sexual Abuse*. Brandon, VT: Safer Society.

Matsakis, A. (1992). *I Can't Get Over It*. Oakland, CA: New Harbinger.

Stark, Evan, and Holly, Marsha. (1999). *Everything You Need to Know About Sexual Abuse*. New York: Rosen.

Sexuality

Madaras, L. (1993). *My Body, My Self for Girls*. New York: New Market.

Madaras, L. (1995). *My Body, My Self for Boys*. New York: New Market.

Sbraga, Tamara Penix, and O'Donohue, William T. (2004). *The Sex Addiction Workbook*. Oakland, CA: New Harbinger.

Shuker-Haines, F. (1992). *Everything You Ever Wanted To Know About Teen Pregnancy*. New York: Rosen.

Sleep Disorders

Ancoli-Israel, S. (1996). *All I Want is a Good Night's Sleep*. St. Louis, MO: Mosby Year Book.

Ferber, R. (1985). *Solve Your Child's Sleep Problems*. New York: Simon & Schuster.

Stress Management

Ayer, E. H. (1994). *Everything You Need to Know About Stress*. New York: Rosen.

Childre, Doc, and Rozman, Deborah. (2005). *Transforming Stress*. Oakland, CA: New Harbinger.

Copeland, M. E. (1998). *The Worry Control Workbook*. Oakland, CA: New Harbinger.

Davis, M., Robins-Eshelman, E., and McKay, M. (2000). *The Relaxation and Stress Reduction Workbook*. Oakland, CA: New Harbinger.

Hipp, E. (1995). *Fighting Invisible Tigers: A Stress Management Guide for Teens*. Minneapolis, MN: Free Spirit.

Matsakis, A. (1998). *Trust After Trauma: A Guide to Relationships for Survivors and Those Who Love Them*. Oakland, CA: New Harbinger.

Rosenbloom, D., and Williams, M. B. (1999). *Life After Trauma: A Workbook for Healing*. New York: Guilford.

Scott-Cameron, N. (2000). *Bad Hair Day?* New York: HarperCollins.

Substance Abuse

Bradshaw, J. (1988). *Healing the Shame That Binds You*. Deerfield Beach, FL: Health.

Fanning, P., and O'Neill, J. T. (1996) *The Addiction Workbook*. Oakland, CA: New Harbinger.

Johnson Institute. (2000). *How to Get Sober and Stay Sober: Steps 1 Through 5*. CenterCity, MN: Hazelden.

Tighe, A. A. (1999). *Stop the Chaos: How to Get Control of Your Life by Beating Alcohol and Drugs*. Center City, MN: Hazelden.

Suicide

Gordon, S. (1994). *When Living Hurts: For Teenagers and Young Adults*. New York: Union of American Hebrew Congregations.

Schleifer, J. (1988). *Everything You Need to Know About Teen Suicide*. New York: Rosen.

VIDEOTAPES

Building Your Child's Self-Esteem. Oakland, CA: New Harbinger.
Self-Esteem Workout for Teenage Girls. Calhoun, KY: Nimco.

SELF-HELP BOOKS FOR PARENTS AND FAMILIES

Abuse

Hagan, K., and Case, T. (1988). *When Your Child Has Been Molested.* New York: Harper & Row.

Alcohol

Althauser, D. (1998). *You Can Free Yourself From Alcohol and Drugs.* Oakland, CA: New Harbinger.
Fanning, P., and O'Neill, J. (1996). *The Addiction Workbook.* Oakland, CA: New Harbinger.
O'Neill, J. and O'Neill, P. (1992). *Concerned Intervention.* Oakland, CA: New Harbinger.
Tanner, L. (1996). *The Mother's Survival Guide to Recovery.* Oakland, CA: New Harbinger.

Anger

Eastman, M. (1994). *Taming the Dragon in Your Child.* New York: Wiley.
McKay, M., and Fanning, P. (1996). *When Anger Hurts Your Kids.* Oakland, CA: New Harbinger.
Namka, L. (1995). *The Mad Family Gets Their Mads Out.* Tucson, AZ: Talk, Trust and Feel Therapeutics.

Anxiety

Bassete, L. (1995). *From Panic to Power.* New York: HarperCollins.
Bodger, C. (1999). *Smart Guide to Relieving Stress.* New York: Wiley.
Bourne, E. J. (1997). *The Anxiety and Phobia Workbook.* 2nd ed. Oakland, CA: New Harbinger.
Bourne, E. J. (1998). *Healing Fear.* Oakland, CA: New Harbinger.
Copeland, M. E. (1998). *The Worry Control Workshop.* Oakland, CA: New Harbinger.

Dacey, J. S., and Fiore, L. B. (2000). *Your Anxious Child: How Parents and Teachers Can Relieve Anxiety In Children*. San Francisco, CA: Jossey-Bass.

Ellis, A. (1998). *How to Control Your Anxiety Before It Controls You*. Secaucus, NJ: Carol Publishing Group.

Gerzon, R. (1997). *Finding Serenity in the Age of Anxiety*. New York: Bantam.

Jacobson, E. (1978). *You Must Relax*. New York: McGraw-Hill.

Jeffers, S. (1988). *Feel the Fear and Do It Anyway*. New York: Fawcett Columbine.

Johnson, S. (1998). *Who Moved My Cheese?* New York: Putnam.

Kopp, S. (1988). *Raise Your Right Hand Against Fear, Extend the Other One in Compassion*. Minneapolis, MN: Compocare.

Wetherill, M. J. (2000). *The Eye of the Storm: Discovering Inner Calm Amidst Inner Pressure*. Holbrook, MA: Adams.

Wilson, R. R. (1996). *Don't Panic: Taking Control of Anxiety Attacks*. New York: HarperCollins.

Ziegler, R. G., and Ziegler, P. (1992). *Homemade Books to Help Kids Cope*. New York: Magination Press.

Attention Deficit Disorder

Barkley, R. A. (2000). *Taking Charge of ADHD*. New York: Guilford.

Christ, J. J. (1997). *ADHD—A Teenager's Guide*. Plainview, NY: Childswork/Childsplay.

Hartman, T. (1995). *Healing ADD: Simple Exercises That Will Change Your Daily Life*. Grass Valley, CA: Underwood.

Hartman, T. (1995). *Success Stories: A Guide to Fulfillment with Attention Deficit Disorder*. Grass Valley, CA: Underwood.

Parker, H. C. (1999). *The ADD Hyperactivity Workbook*. New York: Specialty Press.

Quinn, P. O., and Stern, J. M. (1991). *Putting On the Brakes: Young People's Guide to Understanding ADHD*. New York: Magination Press.

Quinn, P. O., and Stern, J. M. (2000). *The Best of "Brakes": An Activity Book for Kids With ADD*. Washington, DC: Magination Press.

Rief, S. (1998). *The ADD/ADHD Checklist*. Paramus, NJ: Prentice Hall.

Roberts, S., and Jansen, G. J. (1997). *Living with ADD*. Oakland, CA: New Harbinger.

Sears, W., and Thompson, L. (1998). *The ADD Book*. Boston, MA: Little Brown.

Weiner, E. (1999). *Taking ADD to School*. Valley Park, MO: Jayjo.

Behavior Disorders

Bloomquist, M. L. (1996). *Skills Training for Children with Behavior Disorders*. New York: Guilford.
Divinyi, J. (1997). *Good Kids, Difficult Behavior*. Peachtree, CA: Wellness Connection.
Greene, R. W. (1998). *The Explosive Child*. New York: HarperCollins.
Haag, K., Kasper, K., Dziak-Kryst, E., and Young, E. (1982). *Common Solutions for the Uncommon Child*. Danville, IL: Interstate.
Levy, R., and O'Hanlon, W. H. (2001). *Try and Make Me: A Revolutionary Program for Raising Your Defiant Child Without Losing Your Cool*. Emmans, PA: Rosedale.
Tobin, L. *6 Essentials of Discipline*. Audiotape. Duluth, MN: Whole Person Associates.

Bereavement

Caplan, S., and Lang, G. (1998). *Grief's Courageous Journey*. Oakland, CA: New Harbinger.
Fitzgerald, H. (1994). *The Mourning Handbook*. New York: Simon & Schuster.
Jarrat, C. (1994). *Helping Children Cope with Separation and Loss*. Boston, MA: Harvard Common.
Jozefowski, J. (1999). *The Phoenix Phenomenon: Rising From the Ashes of Grief*. Northvale, NJ: Jason Aronson.
Viorst, J. (1986). *Necessary Losses*. New York: Simon & Schuster.
Walsh, F., and McGoldrick, M. (eds) (2004). *Living Beyond Loss: Death in the Family*. Second edition. New York, NY: W. W. Norton & Company.

Bipolar Disorder

Fast, Julie A., and John D. Preton. (2003). *Loving Someone With Bipolar Disorder*. Oakland, CA: New Harbinger.
Lynn, G. T. (2000). *Survival Strategies for Parenting Children with Bipolar Disorder*. Grass Valley, CA: Underwood.

Borderline Personality Disorder

Manson, P. T., and Kreger, R. (1998). *Stop Walking on Eggshells*. Oakland, CA: New Harbinger.

Santoro, J., and Cohen, R. (1997). *The Angry Heart*. Oakland, CA: New Harbinger.

Change

O'Hanlon, W. H. (2000). *Do One Thing Different: Ten Simple Ways to Change Your Life*. New York: HarperCollins.

Defiant Child

Barkley, R. A. (1997). *Managing the Defiant Child: A Guide to Parent Training*. New York: Guilford.

Levy, R., and O'Hanlon, W. H. (2001). *Try and Make Me: A Revolutionary Program for Raising Your Defiant Child Without Losing Your Cool*. Emmaus, PA: Rodale.

Depression/Suicide

Burns, D. (1999). *Feeling Good*. New York: Avon.

Copeland, M. E. (1992). *The Depression Workbook: A Guide for Living with Depression and Manic Depression*. Oakland, CA: New Harbinger.

Dacey, J. S., and Fiore, L. B. (2000). *Your Anxious Child: How Parents and Teachers Can Relieve Anxiety in Children*. San Francisco, CA: Jossey-Bass.

Williams, K. (1995). *A Parent's Guide for Suicidal and Depressed Teens: Help for Recognizing if a Child is in Crisis and What to Do About It*. Center City, MN: Hazelden.

Difficult Child

Greene, R. W. (1998). *The Explosive Child*. New York: HarperCollins.

Greenspan, S. I. (1995). *The Challenging Child*. Reading, MA: Addison-Wesley.

Divorce

Ackerman, M. J. (1996). *Does Wednesday Mean Mom's House or Dad's? Parenting Together While Living Apart*. New York: Wiley.

Ahrons, C. (1995). *The Good Divorce: Keeping Your Family Together When Your Marriage Comes Apart*. New York: HarperCollins.
Garrity, C. B., and Baris, M. A. (1997). *Caught in the Middle*. San Francisco, CA: Jossey-Bass.
Hickey, E., and Dalton, E. (1994). *Healing Hearts: Helping Children and Adults Recover from Divorce*. Carson City, NV: Gold Leaf.
Johnson, J. R., Breunig, K., Garrity, C., and Baris, M. (1997). *Through the Eyes of Children: Healing Stories for Children of Divorce*. New York: Free Press.
Neuman, M. G., and Romanowski, P. (1998). *Helping Your Kids Cope With Divorce*. New York: Ballantine Publishing Group.
Prokop, M. (1986). *Divorce Happens to the Nicest Kids*. Warren, OH: Alegra House.

Eating Disorders

Apple, R. F., and Agras, W. S. (1977). *Overcoming Eating Disorders: A Cognitive-Behavioral Treatment for Bulimia Nervosa and Binge-Eating Disorders*. San Antonio, TX: Harcourt Brace.
Danowski, D., and Lazaro, P. (2000). *Why Can't I Stop Eating?* Center City, MN: Hazelden.
Ebbett, J. (1994). *The Eating Illness Workbook*. Center City, MN: Hazelden.
Edell, D. (1999). *Eat, Drink and Be Merry*. New York: HarperCollins.
Nash, J. D. (1999). *Binge No More*. Oakland, CA: New Harbinger.
Natenshon, A. (1999. *When Your Child Has an Eating Disorder*. San Francisco, CA: Jossey-Bass.
Sandbek, T. (1993). *The Deadly Diet*. Oakland, CA: New Harbinger.
Schroder, C. R. (1992). *Fat is Not a Four-Letter Word*. New York: Chronemed.
Sherman, R. T., and Thompson, R. T. (1996). *Bulimia: A Guide for Family and Friends*. San Francisco, CA: Jossey-Bass.
Zerbe, K. J. (1993). *The Body Betrayed: Eating Disorders and Their Treatment*. Washington, DC: American Psychiatric.

Hypnosis/Visualization

Allen, J. S., and Klein, R. J. (1996). *Ready...Set...R.E.L.A.X*. Watertown, WI: Inner Coaching.
Austin, V. (1998). *Free Yourself from Fear: Self-Hypnosis for Anxiety, Panic Attacks, and Phobias*. London: HarperCollins.
Davis, M., Eshelman, E., and McKay, M. (1988) *The Relaxation and Stress Reduction Workbook*. Oakland, CA: New Harbinger.

Epstein, G. (1987). *Healing Visualizations: Creating Health Through Imagery*. New York: Bantam.

Fisher, S., and Ellison, J. (1991). *Discovering the Power of Self-Hypnosis: A New Approach for Enabling Change and Promoting Healing*. San Antonio, TX: HarperCollins.

Gawain, S. (1982). *Creative Visualization*. New York: Bantam.

Learning Skills

Hernes-Silverman, S. (1998). *13 Steps to Better Gra*des. Plainview, NY: Childswork/Childsplay.

Radencich, M. C. (1988). *How to Help Your Child with Homework*. Minneapolis, MN: Free Spirit.

Medical

Caufield, J., Hansen, M.V., Aubry, P., and Mitchell, N. M. (1996). *Chicken Soup For the Surviving Soul*. FL: Health.

Doka, K. J. (1998). *Living with Life-Threatening Illness: A Guide for Patients, Their Families, and Caregivers*. San Francisco, CA: Jossey-Bass.

Kabat-Zinn, J. (1990). *Full Catastrophe Living: Using the Wisdom of Your Body and Mind to Face Stress, Pain, and Illness*. New York: Dell.

Pitzele, S. K. (2000). *Finding the Joy in Today*. Center City, MN: Hazelden.

Register, C. (2000). *Living with Chronic Illness*. Center City, MN: Hazelden.

Wilens, T. E. (1999). *Straight Talk About Psychiatric Medications for Kids*. New York: Guilford.

Nurturing

Bradshaw, J. (1990). *Homecoming: Reclaiming and Championing your Inner Child*. New York: Bantam Books.

Domar, A., and Dreher, H. (2000). *Self-Nurture: Learning to Care for Yourself as Effectively as You Care for Everyone Else*. New York: Viking-Penguin.

Ford, A. (1994). *Wonderful Ways to Love a Child*. Berkeley, CA: Conari.

Obsessive-Compulsive Disorder

Barlow, D. H., and Craske, M. G. (1994). *Mastery of Your Anxiety and Panic Volume II*. Albany, NY: Graywind.

Foa, E. B., and Wilson, R. (1991). *Stop Obsessing: How to Overcome Your Obsessions and Compulsions*. New York: Bantam.

Hyman, B. M., and White, K. (1990). *The OCD Workbook*. Oakland, CA: New Harbinger.

Roy, C. (2000). *Obsessive-Compulsive Disorder*. Center City, MN: Hazelden.

Parenting

Borba, M. (1999). *Parents Do Make a Difference: How to Raise Kids with Solid Character, Strong Minds, and Caring Hearts*. San Francisco, CA: Jossey-Bass.

Borcherdt, B. (1996). *Making Families Work and What to Do When They Don't*. New York: Haworth.

Briesmeister, J. M., and Schaefer, C. E. (1998). *Handbook of Parent Training*. New York: Wiley.

Butler, B., and Sussman, M. B. (1989). *Museum Visits and Activities for Family Life Enrichment*. New York: Haworth.

Clarke, J. I. (1999). *Time-In*. Seattle, WA: Parenting.

Covey, S. R. (1997). *The 7 Habits of Highly Effective Families*. New York: Golden Books.

Crary, E. (1993). *Without Spanking or Spoiling*. Seattle, WA: Parenting.

Crites-Price, S. (1996). *The Working Parents Help Book*. Princeton, NJ: Petersons.

Edwards, C. D. (1999). *How to Handle a Hard-To-Handle Kid: A Parent's Guide to Understanding and Changing Problem Behaviors*. Minneapolis, MN: FreeSpirit.

Faber, A. (1999). *How to Talk So Kids Will Listen, and Listen So Kids Will Talk*. New York: Avon.

Forehand, R. L. (1996). *Parenting the Strong-Willed Child*. Chicago, IL: Contemporary Books.

Glennon, W. (1995). *Fathering*. Berkeley, CA: Conari.

Greenspan, S. I. (1995). *The Challenging Child*. Reading, MA: Addison-Wesley.

Haag, F. L., Bates-Ames, L., and Baker, S. M. (1955). *Child Behavior*. New York: Harper.

Koplewicz, H. S. (1996). *It's Nobody's Fault*. New York: Times Books.

Metcalf, L. (1997). *Parenting Toward Solutions: How Parents Can Use Skills They Already Have to Raise Responsible, Loving Kids*. Englewood Cliffs, NJ: PrenticeHall.

Nelson, J. (1993). *Positive Discipline A–Z*. Rocklin, CA: Prima.
Newman, S. (1993). *Little Things Long Remembered*. New York: Crown.
Nowicki, S., and Duke, M. P. (1992). *Helping The Child Who Doesn't Fit In*. Atlanta, GA: Peachtree Publishers.
Phalen, T. (1991). *Surviving Your Adolescents*. Glen Ellyn, IL: Child Management.
Renshaw-Joslin, K. (1994). *Positive Parenting From A to Z*. New York: Ballantine Publishing Group.
Schaefer, C. E. (1994). *How to Help Children with Common Problems*. Northvale, NJ: Jason Aronson.
Shapiro, L. E. (2000). *An Ounce of Prevention: How Parents Can Stop Childhood Behavioral and Emotional Problems Before They Start*. New York: HarperCollins.
Tobin, L. (2000). *Parenting on the Go*. Duluth, MN: Whole Person.
Whitham, C. (1994). *The Answer Is No*. Los Angeles, CA: Perspective.
Willens, T. (1999). *Straight Talk About Psychiatric Medications for Kids*. New York: Guilford.
Wilmes, D. L. (1995). *Parenting for Prevention*. Center City, MN: Hazelden/Johnson Institute.
Windell, J. (1994). *8 Weeks to a Well-Behaved Child*. New York: Macmillan.

Personality Disorders

Basco, M. R. (1999). *Never Good Enough: How to Use Perfectionism to Your Advantage Without Letting It Ruin Your Life*. New York: Simon & Schuster.
Kreisman, J. J., and Straus, H. (1999). *I Hate You, Don't Leave Me*. New York: HarperCollins.
Linehan, M. M. (1993). *Skills Training Manual for Treating Borderline Personality Disorders*. New York: Guilford.
Masterson, J. F. (1988). *The Search for the Real Self: Unmasking the Personality Disorder of Our Age*. New York: Free Press.

Phobias

Anthony, M. M., Craske, M. G., and Barlow, D. H. (1995). *Mastering Your Special Phobia*. San Antonio, TX: Harcourt Brace.
Colas, E. (1988). *Scenes from the Life of an Obsessive-Compulsive*. New York: Pocket.
Foa, E. B., and Kozak, M. J. (1997). *Mastery of Obsessive-Compulsive Disorder: A Cognitive-Behavioral Approach*. San Antonio, TX: Harcourt Brace.

Gravitz, H. L. (1998). *New Help for the Family*. Santa Barbara, CA: New Visions.

Robinson, B. E. (2000). *Don't Let Your Mind Stunt Your Growth*. Oakland, CA: New Harbinger.

Schwartz, J. M., and Bigette, B. (1996). *Brain Lock*. New York: HarperCollins.

Zuercher-White, E. (1997). *Taming Panic Disorder and Agoraphobia*. Oakland, CA: New Harbinger.

Post-traumatic Stress Disorder

Alexander, D. W. (1999). *Children Changed by Trauma: A Healing Guide*. Oakland, CA: New Harbinger.

Matsakis, A. (1998). *Trust After Trauma*. Oakland, CA: New Harbinger.

Matsakis, A. (1999). *I Can't Get Over It*. Oakland, CA: New Harbinger.

Matsakis, A. (1999). *Survivor Guilt*. Oakland, CA: New Harbinger.

O'Hanlon, W. H., and Bertolino, B. (2000). *Even from a Broken Web: Brief, Respectful, Solution-Oriented Therapy for Sexual Abuse and Trauma*. New York: Wiley.

Rothblum, B. O., and Foa, E. B. (2000). *Reclaiming Your Life After Rape*. San Antonio, TX: Harcourt Brace.

Relational Problems

Asherson, S. (1992). *Wrestling with Love: How Men Struggle with Intimacy with Women, Children, Parents, and Each Other*. New York: Fawcett.

Basoff, E. S. (1992). *Mothering Ourselves: Help and Healing for Adult Daughters*. New York: Plume Books.

Beck, A. (1988). *Love is Never Enough: How Couples Can Overcome Misunderstandings and Resolve Relationship Problems Through Cognitive Therapy*. New York: Harper Perennial.

Davis, D. (1985). *Something is Wrong at My House*. Seattle, WA: Parenting Press.

Gookin, S. H. (1995). *Parenting for Dummies*. New York: IDG.

Heitler, S. (1997). *The Power of Two*. Oakland, CA: New Harbinger.

Hernes-Silverman, S. (1998). *13 Steps to Help Families Stop Fighting and Solve Problems Peacefully*. Plainview, NY: Childswork/Childsplay.

Lassen, M. K. (2000). *Why Are We Still Fighting?* Oakland, CA: New Harbinger.

Markman, H., Stanley, S., and Blumberg, S. (1995). *Fighting for Your Marriage*. San Francisco, CA: Jossey-Bass.

Schizophrenia

Muesler, K., and Gingerich, L. (1994). *Coping with Schizophrenia*. Oakland, CA: New Harbinger.

School Problems

Caissy, G. A. (1994). *Early Adolescence*. New York: Insight.
Fraiberg, S. H. (1996). *The Magic Years: Understanding and Healing the Problems of Early Childhood*. New York: IDG.
Gookin, S. H. (1995). *Parenting for Dummies*. New York: IDG.
Kindlon, D., and Thompson, M. (1999). *Raising Cain, Protecting the Emotional Life of Boys*. New York: Ballantine Publishing Group.
Martin, M., and Waltman-Greenwork, C. (1995). *Solve Your Child's School Related-Problems*. New York: HarperCollins.
Ramirez-Basco, M. (1999). *Never Good Enough*. New York: Free Press.

Self-Esteem

Clarke, J. I. (1978). *Self-Esteem: A Family Affair*. Center City, MN: Hazelden.
Loomans, D., and Loomans, J. (1994). *Full Esteem Ahead: 100 Ways to Build Self-Esteem in Children & Adults*. Tiburon, CA: H. J. Kramer.
McKay, M., and Fanning. P. (1987). *Self-Esteem*. New York: MJF Books.
Sorensen, M. J. (1998). *Breaking the Chain of Low Self-Esteem*. Sherwood, OR: Wolf.

Sexual Abuse

Anonymous. (1987). *Hope and Recovery: A 12-Step Guide for Healing from Compulsive Sexual Behavior*. Minneapolis, MN: Compcare.
Bolton, F. G., Morris, L. A., and MacEachron, A. E. (1984). *Males at Risk: The Other Side of Sexual Abuse*. Newbury Park, CA: SAGE.
Katherine, A. (1991). *Boundaries: Where You End and I Begin*. New York: Simon & Schuster.

Sleep

Ancoli, I. S. (1996). *All I Want is a Good Night's Sleep*. St. Louis, MO: Mosby.

Ferber, R. (1985). *Solve Your Child's Sleep Problems*. New York: Simon & Schuster.

Huntley, R. (1991). *The Sleep Book for Tired Parents*. Seattle, WA: Parenting.

Ilg, F., Ames, L., and Baker, S. (1981). *Child Behavior: Specific Advice on Problems of Child Behavior*. New York: Harper & Row.

Masurel, C., and Henry, M. H. (1994). *Good Night!* San Francisco, CA: Chronicle.

Waddell, M., and Firth, B. (1988). *Can't You Sleep, Little Bear?* Cambridge, MA: Candlewick.

Substance Abuse

Schaefer, D. (1987). *Choices and Consequences: What to Do When a Teenager Uses Alcohol/Drugs*. Center City, MN: Hazelden/Johnson Institute.

Washton, A. (1990). *Cocaine Recovery Workbooks*. Center City, MN: Hazelden.

Violence

Fall, K. A., Howard, S., and Ford, J. E. (1999). *Alternative to Domestic Violence*. Philadelphia, PA: Accelerated Development.

Garbino, J. (1997). *Lost Boys: Why Our Sons Turn Violent and How We Can Save Them*. Boystown, NE: Boys Town Press.

Karres, E. S. (2001). *Violence-Proof Your Kids Now*. Boystown, NE: Boys Town Press.

VIDEOTAPES

Hazelden Video. (1993). *Quitting Cocaine and Staying Quit*. Center City, MN: Hazelden.

Hazelden Video. (1998). *Alcohol*. Center City, MN: Hazelden.

Hazelden Video. (1998). *Methamphetamine*. Center City, MN: Hazelden.

Hazelden Video. (1999). *Cross-Addiction*. Center City, MN: Hazelden.

Hazelden Video. (2000). *The Voice of Addiction*. Center City, MN: Hazelden.

AUDIOTAPES

Anxiety and Stress

Sanders, Harriett, speaker. (1993). *Body Relaxed, Mind at Ease.* Oakland, CA: New Harbinger.

Sanders, Harriett, speaker. (1995). *Peaceful Body, Quiet Mind.* Oakland, CA: New Harbinger.

Communication Skills

New Harbinger. (1987). *Assertiveness Training.* Oakland, CA: New Harbinger Video.

New Harbinger. (1987). *Effective Self-Expression.* Oakland, CA: New Harbinger Video.

New Harbinger. (1987). *Making Contact.* Oakland, CA: New Harbinger Video.

New Harbinger. (1988) *Becoming a Good Listener.* Oakland, CA: New Harbinger Video.

New Harbinger. (1994). *Expressing Feelings.* Oakland, CA: New Harbinger Video.

Couples

Heitler, Susan, narrator. (1994). *Conflict Resolution for Couples.* Oakland, CA: New Harbinger Video.

Depression

Copeland, Mary Ellen, narrator. (1995). *Living with Depression and Manic Depression.* Oakland, CA: New Harbinger.

Preston, John, narrator. (1993). *Depression and Anxiety Management.* Oakland, CA: New Harbinger.

General

Fanning, Patrick, author. Landis, Jerry, narrator. (1992). *Healing Injuries.* Oakland, CA: New Harbinger Video.

Fanning, Patrick, author. Landis, Jerry, narrator. (1992). *Stress Reduction.* Oakland, CA: New Harbinger Video.

McKay, Matthew, Davis, Martha, and Fanning, Patrick, authors. (1987). *Combating Distorted Thinking*. Oakland, CA: New Harbinger.
McKay, Matthew, Davis, Martha, and Fanning, Patrick, authors. (1987). *Covert Modeling and Covert Reinforcement*. Oakland, CA: New Harbinger.
McKay, Matthew, Davis, Martha, and Fanning, Patrick, authors. (1987). *Pain Control and Healing*. Oakland, CA: New Harbinger.
McKay, Matthew, Davis, Martha, and Fanning, Patrick, authors. (1987). *Systemic Desensitization and Visualizing Goals*. Oakland, CA: New Harbinger.
McKay, Matthew, Davis, Martha, and Fanning, Patrick, authors. (1987). *Thought Stopping*. Oakland, CA: New Harbinger.
McKay, Matthew, and Fanning, Peter, authors. (1997). *Calm Your Mind*. Oakland, CA: New Harbinger.
McKay, Matthew, and Fanning, Peter, authors. (1997). *Improve Your Mood*. Oakland, CA: New Harbinger.
McKay, Matthew, and Fanning, Peter, authors. (1997). *Refresh Your Spirit*. Oakland, CA: New Harbinger.
McKay Matthew, and Fanning, Peter, authors. (1997). *Relax Your Body*. Oakland, CA: New Harbinger.
McKay, Matthew, and Fanning, Peter, authors. (1997). *Relieve Your Worry*. Oakland, CA: New Harbinger.

Hypnosis

Hadley, Josie, and Staudacher, Carol, authors. (1987). *Hypnosis for Coping Before And After Surgery*. Oakland, CA: New Harbinger.
Hadley, Josie, and Staudacher, Carol, authors. (1987). *Hypnosis for Improved Learning*. Oakland, CA: New Harbinger.
Hadley, Josie, and Staudacher, Carol, authors. (1987). *Hypnosis for Motivating Change and Problem Solving*. Oakland, CA: New Harbinger.
Hadley, Josie, and Staudacher, Carol, authors. (1987). *Hypnosis for Non-Smoking*. Oakland, CA: New Harbinger.
Hadley, Josie, and Staudacher, Carol, authors. (1987). *Hypnosis for Overcoming Depression*. Oakland, CA: New Harbinger.
Hadley, Josie, and Staudacher, Carol, authors. (1987). *Self-Hypnosis*. Oakland, CA: New Harbinger.
Hadley, Josie, and Staudacher, Carol, authors. (1987). *Hypnosis for Sleep*. Oakland, CA: New Harbinger.
Hadley, Josie, and Staudacher, Carol, authors. (1987). *Hypnosis to End Anxiety and Panic Attacks*. Oakland, CA: New Harbinger.
Hadley, Josie, and Staudacher, Carol, authors. (1987). *Hypnosis for Weight Control*. Oakland, CA: New Harbinger.

18
SELF-HELP GROUPS AND 800 NUMBERS

ALCOHOL

Al-Anon and Alateen: 1-898-425-2666
Alcohol and Drug Abuse Testing Center: 1-900-942-3784
American Council on Alcohol Addiction: 1-800-527-5344
National Clearinghouse for Alcohol and Drug Information:
    1-800-729-6686
National Council on Alcohol Addiction: 1-800-622-2255
National Council on Alcoholism and Drug Dependence:
    1-800-475-HOPE

CHILD ABUSE

If a child is in immediate danger or risk, Call: 1-800-THE-LOST
National Child Abuse Hotline: 1-800-25-ABUSE

DEPRESSION

DAD (Depression After Delivery): 1-800-944-4773
National Depressive And Manic Depressive Association:
    1-800-826-2632
National Foundation For Depressive Illness: 1-800-926-3632

DIVORCE

Association For Children For Enforcement Of Support (ACES): 800-537-7072
Children's Rights Council: 202-547-6227
Joint Custody Association: 310-475-6962
North American Conference of Separated and Divorced Catholics: 401-943-7903
Rainbows: 708-310-1880

DRUG ABUSE

Marijuana Anonymous: 1-800-766-6779
Narcotics Anonymous: 1-888-994-9484
National Cocaine Hotline: 1-800-COCAINE
National Council on Alcoholism and Drug Dependence Inc.: 1-800-622-2255
National Parents Resource Institute For Drug Education (PRIDE): 1-800-668-9277
National Substance Abuse Hotline: 1-800-Drug-Help
Office of Substance Abuse Prevention: 1-900-638-2045
Schick Shadel Hospital: 1-800-Craving (1-800-272-9464)
Teen Help Adolescent Resources: 1-800-637-0701

MENTAL HEALTH

National Alliance for the Mentally Ill: 1-800-950-NANG (6264)

SEXUAL ADDICTION

S-Anon Family Groups: 818-990-6910
Sex Addicts Anonymous (SAA): 713-869-4902
Sexaholics Anonymous (SA): 615-331-6230
Sex and Love Addicts Anonymous (SLAA): 617-332-1845
Sexual Compulsives Anonymous (SCA): West Coast: 310-859-5585; East Coast: 212-439-1123

19
ONLINE RESOURCES

(From *How To Use Computers and Cyberspace in the Clinical Practice of Psychotherapy*. Copyright ©1999 by Jason Aronson and used with permission.)

GENERAL

Child welfare home page
   http://www.childwelfare.com/
Internet mental health
   http://www.mentalhealth.com/
Internet mental health
   http://www.openmarket.com
Mental health net
   http://www.cmhc.com/
NIMH home page
   http://www.nimh.nih.gov/
Pharmaceutical information network home page
   http://pharminfo.com
Psychology organizations on the web
   http://www.wesleyan.edu/spn/psych.htm
Psychscapes worldwide
   http://www.mental-health.com
Psyjourn, Inc.
   http://www.psyjourn.com
Search page for articles in psychology and social science journals
   http://www.shef.ac.uk/~psych/journals/jsearch.html
Social work and social services websites
   http://www.gwbweb.wustl.edu/websites.html

The shrink tank bbs website
   http://www.shrinktank.com/testing.htm
The social statistics briefing room
   http://www.whitehouse.gov/fsbr/ssbr.html

PROFESSIONAL ORGANIZATIONS

American Academy of Child and Adolescent Psychiatry home page
   http://www.aacap.org/web/aacap/
American Psychiatric Association online
   http://www.paych.org/
American Psychoanalytic Association online
   http://apsa.org/
American Psychological Association psychnet
   http://www.apa.org
California Coalition for Ethical Mental Health Care
   http://www.pw1.netcom/~mastery/coalitionMain.html
Clinical Social Work Federation
   http://www.cswf.org
NASW online
   http://www.socialworkers.org/main.htm

SELF-HELP AND SUPPORT GROUP RESOURCES

Adult Children of Alcoholics
   http://www.adultchildren.org
Alateen And Al-Anon Family Groups
   http://www.al-anon.org or http://www.alateen.org
Alcoholics Anonymous
   http://www.alcoholics-anonymous.org
American Council on Alcoholism
   http://www.aca-usa.org
Emotional support on the Internet
   http://www.cix.co.uk/~net-sercvices/care
Mental health net-self-help questionnaires
   http://www.cmhc.com/guide/quizes.htm
Mental health net-self-help resources index
   http://www.cmhc.com/selfhelp.htm
Support-group.com
   http://support-group.com

SPECIFIC DISORDERS

ADHD:

Children and adults with attention deficit disorders (C.H.A.D.D.)
   http://chadd.org/

Anxiety:

Anxiety-panic
   http://www.algy.com/anxiety/

Alcoholism:

Adult children of alcoholics
   http://www.couns.uiuc.edu/adukt.htm
Al-Anon and Alateen
   http://www.Al-Anon-Alateen.org
Alcohol–an interactive assessment
   http://www.mayohealth.org//mayo/9707/htm/alcohol.htm
Alcohol dependence
   http://www.mentalhealth.com/dx/fdx-sb01.html
Alcoholics Anonymous
   http://www.alcoholics-anonymous.org/
Another empty bottle
   http://www.alcoholismhelp.com
Concerned about your drinking?
   http://www.carebetter.com
Habitsmart (alcohol)
   http://www.habitsmart.com
JACS—Jewish Alcoholics, Chemically Dependent Persons, and Significant Others
   http://www.jacsweb.org
Mothers Against Drunk Driving
   http://www.madd:org
National Institute on Alcohol Abuse and Alcoholism
   http://www.niaaa.nih.gov
Secular Organization for Sobriety/Save Our Selves
   http://www.unhooked.com/toolbox/index.html

Bipolar Disorder:

Bipolar and other mood disorders: pendulum resources
   http://www.pendulum.org

Co-dependency:

The issues of co-dependency
   http://www.soulselfhelp.on.ca/coda.hml

Death:

Death, dying, and grief resources: the webster
   http://www.cyberspy.com/%7Ewebster/death.html

Depression:

Depression central
   http://www.psycom.net/depression.central.html

Dissociation:

International Society for the Study Of Dissociation
   http://www.issd.org/

Drugs:

Addiction resource guide
   http://www.addictionresourcegguide.com
Cocaine abuse and addiction
   http://www.nida.nih.gov/researchreports/cocaine/cocaine.html
Cocaine Anonymous
   http://www.ca.org
Cola-center for online addiction
   http://netaddiction.com/
Commonly abused drugs
   http://www.nida.nih.gov/drugpages.html
Drug/alcohol brochures
   http://www.uiuc.edu/departments/mckinley/health-info/drug-alc/drug-alc.html

National Inhalant Coalition
http://inhalants.org
National Institute on Drug Abuse
http://www.nida.nih.gov
Web of addictions
http://www.well.com/user/woa

Eating Disorders:

Cyber-psych: Eating Disorders
http://www.cyber-psych.com/eat.html

Gambling:

Compulsive gambling
http://drkoop.com/wellness/mental_health/compulsive_gambling
Debtors Anonymous
http://www.gamblersanonymous.org
Pathological gambling
hsttp://www.cme-reviews.com/pathologicalgambling.html

General medical:

Quick docs:
http//www.health.org/pubs/qdocs/index.htmex.html

Obsessive-Compulsive Disorder:

Obsessive-Compulsive Disorders
http://www.cmhc.com/guide/ocd.htm

Psychosis:

Futur.com (Schizophrenia and other psychoses)
http://www.futur.com/

Recovery:

Moderation management
   http://moderation.org
Rational recovery
   http://www.rational.org/recovery
Recovery online
   http://www.recovery.alano.org
SMART: Self-Management And Recovery Training
   http://www.smartrecovery.org
Software for recovering people
   http://Christians-in-recovery.org/software

Suicide:

The Samaritans (suicide)
   http://www.samaritans.org.uk/

PART IV
APPENDIX

20
PRACTICE MANAGEMENT REPORTS

In addition to the Outpatient Treatment Report, there are a number of other written reports you may find helpful in managing your practice. These include the Psychosocial Intake Report, the Outpatient Medical Management (Psychiatrist's) Report, the Payment and Session Monitor, a Progress Notes form, a list of current CPT codes, and a Discharge Summary.

PSYCHOSOCIAL INTAKE REPORT

[To be completed at intake and retained for the therapist's records]

Date: _____

First name:	Last name:
Address:	
SS#:	Birth date:

Presenting problem:

Assessment of mental status:

Affect: (*Check*)	☐ Poor	☐ Okay	☐ Good
Explain:			

Mood:	☐ Poor	☐ Okay	☐ Good
Explain:			
If suicidal:	☐ With plan	☐ Ideation	

Speech	☐ Poor	☐ Okay	☐ Good
Explain:			

Thought content:	☐ Poor	☐ Okay	☐ Good
Explain:			

Judgment:	☐ Poor	☐ Okay	☐ Good
Explain:			

Insight	☐ Poor	☐ Okay	☐ Good
Explain:			

Concentration:	☐ Poor	☐ Okay	☐ Good
Explain:			

Memory:	☐ Poor	☐ Okay	☐ Good
Explain:			

Relevant medical conditions:

Provider: Name: _____

Signed: _____ Date: _____

OUTPATIENT MEDICAL MANAGEMENT OTR—
Psychiatrist's Report

[To be completed by psychiatrist and submitted to the insurance company. The referring therapist, if any, should receive a copy.]

PATIENT INFORMATION:	PROVIDER INFORMATION:
Name: DOB:	Name:
Case #:	Title:
Treatment Start Date:	Address:
Treatment End Date:	State: Zip:
SS#:	Telephone:
Employer:	Tax ID: SS#

DSM-IV MULTI-AXIAL DIAGNOSIS: based on current symptoms.

Axis I:

Axis II:

Axis III:

Axis IV:

Axis V: GAF: Current: At treatment start: Highest last year:

CURRENT MEDICATION:

Medication	Dosage/frequency	Start date	Reaction

SUBSTANCE ABUSE:

Current problem: ☐ Yes   ☐ No   Past problem: ☐ Yes   ☐ No

CLINICAL SYNOPSIS:

Page 1

RISK:
☐ Suicidal ☐ Violent ☐ None
☐ Homicidal ☐ Other

SAFETY PLAN IN PLACE? If so, please describe:

Medication Management CPT Code: **Frequency:**
Start date: **End date:**

I certify that I personally direct treatment to this patient and that the above information is accurate to the best of my knowledge.

Signature: Date:

PAYMENT AND SESSION MONITOR

It is well worth your time and effort to use the Basic Session Monitor for all managed care patients. It is designed to organize all critical information in one place, and advises you when future Outpatient Treatment Reports (OTRs) are due. In addition to client data, it provides space to track client sessions and payments. The form should be started right from the initial telephone referral from an insurance company. It can be entered into your computer or kept in a notebook for manual notation.

The form also provides space to enter the telephone numbers and contacts for the client's insurance company. This eliminates the need to pore through a lengthy provider manual every time you must contact the insurer to confirm coverage, co-pay amounts, and treatment authorizations. It is recommended that the completed form be checked weekly.

Recordkeeping can be a nightmare, and the requirements are a lot more extensive than many providers realize. However, the more complete your documentation and the more behavioral it is, the better your chances of getting the authorized sessions your client needs.

This section, including the form that follows, is from *The Psychotherapists' Guide to Managed Care in the 21st Century* by S. Tuckfelt, J. Fink, and M. P. Warren. Copyright © 1997 by Jason Aronson and used with permission.

PAYMENT AND SESSION MONITOR

CLIENT NAME:	PRIMARY INSURANCE CO.:
Address:	Billing Address:
City, State, Zip:	City, State, Zip:
Tel. Home: Work:	Telephone: Fax:
SS#: DOB:	Contact:
Ins. Member #:	Your Provider #:
Date of First Visit:	SECONDARY INSURANCE CO.:
CPT 1st Visit – 90801	Billing Address:
90806 individual; 90847 couples/family	City, State, Zip:
90856 – parents without patient	Telephone: Fax:
Managed Care Protocol:	Contact:
	Your Provider #:
	PCP:
	Address:
	City, State, Zip:
Authorizations:	Telephone: Fax:
No. # of Visits Date:	Psychiatrist:
	Address:
	City, State, Zip:
	Telephone: Fax:

(PAYMENT AND SESSION MONITOR—continued)

OTR alert #	Auth. start	Auth. end	Visit #	Date of visit	Date OTR filed	Ins. amt.	Date paid	Co. pay amt.	Date paid	Ins. bal.	Pt. Bal.
			1								
			2								
			3								
			4								
			5								
			6								
			7								
			8								
			9								
			10								
			11								
			12								
			13								
			14								
			15								

PROGRESS NOTES

These guidelines for Progress Notes have been recommended by the National Committee On Quality Assurance (NCQA), and are required by many insurance companies, including Magellan. Progress Notes must be kept for each session. The notes must include the name of the client, the date, a summary of what transpired in the session, including your intervention, and an evaluation of progress toward a treatment goal. The provider must sign the Progress Notes for each session. Dictated notes are considered preliminary until the transcription is reviewed and signed.

PROGRESS NOTES

Client:	Date:
Address:	Insurance co.
City, State, Zip:	
SS#:	ID#

Session summary:
Intervention:
Behavioral goals:

Provider: _____ Date: _____

Signed: _____

CPT CODES

Current procedural terminology (CPT) codes represent the procedure and services performed by providers. They are followed by modifiers that indicate the provider's specialty, AH for licensed psychologist, and AJ for clinical social worker. The current codes for psychiatric treatment procedures include:

DESCRIPTION OF SERVICES	CPT CODE
Initial diagnostic interview	90801
Individual psychotherapy, 23–30 minutes	90804
Individual psychotherapy, 35–50 minutes	90806
Individual psychotherapy, 75–80 minutes	90808
Family psychotherapy—without patient present	90846
Family/conjoint psychotherapy therapy—with patient present	90847
Group psychotherapy (other than multiple family group)	90853
Interactive group psychotherapy	90857
Pharmacological management	90862

DISCHARGE SUMMARY

Some, but not all, insurance companies require a Discharge Summary. Since many companies are tracking your success rate and duration of treatment, it is a good idea to submit a Discharge Summary even if you suspect the client may return to treatment and you have authorized sessions left. You can always open the case again.

DISCHARGE SUMMARY

CLIENT:	DATE:
SS#:	INSURER:
DATE OF FINAL VISIT:	

REASONS FOR DISCHARGE: (Check)	
☐ Treatment objective achieved	☐ Client Relocated
☐ Treatment regarded as ineffectual by therapist	☐ Referred to new therapist
☐ Treatment regarded as ineffectual by client	☐ Quit treatment
☐ Substantial progress made and client satisfied	☐ Other:
☐ Client no longer eligible for service	

Describe Situation at Discharge:

DESCRIBE AT DISCHARGE:

Axis I:

Axis II:

Axis III:

Axis IV:

Axis V:

GAF (at discharge):

GAF (at start of treatment):

CLIENT ATTITUDE TOWARD TREATMENT:

☐ Well motivated   ☐ Somewhat motivated   ☐ Unmotivated   ☐ Uncooperative

PROGNOSIS:

Provider: Name: _____

Signed: _____ Date: _____

REFERENCES

Agre, L. G. (1999). Bad Dreams. In H. Kaduson and C. Schaefer (eds). *101 Favorite Play Therapy Techniques*. Northvale, NJ: Jason Aronson.

Allen, F. H. (1942). *Psychotherapy with Children*. New York: Norton.

American Psychiatric Association. (1994). *Diagnostic and Statistical Manual of Mental Disorders*. 4th edn. Washington, DC: Author.

Axline, V. (1969). *Play Therapy*. New York: Ballantine.

Azrin, N. H., and Foxx, R. M. (1974). *Dry-Bed Training: Rapid Elimination of Childhood Enuresis*. New York: Simon & Schuster.

——— (1974). *Toilet Training in Less Than a Day*. New York: Simon & Schuster.

Bandler, R. (1985). *Using Your Brain—for a Change*. Moab, UT: Real People Press.

Bandler, R., and Grinder, J. (1982). *Reframing—Neuro–Linguistic Programming and the Transformation of Meaning*. Moab, UT: Real People Press.

Barbe, W. B. (1979). Observable Characteristics Indicative of Modality Strength. In R.H. Swassing, and W. B. Milove (eds). *Teaching Through Modality Strengths: Concepts and Practices*. New York: Zanner-Blosser.

Bourne, E. J. (1997). *The Anxiety and Phobia Workbook*. 2nd edn. Oakland, CA: New Harbinger.

Bourne, E. J. (1998). *Overcoming Specific Phobias*. Oakland, CA: New Harbinger.

Bradley, S., and Zucher, K. (1995). *Gender Identity Disorder and Psychosocial Problems in Children and Adolescents*. New York: Guilford.

Bruce, T. J., and Sanderson, W. C. (1998). *Specific Phobias: Clinical Applications of Evidence-Based Psychotherapy*. Northvale, NJ: Jason Aronson.

Carkhuff, R. R. (1969). *Helping and Human Relations*, Vol. 1. New York: Holt, Rinehart & Winston.

Carnes, P. (1992). *Out of the Shadows: Understanding Sexual Addiction*. Center City, MN: Hazelden.

Dacey, J. S., and Fiore, L. B. (2000). *Your Anxious Child: How Parents and Teachers Can Relieve Anxiety In Children*. San Francisco, CA: Jossey-Bass.

Davis, M., Eschman, E. R., and McKay, M. (1994). *The Relaxation and Stress Reduction Workbook*. Oakland, CA: New Harbinger.

Diceglia, D. (2000). Gender Disorder in Young People. *Psychiatric Treatment*. 6: 458–66.

Dodds, J. B. (1985). *A Child Psychotherapy Primer*. New York: Human Sciences.

Emery, G. (2000). *Overcoming Depression*. Oakland, CA: New Harbinger.

Erickson, E. H. (1950). *Childhood and Society*. New York: Norton.

Fink, J. (1999). *How to Use Computers and Cyberspace in the Clinical Practice*. Northvale, NJ: Jason Aronson.

Frager, S. (2000). *Managing Managed Care: Secrets from a Former Case Manager*. New York: Wiley.

Freud, A. (1965). *Normality and Pathology in Childhood*. New York: International Universities Press.

Freud, S. (1920). *Beyond the Pleasure Principle*. New York: Norton.

Gardner, R. A. (1971). The Mutual Storytelling Technique in the Treatment of Anger Inhibition Problems. *International Journal of Child Psychoanalysis*. 1: 34–64.

Goldstein, A. P., and Glick, B. (1987). *Aggression Replacement Training—A Comprehensive Intervention for Aggressive Youth*. Champaign, IL: Research Press.

Gottman, J. M., Gonso, J., and Shuler, P. (1976). Teaching Social Skills to Isolated Children. *Journal of Abnormal Psychology*. 4: 179–97.

Gresham, F. M. (1986). Conceptual Issues in the Assessment of Social Competence in Children. In P. S. Strain, M. J. Gurainick, and H. M. Walker (eds). *Children's Social Behavior—Developmental, Assessment, and Modification*. Orlando, FL: Academic.

Guerin, P. J., Jr. (ed.). (1976). *Family Therapy: Theory and Practice*. New York: Gardner Press.

Halberstadt-Freud, I. (1975). Technical Variations in the Psychoanalytic Treatment of a Pre-School Child. *Israel Annals of Psychiatry and Related Disciplines*. 13: 162–76.

Harter, S. (1977). A Cognitive-Developmental Approach to Children's Expression of Conflicting Feelings and a Technique to Facilitate Such Expression in Play Therapy. *Journal of Consulting and Clinical Psychology*. 45: 417–32.

Hendricks, G., and Wills, R. (1975). *The Centering Book*. Englewood Cliffs, NJ: Prentice-Hall.

Horney, K. (1945). *Our Inner Conflicts*. New York: Norton.

Irwin, E. C. (1983). The Diagnostic and Therapeutic Use of Pretend Play. In C. E. Schaefer and K. J. O'Connor (eds). *Handbook of Play Therapy*. New York: Wiley.

Jacobs, E. H. (2000). *ADHD: Helping Parents Help Their Children*. Northvale, NJ: Jason Aronson.

Jacobson, E. (1938). *Progressive Relaxation—A Physiological and Clinical Investigation of Muscular States and Their Significance in Psychology and Medical Practice*. 2nd edn. Chicago: University of Chicago Press.

Jozefowski, J. (1999). *The Phoenix Phenomenon: Rising From the Ashes of Grief*. Northvale, NJ: Jason Aronson.

Kadusen, H. and Schaefer, C. E. (eds). (1997). *101 Favorite Play Therapy Techniques*. Northvale, NJ: Jason Aronson.

Kelly, G. A. (1955). *The Psychology of Personal Constructs: Vol. 2. Clinical Diagnosis and Psychotherapy*. New York: Norton.

Kendall, P. C. (1991). *Child and Adolescent Therapy: Cognitive Behavioral Procedures*. New York: Guilford Press.

Kendall, P. C., and Braswell, L. (1985). *Cognitive Behavioral Therapy for Impulsive Children*. New York: Guilford Press.

Klein, M. (1975). *The Psychoanalysis of Children*. New York: The Free Press.

Klosko, J. S., and Sanderson, W. C. (1999). The Steps to Constructing a Rational Response. *Cognitive–Behavioral Treatment of Depression*. Northvale, NJ: Jason Aronson.

Knell, S. M. (1993). *Cognitive–Behavioral Play Therapy*. Northvale, NJ: Jason Aronson.

Krumholtz, J. D., and Thoresen, C. E. (1969). *Behavioral Counseling: Cases and Techniques*. New York: Holt, Rinehart & Winston.

Kubler-Ross, E. (1997). *On Death and Dying*. New York: Simon & Schuster.

Kurdek, L.A. (1986). Custodial Mothers' Perceptions of Visitations and Payment of Child Support by Non-Custodial Fathers in Families with Low and High Levels of Preseparation Interparent Conflict. *Journal of Applied Developmental Psychology*. 9: 315–28.

La Greca, A. M. (1983). Interviewing and Behavioral Observations. In C. E. Walker and M. C. Roberts (eds). *Handbook of Clinical Child Psychology*. New York: Wiley.

Lazarus, A. A. (1971). *Behavior Therapy and Beyond*. New York: McGraw-Hill.

Lazarus, A. A., and Abramovitz, A. (1962). The Use of Emotive Imagery in the Treatment of Children's Phobias. *Journal of Afentat Science*. 108: 191–5.

Linehan, M. M. (1993). *Skills Training Manual for Treating Borderline Personality Disorder*. New York: Guilford.

McGinn, L. K., and Sanderson, W. C. (1999). Automatic Thought Log. *Treatment of Obsessive-Compulsive Disorder*. Northvale, NJ: Jason Aronson.

McGuire, W. J. (1961). The Effectiveness of Supportive and Refutational Defenses in Immunizing and Restoring Beliefs Against Persuasion. *Sociometry, 24*, 184–97.

McKay, M., Fanning, P., and Paleg, K. (1994). *Couples Skills*. Oakland, CA: New Harbinger.

Moreno, J. (1969). *Psychodrama*. New York: Beacon House.

Moustakas, C. E. (1953). *Children in Play Therapy*. New York: McGraw-Hill.

New York State Department Of Civil Services. (1999). *Value Options Provider Handbook: More Choices For More People*. New York: Author.

O'Connor, K. (1991). *The Play Therapy Primer*. New York: Wiley.

O'Hanlon, W. H. (2001). How to Change 101. In *Possibilities E-mail*, April 2001.

Piaget, J. (1952). *The Origins of Intelligence*. New York: Norton.

Ramey, C. T., Campbell, F. C., and Ramey, S. L. (1998). *Early Intervention: Successful Pathways to Improving Intellectual Development*. Paper presented at the Conference on Dendritic Mechanisms of Mental Retardation and Developmental Disabilities, National Institute for Child Health and Human Development, Bethesda, MD. (June 1998).

Rapee, R. C., and Sanderson, W. C. (1998). *Social Phobia*. Northvale, NJ: Jason Aronson.

Rathus, J. H., and Sanderson, W. C. (1999). Challenging Cognitions Worksheet and Common Cognitive Distortions. *Marital Distress*. Northvale, NJ: Jason Aronson.

Reinecke, M. A., Dottilio, F. M., and Freeman, A. (eds). (1996). *Cognitive Therapy with Children and Adolescents*. New York: Guilford Press.

Reisman, J. M. (1973). *Principles of Psychotherapy with Children*. New York: Wiley.

Rychlak, J. F. (1973). *Introduction to Personality and Psychotherapy—A Theory-Construction Approach*. Boston: Houghton Mifflin.

Sarnoff, C. (1976). *Latency*. New York: Jason Aronson.

Schaefer, C. E. (1993). *The Therapeutic Powers of Play*. Northvale, NJ: Jason Aronson.

Schaefer, C. E., and Conglosai, D. M. (eds) (1997). *Play Therapy Techniques*. Northvale, NJ: Jason Aronson.

Schaefer, C. E., and Millman, H. L. (1977). *Therapies for Children*. San Francisco: Jossey-Bass.

Schwebel, A. I., and Fine, M. A. (1994). *Understanding and Helping Families: A Cognitive–Behavioral Approach*. NJ: Lawrence Erlbaum Associates.

Sketekee, G. (1998). *Overcoming Obsessive–Compulsive Disorder*. Oakland, CA: New Harbinger.

Smith, C. D. (1977). Counter Attitudinal Role-Playing and Attitude Change in Children, *Dissertation Abstracts International*. 39: 400B.

Steinberg, M., and Schnell, M. (2000). *The Stranger in the Mirror: Dissociation, the Hidden Epidemic*. New York: HarperCollins.

Swassing, R. H., and Barbe, W. B. (eds) (1979). *Teaching Through Modality Strengths: Concepts and Practices*. New York: Zaner Bloser.

Tobin, L. (1999). *What Do You Do with a Child Like This?* Los Angeles, CA: Western Psychological Services.

Tuckfelt, S., Fink, J., and Warren, M. P. (1997). Payment and Session Monitor. *The Psychotherapists' Guide to Managed Care in the 21st Century*. Northvale, NJ: Jason Aronson.

Waelder, R. (1933). The Psychoanalytic Theory of Play. *Psychoanalytic Quarterly* 2: 208–24.

Warren, M. P. (2001). *Behavioral Management Guide: Essential Treatment Strategies for Adult Psychotherapy*. Northvale, NJ: Jason Aronson.

White, J. (1998). *Overcoming Generalized Anxiety Disorder*. Oakland, CA: New Harbinger.

Woody, R. H. (1971). *Psychobehavioral Counseling and Therapy: Integrating Behavioral and Insight Techniques*. New York: Appleton–Century–Crofts.

Zuercher-White, E. (1998). *Overcoming Agoraphobia and Panic Disorder*. Oakland, CA: New Harbinger.

INDEX

abuse or neglect *see* child abuse or neglect
acute stress disorder
   diagnosis 37
   treatment plan 39
agoraphobia 83, 95, 96
   social phobia 95
   specific phobia 108
alcohol abuse 351, 420
   see also drug abuse
amnesia *see* dissociative amnesia
anger, behavioral techniques 359
anorexia nervosa
   bibliotherapy 386
   diagnosis 201
   treatment plan 204
anxiety
   audiotapes 403, 405
   bibliotherapy 398
   online resources 410
   therapeutic games 374
anxiety disorders 37
   acute stress disorder 37
   critical incident stress management 15
   generalized anxiety disorder 50
   obsessive-compulsive disorder 61
   post-traumatic stress disorder 71
   social phobia 95
   specific phobia 108
attention deficit/hyperactivity disorder (AD/HD)
   bibliotherapy 384
   diagnosis 121
   online resources 410
   treatment plan 123
audiotapes 403
Axis (I–IV), multiaxial assessment documentation 4, 15

bad dreams, behavioral techniques 359
behavioral techniques 359
   anger 359
   bad dreams 359
   change 361
   diaphragmatic breathing and relaxation exercise 367
   family sculpturing 362
   genograms 363
   hypnosis 365
   life maps 182
   role playing 369
behavior disorders 121
   attention deficit/hyperactivity disorder (AD/HD) 121
   bibliotherapy 384
   conduct disorder 133
   disruptive behavior disorder NOS 136, 137
   oppositional defiant disorder 135, 137
   therapeutic games 374
bereavement 187
   bibliotherapy 384
   online resources 411
   therapeutic games 375
   treatment plan 188
bibliotherapy 382
   audiotapes 403
   videos 403, 404
billing 12
bipolar disorder(s) 146
   bibliotherapy 395
   bipolar disorder NOS 151
   bipolar I disorder 146
   bipolar II disorder 151
   cyclothymic disorder 153
   online resources 411
bipolar disorder NOS
   diagnosis 151
   treatment plan 152
bipolar I disorder
   diagnosis 146
   treatment plan 150

depressed 148
hypomanic 149
single manic episode 147–8
bipolar II disorder
   diagnosis 151
   treatment plan 152
      depressed 151
      hypomanic 151
borderline personality disorder
   bibliotherapy 395
bulimia nervosa
   bibliotherapy 387, 397
   diagnosis 203
   treatment plan 204

change
   behavioral techniques 361
   bibliotherapy 396
child abuse or neglect
   bibliotherapy 382, 393
   diagnosis 308
   self-help groups 406
   therapeutic games 376
   treatment plan 309
child psychotherapy, role playing 369
children of divorce or separation 294
   bibliotherapy 397
   diagnosis 294
   self-help groups 407
   therapeutic games 375
   treatment plan 295
co-dependency, online resources 411
cognition
   audiotapes 403–5
   bibliotherapy 389, 397, 400, 401, 430
   challenging 380
   distortions 381
   worksheet 380
cognitive skills
   homework assignments 377
   therapeutic games 374
communication
   audiotapes 404
   therapeutic games 374
   videos 404
conduct disorder
   diagnosis 133
   treatment plan 137
conflict resolution
   audiotapes 404
   bibliotherapy 385
crisis management, bibliotherapy 385
critical incident stress management
   diagnosis 15
   bibliotherapy 385
   online resources 408–13

treatment plan 18
current procedural terminology (CPT)
   codes 426
cyclothymic disorder
   diagnosis 153
   treatment plan 155

death *see also* bereavement
   bibliotherapy 384
   online resources 411
   therapeutic games 375
   treatment plan 188
defiant child *see* oppositional defiant
   disorder NOS
depersonalization disorder 37, 96
depression
   audiotapes 404
   bibliotherapy 383, 385–6, 396, 405
   major depressive disorder 170
   online resources 411
   self-help groups 406
   therapeutic games 374–6
depressive disorder NOS
   diagnosis 173
   treatment plan 174
depressive episodes 148
developmental disorder
   pervasive 83
Diagnostic and Statistical Manual of
   Mental Disorders (DSM-IV) 4, 429
diaphragmatic breathing 367
discharge summary 12, 426–7
disorder of written expression *see*
   learning disorders
disruptive behavior disorder
   diagnosis 136
   treatment plan 137
dissociative
   amnesia 37
   disorder, bibliotherapy 386
   symptoms 217
dissociative disorders
   depersonalization disorder 37, 96
   dissociative amnesia 37
   dissociative disorder, bibliotherapy 386
   online resources 411
divorce *see* children of divorce or
   separation
documentation
   multiaxial assessment 4, 11, 187
   Axis (I– IV) 4, 15
   outpatient treatment report 11
domestic violence
   bibliotherapy 386
   see also child abuse or neglect
dreams 359

drug abuse
  online resources 411–12
  self-help groups 407
  see also alcohol abuse
dyssomnias 326
  see also sleep disorders
dysthymic disorder
  diagnosis 172
  treatment plan 174

eating disorders, 260–282
  anorexia nervosa 201
  bibliotherapy 397
  bulimia nervosa 203
  online resources 412
elimination disorders 294, 295

family issues 375
family sculpturing 362
feelings
  bibliotherapy 385, 404
  therapeutic games 375

gambling (pathological/compulsive)
  diagnosis 258
  bibliotherapy 387
  online resources 412
  treatment plan 259
generalized anxiety disorder
  diagnosis 50
  treatment plan 51
general medical conditions 216
genograms 363

Health Care Financing Administration (HCFA) (billing) 10, 12
homework assignments 377–81
hypersomnia 148, 151, 153, 154, 171, 172, 326
  see also sleep disorders
hypnosis 365
  audiotapes 405
  bibliotherapy 397

impulse control disorders (trichotillomania)
  diagnosis 272
  treatment plan 273
insomnias 326
  see also sleep disorders
insurance companies *see* managed care
integration, behavioral techniques 373

kleptomania
  diagnosis 246
  treatment plan 247

learning 365
  audiotapes 405
  disability, bibliotherapy 388
  skills, bibliotherapy 398
  style 366

major depressive disorder
  diagnosis 170
  treatment plan 174
managed care
  child psychotherapy and 3
  outpatient treatment report (OTR) 11
manic episode, single 147–8
medical necessity 5
mental disorder due to medical condition 217
motivation, therapeutic games 375
multiaxial assessment documentation, Axis (I–IV) 4, 15
Multiaxial Assessment System 187
mutism 95

narcolepsy 326
  see also sleep disorders
National Association of Insurance Commissioners (NAIC), appeal process 6–7
neglect or abuse *see* child abuse or neglect
nurturing, bibliotherapy 398

obsessive-compulsive disorder
  bibliotherapy 398, 399, 400
  diagnosis 61
  online resources 412
  treatment plan 62
online resources 408–13
oppositional defiant disorder NOS
  diagnosis 135
  treatment plan 137
outpatient treatment report (OTR) 11

panic attack
  bibliotherapy 381, 387, 397, 405
  social phobia 95
  specific phobia 108
paper trail 10
parasomnias 326
  see also sleep disorders
parent–adolescent relational problem
  diagnosis 285
  treatment plan 288
parenting
  bibliotherapy 389, 399–400, 401, 402
personality change due to general medical condition
  diagnosis 216
  treatment plan 219

personality disorders, bibliotherapy 400
pervasive development disorder 83
phobia *see* social phobia; specific phobia
play therapy
    behavioral techniques 359
    role-playing 369
post-traumatic stress disorder
    bibliotherapy 401
    diagnosis 71
    treatment plan 73
practice management reports, examples of 417
problem solving, bibliotherapy 390
professional organizations, online resources 409
project management 3
psychological factor affecting general medical condition
    diagnosis 218
    treatment plan 219
psychosis, online resources 412
psychosocial problems 121, 369

record keeping *see* documentation
recovery, online resources 413
relational problems 285
    bibliotherapy 401
    children of divorce or separation 294
    parent–adolescent relational problem 285
    sibling relational problems 287
relaxation 367
    bibliotherapy 387, 392, 397
role-playing 369

schizophrenia 83
    bibliotherapy 390, 401
    online resources 412
school problems, bibliotherapy 402
selective mutism, 95
self-confidence, therapeutic games 375
self-control, therapeutic games 375
self-esteem
    bibliotherapy 390, 391, 401, 402
    therapeutic games 375
self-help 5
    groups listing of 406–7
    online resources 408–13
separation *see* children of divorce or separation
sexual abuse *see* child abuse or neglect
sexuality 317, 318
sibling relational problems 287
sleep disorders
    bibliotherapy 392
    diagnosis 326
    treatment plan 328

social phobia
    diagnosis 95
    treatment plan 97
specific phobia
    behavioral techniques 368n
    bibliotherapy 389
    diagnosis 108
    treatment plan 110
state insurance departments 7
stress management, critical incident 15
    bibliotherapy 392
    therapeutic games 376
substance abuse
    bibliotherapy 392, 403
    see also alcohol abuse; drug abuse; self-help groups
suicide
    bibliotherapy 392, 396, 413
support groups *see* self-help groups

terminology 11, 426
therapeutic alliance 4
therapeutic games 374
treatment aids *see also* behavioral techniques; homework assignments
    behavioral techniques 359
    homework assignments 377
    self-help groups 406
    therapeutic games 374
treatment plan *see also* main heading
    anxiety disorders 37
    behavior disorders 121
    bereavement 187
    bipolar disorders 146
    depressive disorders 170
    dissociative disorders 386, 411
    eating disorders 201
    elimination disorders 294–5
    general medical conditions 216
    impulse control disorders 232
    personality disorders 4, 7, 246, 285, 400
    relational problems 285
    separation anxiety disorder 83
    sleep disorders 326
trichotillomania
    diagnosis 272
    treatment plan 273

videos 403, 404
videotalk 361, 361n
videotape 361n, 393, 403
violence 9, 130, 141, 244, 302
    bibliotherapy 386, 403
visualization 182, 252, 267, 278, 318, 334, 352, 365
    bibliotherapy 387–8, 397